The Violent E

and Other Tricky Sounds

Learning to Spell from
Kindergarten Through Grade 6

Margaret Hughes and Dennis Searle

Stenhouse Publishers
York, Maine

Pembroke Publishers Limited
Markham, Ontario

Stenhouse Publishers, 431 York Street, York, Maine 03909

Library of Congress Cataloging-in-Publication Data
Hughes, Margaret.
   The violent E and other tricky sounds : learning to spell from kindergarten through grade 6 / Margaret Hughes and Dennis Searle.
      p.   cm.
   Includes bibliographical references (p. `   ).
   ISBN 1-57110-034-2 (alk. paper)
   1. English language—Orthography and spelling—Study and teaching (Elementary). I. Searle, Dennis. II. Title.
LB1574.H92   1997
372.63'2'044—dc21   97-16201
                                               CIP

Published simultaneously in Canada by
Pembroke Publishers Limited
538 Hood Road
Markham, Ontario L3R 3K9
ISBN 1-55138-088-9

Canadian Cataloging-in-Publication Data
Hughes, Margaret A., 1941–
   The violent E and other tricky sounds : learning to spell from kindergarten through grade 6
Includes bibliographical references.
ISBN 1-55138-088-9
1. English language—Orthography and spelling—Study and teaching (Elementary). I. Searle, Dennis. II. Title.
LB1574.H83 1997   372.63'2   C97–931059–8

Cover and interior design by Cathy Hawkes

Manufactured in Canada on acid-free paper
01 00 99 98 97 9 8 7 6 5 4 3 2 1

The Violent E
and Other Tricky Sounds

To Maija and Gethin

Contents

Acknowledgements

We thank the children, parents, teachers, principals, and support staff at Hampton Park Elementary School, Fulham Public School, and Black Ravine Public School, whose involvement and generous support made this project possible. We further acknowledge the invaluable assistance provided by Deirdre Whitfeld at the Faculty of Education, York University. We are also indebted to our many research assistants, who moved in and out of the project over the years, and to our families, who elected not to move out over the long years of the study.

Portions of the research presented in this book were supported by grants from the Social Sciences and Humanities Research Council of Canada, for which we are grateful.

Listening to Children

MARGARET: *Now what if you came across a word in your own writing that you don't know how to spell? Then what do you do?*

LORNA: *I think about it and I sound it out.*

MARGARET: *What do you think about when you're thinking about it? […] Have you had a word lately that you didn't know how to spell, that you wanted to write in a story?*

LORNA: *Yes, the word invention and avalanche.*

MARGARET: *O.K., so you got to avalanche. What did you do?*

LORNA: *I guessed Eve and I know how to spell Eve so I just changed the "eh" to "av" [AVE] and then I did l and then I know how to spell ranch, so I did it without the r.*

From the very beginning of our study of spelling, children showed us that, if we gave them the opportunity, they would teach us about spelling development. Lorna gave us our first lesson when she shared with us early in grade 1, in the conversation above, how she spelled very difficult words in her writing.

Although Lorna was easily identified as an advanced speller, we were surprised by the sophistication of her reasoning about spelling, and also that she could so clearly recall and explain her process. Initially, we were sceptical about whether the other children, whose progress we were studying but who did not show Lorna's precociousness in spelling, would

1

be able to give us clear insight into what they were doing. Our curiosity led us to ask all the children about how they worked out their spellings; we found that children can be wonderful informants about their approaches.

Although few children were at first as forthcoming or as elaborate in their explanations as Lorna, from the beginning we found that most children were willing to try to spell new words and talk about what they were doing even when, like Joe, they knew how to print relatively few letters.

MARGARET: How are you going to write *rag*?
JOE: I think I do it with *t-o-o*. It might be that. [*Joe actually proceeded to write* JLO.] I think I've done it.

Early in grade 1, Linda wrote in her daily journal that she and her family were going to MOVEH. We asked her how she had worked out that spelling. "I sounded it out," she told us. When we replied, "Show us how you did that," she demonstrated: "Mmm—ooo—vvv—uh." Linda accounted for each of the sounds she had represented in her spelling.

In talking with the children we increasingly came to understand the reasons behind even the most bizarre spellings. Adam, for example, filled his words with strings of vowels, as in KAEIS (*kiss*) and YEALEEO (*yellow*). What could he be doing to create such strings? We listened and found that, like Linda, he used exaggerated pronunciations of each sound and then strung these exaggerations together with no concern for how the resulting word might look:

MARGARET: How do you know that *kiss* has so many letters in it?
ADAM: Sound it out.
MARGARET: Show me how you did that.
ADAM: Ka-eh-is.
MARGARET: So that's how you do your spelling, is it? Do you ever do anything else?
ADAM: Not really.

Even though Adam had great trouble reading his own writing, he proceeded resolutely with this strategy.

As we continued to observe the children, their conversations included reasons besides sound. Suddenly *e*'s appeared at the end of the strangest words and we were assured that the word needed either a silent *e* or, as Starr put it, a "violent *e*." Julian's YELOWE and JOBE are typical examples. At the end of grade 1, Saul added *e*'s to almost every spelling, some of which, such as FIVE and WIFE, produced the conventional spellings, while many others, including LIDE, SIXSE, VUWE, DOCDRE, MAFNE, CAPE (*camp*) and YELLE (*yell*), did not. Interestingly, he did not add *e* to his GAM! In the following discussion of those spellings Saul demonstrated that he was beginning to understand the use of the *e*, but knowledge and the application of that knowledge do not come in a complete package.

MARGARET: Now, I also see that sixteen words all end in *e*. How did you know that? How did you know that they ended in *e*?
SAUL: Well, most words end with *e*.
MARGARET: Do you know what the little *e* on the end does?
SAUL: It's the same kind of letter as—as—*a* and those kinds of letters. They're sticking to lots of sounds—about three sounds—just like their name.
MARGARET: Ah, I see. An *a*, an *e*. Are there any others like that?
SAUL: *A*, *e*, and *b* and *c*, and I can't remember any other ones. I think *y* is one. *W*, I guess. That's all.

Overgeneralizations and misapplications such as Saul's usually signalled that the children were beginning to experiment with new learnings, even though they were not yet able to explain them fully or to apply them correctly in all instances. As their understanding became more correctly applied, explanations became more coherent. In grade 3, Thomas linked the use of the silent *e* to the long vowel sound in the following concise explanation:

MARGARET: How did you know about all those *e*'s?
THOMAS: Because if the second letter makes its own sound, like if it was an *a* and it made an *a* sound, you'd put an *e* at the end.

As the children brought more knowledge of text from their reading to their writing, we heard references to word's "looking right." Elly, for example, explained how she had come to her final spelling of *drive*:

MARGARET: You put an *e* very lightly, then you filled it in. How did you know to do that?
ELLY: I tried to see if it looked right or not.

It also became common for the children to borrow words they already knew to spell new words. For example, many borrowed *joy* or *Joyce* and *sigh* or *sight* to produce REJOYCE and SIGHN. Kareem, at the beginning of grade 6, explained this borrowing process to us:

MARGARET: How did you work out *sign*?
KAREEM: Like, the "sigh" part, that, looking, I can just tell with the *s* and the *i*, but the *g-h-n* part at the end, like—ah—like, I sort of know, 'cause in words like *sign* or, like, *sight* that always happens.
MARGARET: Ah, so you thought about *sight*, did you?
KAREEM: Yeah.

MARGARET: I wondered where the *h* came from.

KAREEM: Yeah. Because it's *g-h-t*. So I figured that instead of *g-h-t*, like, it's not *sight*—the whole word—it's actually *sign*, so I just took off the *t* and put in the *n*.

From these and many other examples, we became convinced that all children have reasons for spelling the way they do. Once we realized this, it made our study of children's spellings a problem-solving activity with the fun and challenge of figuring out a fascinating puzzle. This realization can also help teachers learn how to help children become successful spellers.

We suspect that the children were encouraged to tell us so much about their thinking because they sensed our confidence that they have good reasons for their spellings, and they were convinced that we asked out of a real interest in exploring what they were doing. You can't fake that. If you don't believe that children are busily making sense of how print works and if you aren't genuinely interested in their process, the children are likely to sense a lack of authenticity in your questions and are unlikely to share their thinking. Children need to see that they are experts in their own spelling and that their expertise is valued. Our emphasis in questioning was very rarely on correctness and more often on how a child engages with the challenge. Children have far less to lose responding to the second issue.

Wouldn't it be great if all we had to do is ask children what they did and they'd tell us? It doesn't always work that way. If you ask a young child, "How did you figure out how to spell that word?" chances are pretty good that the child will answer, "I sounded it out." This response shouldn't surprise us. Maybe that's exactly what the child did. Once a child has established that sounds and letters are related in some way, "sounding out" isn't a bad way to get started. In fact, all the children at some point used their knowledge of letter names to spell, and such spellings as GAM, YLO, VU, SIN, and CRPT (or HRPT—you can hear a "ch" sound in the letter name "aitch") were common results. At home and at school children are often encouraged to "sound it out." So if an adult asks, "How did you figure out how to spell that word?" it seems reasonable that a child would give back the solution most adults have offered. In many cases, however, that answer just can't provide the whole explanation, and you need to probe further, as was done in the following conversations with Braden, Toshi, and Julian.

Braden, for example, had just stated that he spelled most of his words by "sounding them out."

MARGARET: What about *buzz*? Did you sound that out?

BRADEN: I sounded it out.

MARGARET: Well, how did you know there were two *z*'s in it? Did you hear two *z*'s in it?

BRADEN: Bu*zzz*. Yeah, I sounded out bu*zzz*, bu*zzz*.

Toshi wrote KNOCKED with the *-ed*, but then wrote LEARND and STAIND.

MARGARET: How did you decide whether to use *d* or *ed*?

TOSHI: I don't know. I just put it. [*Margaret continues to press for a reason.*] Well, because in *knocked* it goes "knock*t*," so there's a *bit* of the sound of *e* there, and with *learned*, it just goes "ern*d*."

In grade 3, Julian had initially spelled TRIAND, PEEKD, STAIND, LERNT, JUMPT, and CHIRPED, but then immediately changed his spelling to produce the correct *ed* ending in all cases.

MARGARET: I want to know how you know about *ed* because you didn't know about it and now you've started to put them in.

JULIAN: I just sounded it out. I did *jump*, then *jumped* [*he spelled it JUMPT*]. Then I couldn't find it so I just thought, I know, I'm missing something and it couldn't be "jump-*ad*" or "jump-*id*" so it must be *e*. And then I just sounded out that anything would be under the *d*.

MARGARET: Yes, but how can that be? How come a word that sounds as if it ends in a *t* ends in *ed*? How do you know about that? Because that isn't how it sounds, is it?

JULIAN: No, but I just worked it out.

MARGARET: "Jumped" sounds like a *t* to me. So why is it an *ed*?

JULIAN: Because it's "*jummmed*."

In a later interview, still unwilling to give up on the primacy of sound, Julian offered the following explanation for the discrepancy between sound and spelling in *jumped*.

JULIAN: When I say "jumped" it sounds like a *t*, but in my head it keeps echoing after *d*.

At other times, explanations demonstrate children's different understandings of what is meant by particular approaches. In their discussions, Lorna and Jamal show different understandings about how word meanings can be used to generate spellings.

MARGARET: What about *sign*?

LORNA: I always used to get that word mixed up and put a *h* after the *g*.

MARGARET: Why?

LORNA: Well, because that looks sort of abrupt.

MARGARET: When did you figure out there wasn't an *h* there?

LORNA: When it didn't look right. At the beginning neither of them looked right to me.

MARGARET: O.K. Try *signal.* [*Lorna wrote* SIGNAL.] Now, was there a time when you put an *h* there as well?

LORNA: No, just in *sign.*

MARGARET: O.K., why would *signal* and *sign* be so similar? They don't sound like each other, but why are they—are they connected in any way?

LORNA: Yeah, I think so, because a sign sometimes is a signal to do something or not to do something.

MARGARET: So would that have anything to do with the spelling?

LORNA [*after a long pause*]: I don't think so.

MARGARET: Why not?

LORNA: Because *signal* can mean a whole bunch of other things and *sign* can mean a whole bunch of other things, so I don't think they are together at the beginning, and I don't think they use *sign* to make *signal* and *signal* to make *sign.*

MARGARET: Don't you?

LORNA: I don't think so. They might have the same beginning, first two words—letters, but I don't think they use one to make the other.

Lorna suggested that the multiple meanings possible in English made spelling based on meaning unreliable. But Jamal, like many other children, was less flexible in his concept of root words and was unwilling to adapt root words when necessary, as in the following example.

MARGARET: How do you know it's spelled *r-e-m-e-m-b-e-r-a-n-c-e?*

JAMAL: I'm sure that this part of the word [*pointing to* REMEMBER] is right because it's the part that's the *root* word.

Later, when challenged with the inconsistency between the pronunciation of the word and his spelling of it, he insisted that it could not be spelled *remembrance* "because I'd have to break the *root* word."

Sometimes the rationale behind a child's spelling seems almost impossible to determine. In grade 2, Joe spelled *muffin* as MUSSA and, in a second attempt, MUEER. His explanation, "I sounded it out," certainly didn't clarify why he had placed SSA and EER at the end. At the time, we wondered whether Joe was representing just the first two sounds and then throwing random strings of letters onto the page. Over the years, however, we began to appreciate that Joe always had a reason for his spellings and took spelling very seriously. We also came to understand that he had a very strong sense of the appearance of words. *Muffin* was a word Joe saw regularly on "Muffin Sale" signs at school once a week (each classroom was responsible for raising money for the school by selling muffins). Eventually we realized that the curves of the printed letters *s* and *e* have a lot in common with the printed letter *f*. Visually Joe's spellings of *muffin* were very close to the actual word and, given this perspective, made sense.

As we sought the reasoning behind particular spellings, the children were helping us identify a variety of strategies that both they and adults use to spell words. A strategy for spelling is really a principle about language put into operation. Over time we found that the children in the study used a variety of principles that helped them understand the names and sounds of letters, the different ways sound can be represented, how words should look, how words are changed for syntactic reasons, and how words may share characteristics of sound and meaning.

All of these principles, even the simplest—that a letter says its name (for example, "I")—can produce correct spellings. Even before they could read, with a minimal understanding of letter-sound relationships, most of the children could spell *rag* correctly. In addition, we found that children may achieve correct spellings using different principles, as Julian and Toshi did in formulating past tense. And every principle, at one time or another, has led to a misspelling. By grade 6, Saul and Najali had both realized the uncertainty of relying on even their most effective principles and sometimes turned in frustration to the dictionary. Saul, who like Jamal had an emerging concept of root words, abandoned this strategy because it was "too complicated." He explained, "Sometimes it's confusing, like *terrify, terrified,* and *terror*...It's kind of like you have to drop certain letters in some of them, so it's just confusing." Najali used to write words out and then check to see how they looked. She told us, "Before I used to do that a lot more, but now I look in the dictionary a lot more...because my looks could be wrong, but the dictionary *can't* be wrong." As the many spellings in this chapter show, no strategy can be relied on exclusively, so children must learn to monitor and control their repertoire of strategies as they correct their spelling. It seems useful to think of children expanding their repertoire of strategies rather than moving from one strategy to another as they mature.

When we surveyed the children's spelling over time, it became apparent that, even though growth is hard to predict and difficult to characterize in the abstract, it is easy to recognize in individuals. Certainly, we had assumed that we would see changes over time as individual children learned and applied more knowledge about print, but we had not assumed any particular pattern of growth or even that there might be a common pattern. We were not prepared for the high degree of commonality across individual spellers that we saw. Different children often used the same knowledge in similar ways. Initially it surprised us that many children would produce similar misspellings. But as we came to see the logic in these spellings and to understand that there are a limited number of approaches to spelling a word, we understood why many children would adopt a similar, logical approach to spelling a particular word. There were patterns in how and when that knowledge was developed and when it appeared in many children's spelling.

At the same time, we believe there are dangers in overgeneralizing, either about how children apply principles or about how individuals grow. Certainly, we found early evidence in some children of awareness of as yet seldom used strategies. For example, there might have been times when a child showed a new awareness of a spelling rule, but though the rule might well be the significant new feature in that child's work, he or she would still rely on established principles. Clearly, there is more than one route to becoming a good speller. Children focussed on different things and used different knowledge at different times. Individual children would at times appear to ignore various features, such as sound, sight, or the influence of meaning, that many adults would consider to be essential in learning how to spell, yet managed to succeed.

Looking at how children spelled individual words over several years made us aware of the knowledge children used to become increasingly proficient. We began to better understand how this knowledge related to children's overall growth when we were able to look at the spelling of individual children over time and in relationship to their growth as readers and writers.

Observing the same children over eight years convinced us that learning to spell is indeed a developmental process in that the learner continually applies and refines knowledge and expands that knowledge base through interaction with text. Thinking of learning as occurring in stages of a continuing journey can be useful. Stages provide a language for talking about common, but not required, patterns of growth. However, stages become less useful when they are used to set goals for learners or to limit our understanding of the range of strategies a speller is actually using. Our focus on listening to the learner in this first chapter is meant to encourage you to use knowledge provided by the children, combined with an understanding of how the ability to spell develops over time, in order to support and extend children's learning.

Studying Spelling

Why are nice people like you studying spelling?

The question above—"Why are nice people like you studying spelling?"—was one we had to answer for ourselves and others as we set out on what was to be an eight-year study of how young children learn to spell. Nobody really prepares to devote nearly a decade to researching spelling. After all, reading and writing are the real pillars of literacy; these are what give children access to meaning and the power to make and share their own meaning. For many, including ourselves, spelling is seen as a trivial problem relating to the mastery of particular conventions, more the table manners of writing than the meal itself. Many people seem to believe that correct spellers are born, not made, as if there is a spelling gene distributed randomly through the population making some destined for spelling greatness and others doomed to devising strategies for hiding the shameful secret of their lack of ability. Others boldly claim that learning to spell is "just natural" and, if left on their own, all would develop the ability to spell.

As literacy educators, we were influenced by views of reading (Goodman 1970; Smith 1978) and writing (Graves 1983) that emphasized meaning making as the focus of literacy and that drew parallels between literacy learning and the understandings of language learning that had emerged during the 1960s and '70s (Brown 1973; Halliday 1973). We had spent a lot of time working with teachers and student teachers to help them develop a "process approach" to writing, but we felt unable to give definitive answers when we were asked questions about how spelling develops, how it relates to reading and writing, how it could be taught, or even what makes a good speller. Increasingly we came to see that spelling was becoming the lightning rod for criticisms of what has been called whole-language teaching.

The impact of this criticism was hard to miss. While attending a parents' night at his children's school, Dennis noticed a display of books written by grade 1 children and published by the school. The first comment he saw written on the response page was, "This is not your best effort. Watch your spelling next time. Love, Mommy and Daddy." Clearly, spelling counts for a great many parents and educators. Often, when discussing writing instruction with principals and teachers, we found that process approaches would be considered only as long as some assurance about spelling could be given. As a result, we began to feel that if we couldn't answer the basic questions about spelling that we knew parents and principals would ask the teachers we were working with, we wouldn't be much help and couldn't expect them to get on with the difficult task of implementing and using sound contemporary approaches to literacy instruction. Indeed, some schools, motivated in part by the concerns of parents, but also by the failure of the research to suggest alternatives, have returned to various programmed approaches to the teaching of spelling. We decided that we needed to confront the issue of spelling within the context of literacy development head on. If spelling was to be the litmus test of what we felt was good instruction, then we had to know more about spelling and literacy development.

We knew that research had begun to address questions about the nature of spelling and spelling instruction. The work of Hanna and his colleagues (Hanna et al. 1966) and Hodges (1981), among others, had caused people to view English orthography as a more logical system than had been previously thought and to consider that learning to spell need not be a matter of drill and rote memorization aimed at mastering individual words. Read (1975) demonstrated that even very young children approach writing with a set of tacit hypotheses about the relationship between the phonology and orthography of English and use their phonetic knowledge and knowledge of letters to "invent" spellings. These insights into the nature of the spelling system and the approaches children make to learning it made the study of spelling more interesting and more a part of the general investigation of how children achieve literacy. Henderson and his colleagues (Henderson and Beers 1980; Henderson and Templeton 1986) went further, showing how children's early invented spellings become more refined and suggesting varying, but related, developmental schema from beginning to correct spelling. Researchers such as Morris (1983), Ehri (1985), and Zuttell and Rasinski (1989) added to our understanding by studying the relationship of reading to spelling and the development of orthographic awareness.

This work was extremely valuable, but it raised other questions and even created some problems as teachers tried to make sense of it in their classrooms. One problem was the apparent dichotomy between "invented" and "correct" spelling. The term "invented spelling" has the advantage of suggesting the purposefulness of the writer's thinking process, but it perhaps too easily implies the continued acceptance by teachers of a greater degree of randomness in spelling than most people can tolerate. (Alternate terms such as "temporary" or "approximate" spelling have been used to allay this fear.) Many teachers of young children began to identify what their children did as "invented" spelling and to assure parents that the children would move to "correct" spelling in later grades. While this approach may have freed children for the (in our view) necessary step of moving into composing, it suggested that invented spelling is a stage of development that passes in time, when in fact inventing is used by anyone, young or old, when attempting to spell unfamiliar words. The idea that children would eventually stop inventing and adopt some other process for spelling was misleading. All spellers invent spellings—that is, develop strategies that allow them to generate words. Correct spellers, in essence, have better informed inventing processes.

Another problem was that what came to be called the "transitional" stage of spelling was used as a catch-all term for much that was unknown about what spellers did as they developed. Descriptions of early developmental stages were characterized by details of what children actually do when they spell words, but those of later stages tended to be based on children's errors—what they did not do in their spelling. It was also very clear that many children never reached the "correct" stage of spelling. Clearly, it wasn't enough just to say that spelling would take care of itself.

Early research necessarily focussed on how spelling is learned rather than on how instruction might facilitate that learning. Nevertheless, it raised issues relating to the role of instruction. It was evident that, when learning to spell, children use the same natural learning processes that they use to learn other aspects of language and literacy. But the fact that they use a natural process should not be interpreted to mean that instruction is unnecessary or even intrusive. The aim in identifying and understanding natural learning processes is to make instruction complementary with these processes—that is, to work with natural learning. It is one thing, for example, to know what children's spelling looks like at various stages; for instruction, it is equally important to know what the key learnings are at particular stages of children's development and, more important, to know which ones will facilitate or inhibit further growth.

In the end, it was some very simple, and possibly naive, questions that prompted us to study spelling. For example, why do some people become good spellers while others don't? It seemed relatively easy for teachers of older children to identify good and poor spellers. We thought it would be interesting if, having made such a determination, we could go back in time and look at how good and poor spellers approached spelling from kindergarten on, seeing how they developed as readers, the kinds of writing they tried, what formal and informal instruction they received, and what they had to say about spelling through the years. What did good spellers know about spelling that poor spellers didn't? How did they learn that? Were poor spellers just underdeveloped, or had they taken a different path from good spellers somewhere along the way? When were differences apparent so that potentially poor spellers could be identified early and helped? We also wanted to know how spelling related to other aspects of literacy. Does reading help spelling? If so, how? Where does writing fit in? Does poor spelling inhibit writing? Does success in writing help develop an awareness of audience that encourages a concern for improved spelling? How do children approach spelling in their own writing as opposed to when teachers involve them in specific spelling tasks? We wound up with three research questions:

1. What is the nature of spelling development over time, and are there differences and similarities in the development of good and poor spellers?

2. What is the relationship between spelling development and reading and writing development?

3. How can instruction, including literacy instruction, contribute to children's learning to spell?

The questions we asked committed us to some very specific constraints. The first was that our study would have to be longitudinal. If we were going to look back at the history of good spellers and poor spellers, we would have to observe that history and collect evidence of it along the way. Originally we planned to organize the study and collect the first data on children at the end of their kindergarten year and continue the study until they had completed grade 5, because research (Pringle and Freedman 1985) indicated that the overall spelling performance of fifth-grade children did not differ significantly from that of eleventh-grade adolescents. Also, because of our interest in the relation of growth in spelling with overall literacy development, we were committed to the idea of working in a context in which the children had ample opportunities for reading and writing. At a minimum, there should be daily opportunities for personal reading and writing in the classrooms where we worked. This would give us an opportunity to observe and monitor children's literacy development and would also ensure that they had frequent and regular opportunities to interact with print.

The demands of a longitudinal study and the desire that our study reflect our area's population affected our choice of schools. We needed schools with relatively stable populations and, because we would eventually be involved with every classroom in the school, we also needed schoolwide acceptance of the study, including significant administrative support. Also, given the fact that our community is one that prides itself on its cultural and ethnic diversity, if our study was to have any credibility with teachers in our area we had to make sure that such diversity was reflected in our study. It was hard to find one school that reflected this diversity. In addition, the demand for stability seemed to favour our working in a school that served a well settled and possibly less diverse community. We decided to work in two schools that served two quite different communities.

The first school we selected, Hampton Park Elementary School, was located in a large city and served an established neighbourhood of urban professionals, including many in the media and the arts. Relative to the city, the population was ethnically homogeneous, and English was the first language spoken in most homes. Soo, a young Chinese girl, and Hana, whose family was originally Korean, were the only children from Hampton Park in our study for whom English was not their first language, although three of the other girls had East Asian family backgrounds. Hampton Park was sought out by parents from outside the immediate community. It was well supported by parents, and parent volunteers were regularly seen working with the children.

The second school we chose to work with, Fulham Elementary School, was located outside the same city in a suburban community of newer, relatively affordable homes. The parents were mainly nonprofessional; many were involved in small-scale entrepreneurial ventures. Many ethnic groups were represented, and for over half the participants, English was not the only language in the home.

Having just described the two schools, we are reluctant to overgeneralize. Each school had some parents who were professionals and some who were not. Some children in both schools came from homes where a language other than English was used as the first language. In fact, in each school we encountered one child who had no expressive English abilities in kindergarten; Soo and Vang would both smile at us patiently as we gamely tried to elicit from them clues to their understanding of literacy. In both schools, parents were supportive of their children. In both schools we encountered children who were experiencing family breakdown and poverty. The most significant single difference between the parents of each school as a group was the relatively recent immigration of many of the families in Fulham.

Both schools shared many features in their overall programmes. Both put language and literacy development at the centre of their programmes. Beginning in kindergarten, both schools provided frequent opportunities for the children to engage in literacy activities. Regular visits to the school libraries were an important part of all classroom programmes. In the primary grades, children in both schools wrote daily for periods of forty to sixty minutes, including conferences with teachers and peers and regular in-class sharing. In some of the higher grades the writing, though still frequent, was more related to ongoing projects or assignments. Each day, teachers read to the class and provided time for personal reading. Trade books or basal readers were used for individual or small-group reading instruction. No series-based spelling programme was used in the primary grades in either school. Spelling was approached as a part of reading and writing instruction and through specific spelling activities, including in some classes word lists and tests. But as the children in both schools moved through grades 4, 5, and 6, the teachers included a specific spelling programme in the classrooms, in some cases using a commercial spelling text. Teachers who did not use such a text tended to follow a pattern of conducting a regular weekly spelling test and including the kinds of activities that are common in such "spellers." In Hampton Park, the children were placed with one teacher for two years, and in one case for three years, although changes in personnel and student movement sometimes resulted in individual children's deviating from this pattern.

Inevitably, as the children proceeded through the grades, they were placed in a wide variety of classrooms. Working as we did in two settings, we found that in any given year we were involved in from eight to twelve classrooms. Although there were some similarities among programmes in these classrooms, there was considerable variation from class to class. Some teachers identified themselves as being very traditional, while others identified strongly with whole-language approaches. Even within such labels, reading and writing were approached differently. In some classes students kept spelling books and studied lists provided by the teacher. Sometimes teachers presented lists relating to themes being studied. Some teachers closely proofread their students' work and required "good copies" to keep in files; others were content with draft copy. From our point of view, what was interesting about this was that in the end it was impossible to isolate any specific spelling, composing, or reading behaviour with any particular instruction. Children who had shared almost the same instructional experiences were as different from each other as if they had been in different classrooms. Even when children had shared the first three years of elementary school with one teacher we couldn't pick out any common characteristic. It seems to us that the sense that children make of any instruction is much more important than the specific instruction given.

We planned to work with two groups of twenty-four children each. We chose the children at random, but checked our list with teachers at each school to get their sense that the selected group was representative of the range of abilities and backgrounds of the children in the school. At the beginning of grade 1 in Hampton Park we had twenty-four children, but four left the school that year so we added four new children at the beginning of second grade. In Fulham School we had twenty-four children at the end of kindergarten, but two left the school over the summer. We added five to the study at the beginning of grade 1, but three more left the school during that year. Ultimately we followed twenty-eight children at Hampton Park, of whom eighteen were in the study for a minimum of five grades, and ended the study with sixteen children. We followed twenty-nine children from Fulham, of whom nineteen were present at the end of the study. At Fulham we had to follow a small group who moved to Black Ravine School, a school with a similar approach to literacy that opened in their neighbourhood.

These children presented a wide range of ability. Each school had children who became successful spellers early and easily. You have already met Lorna, a Hampton Park pupil, who was reading and writing at the beginning of grade 1. We also got to know Chan, a student at Fulham, who eventually won the spelling championship in her school district. Lorna and Chan, along with Hana, another child at Hampton Park, were all into what Gentry (1982) has called the transitional stage of spelling by the time they entered grade 1; that is, they included features in their spellings that could not be explained by sound alone. In fact, except for the word *doctor*, Lorna was able to spell correctly all the words we dictated to her in kindergarten and was spelling correctly such words as *family*, *machine*, *picture*, *pushing*, *honey*, *candy*, and *barber* in her unedited kindergarten stories. During kindergarten, seven children in Hampton Park and twelve in Fulham were presound spellers, and the rest of the children in both schools were at various stages of using sound in their spelling. By the end of the study, we had followed many children who were given special assistance inside and outside their classrooms and two who were held back a year. We saw children who loved to read and write and others who hated it, some who cared about correct spelling and others who seemed either indifferent or defeated by it.

Three times a year, we collected the children's attempts at the spelling list we had developed and interviewed them about how they approached those words. The words were selected to help us monitor the children's understandings of particular spelling features over time. (In Chapter 9, we explain how such a list might be constructed and used in a classroom.) We also conducted informal reading assessments with each child until we felt they had become mature, independent readers. We tried to observe them during in-class writing time a few times each year and to collect copies of their writing throughout their school experience. We also interviewed them near the end of the study about their approaches to writing. In addition, we interviewed their teachers each year to gain insight into the teachers' literacy programmes and to learn the teachers' perceptions of the children as readers, writers, and spellers. We also gave parents opportunities to meet with us to discuss their child's background and progress through school and to share our observations.

We set up our study so that we would begin in Hampton Park in June 1987; two years later, in February 1989, we would begin to study the children in Fulham. This plan was deliberate, as we wanted to use what we were learning in one setting to help us clarify and refine our approaches at the second site. This approach led to a few significant changes in what we did in the two schools. Originally we began our study at the end of kindergarten. However, we felt we missed a few key early learnings in this way, so when we began working in Fulham we started in the middle of the kindergarten year. We had originally intended to work with the children through grade 5, but as we approached the end of grade 5 at Hampton Park it was clear that there was still much significant learning going on, so we extended the study in both schools to the end of grade 6. Originally we felt that classroom observation and analysis of written work would be the most important aspects of data collection, but early in our work at Hampton Park, as we listened to what the children were telling us, we learned the importance for our study of the individual spelling dictations and interviews. In our interviews at Hampton Park we began to get conflicting answers on the role of meaning in generating spelling. We wished we had been more systematic earlier in collecting information about the children's understanding of how meaning relates to spelling, though we were able to make the necessary changes in our word lists and interviews at Fulham.

A longitudinal study has its risks and drawbacks. For one thing, we did lose children, sometimes at points where we sorely wished we could continue to follow them to see how a particular situation worked out. Inevitably, in such a long-term study our own professional lives also had an impact on the attention we could give the study. Both of us were pressed into administrative duties during the course of the study and had to weigh competing commitments. The funding for a longitudinal study is also difficult to arrange evenly, and while we did receive excellent support for the study at times, there were other times when we scrambled for both resources and time, and relied on the kindness of friends to keep the study going. In addition, research assistants come and go, bringing different skills and understandings to the project. Also, like a do-it-yourself project, where you see how much you've learned by the time you finish, we can see how we asked better questions and were more observant as we progressed through the study. Ironically, the more we learned, the more we discovered questions that needed to be addressed. As a result, in spite of all the data we have—all the writing, reading analyzes, observations, spelling lists, taped interviews—we can still say, "If only we'd got that!" or "Why didn't we ask about that?" Still, we believe that as a result of our study we can answer key questions about the teaching and learning of spelling, and we think you will see throughout the book the advantages gained by working in depth with a group of children over time.

Early Spellings:
"Just Sound It Out"

In February of first grade, when asked how he knew how to spell words, Saul told us, "Sound it out...like, you think about what sound each [letter] makes and then you sound it out, and then you're an expert at spelling that word."

Saul's bold description of how he became an expert was typical of the children's confidence in sound as the route to spelling as they moved into literacy. From observing and talking with the children in our eight-year study we were able to observe and understand distinct trends in the process of learning to spell. At the same time, within these general trends, individual children develop differently. These differences may be in the rate of learning, in the significance of different aspects of the spelling system for different individuals, in the control children may feel over the process, in their confidence in spelling as a system, and in their ability to apply instruction in spelling and literacy to their own spelling. It is important that we, as teachers, have a sense of developmental trends and the factors that influence children as they learn to spell. It is equally important that teachers understand how to apply this knowledge to the individual children they work with.

As we pointed out in the last chapter, before we began our study in 1987, children's early understandings of spelling had been well documented, and there had been a change in how spelling was thought of, from mainly a rote-learning activity to a complex developmental process closely related to language and literacy learning. This earlier work generated useful descriptions of spelling development; when we began to study spelling, we found Gentry's (1982) and Henderson's (1985) classification systems helpful starting points for talking about growth in spelling. In saying this, we caution again against seeing stages as a required route for growth, or as providing an all-inclusive vehicle for understanding what children are doing or what they will be doing next.

One problem with considering stages of development is that each stage focusses on particular dominant strategies, such as children's use of sound in early spellings. Such a focus may lead us to forget that what children actually do is much more complex than applying a particular strategy to every word in every situation. When most of her spellings were still representing only two sounds (VU, *view*; KS, *kiss*; BS, *buzz*; SN, *nice*), Dhara's list of words she felt she knew how to write included correctly spelled versions of *orange, green, yellow, blue, talk, two, three, book,* and *house*. Starr correctly spelled *kiss* when the rest of her spellings represented only one or two sounds in such spellings as O for *yellow*, RG for *rag*, DA for *doctor*, and GM for *game*. In kindergarten, almost all the children, even those who were barely using print, were able to spell their own names correctly. In addition most knew *mom*, and many knew such common words as *stop, yes,* and *no*. Children included correct features in otherwise "sounded out" words, which suggested a use of rules and generalizations about how words are spelled that go beyond only understandings of sound, as was evident in Parviz's *tion* in ETRACKTION for *attraction* and COMPATION for *competition* and Catrina's *ure* in FEACHURE and NACHURE in grade 3.

At the same time it was common to see the children use strategies associated with earlier development as they struggled with unfamiliar vocabulary or a challenging new feature in a word. For example, several children returned to letter-name spellings of *chirp* or *learn* when they were trying to understand the past tense marker *ed* and produced CHRPED and LRNED. Parviz, by the end of grade 3, had abandoned *tion* and now wrote ATACSHON, COMPETISHON, and NASHON.

Another concern with early descriptions of spelling development is that they are predicated on a sound-based approach to spelling by all children. This conforms to the observed approach of most children, but there were children in our study for whom sight, more than sound, was a more powerful and useful entry into spelling. There is also a whole group of children who are hearing impaired, for whom sound is not the route to understanding spelling.

Given these reservations, we do see some common patterns and trends and, more important, some basic understandings about literacy and spelling that are part of children's development as spellers. In very simple terms, these patterns suggest that most children's development proceeds from a time when sound is not part of their writing system, to a period in which sound is the most dominant feature, to a realization that while sound is important, there are several logics that influence how words are spelled and the look of words is a useful means of monitoring the relationships among these logics. In this chapter and the next two, we describe the nature of that spelling journey, beginning in this chapter with children's development from pre-sound logic to one based on letter-sound matching.

Pre-Sound Logic

During kindergarten, several children (seven in Hampton Park and twelve in Fulham) used a pre-sound logic when they generated spellings. When they represented the words we dictated to them, and when they added print to their story drawings, their spellings bore no relationship to the sound or look of the words they were spelling. In all but their "known" words, and those they copied, they represented words by strings of letters or letterlike shapes, with sometimes a numeral or other symbol thrown in for good measure. Even at this stage, most children were confident that they could write the words we dictated to them. Only a very few, mostly children for whom English was not the language of the home, declined to write something. Indeed, some words they actually did know how to spell and others they believed they knew. For example, Monali said, "I know how to write *forest*" (and proceeded to write YRIZOEBeYU) "and *love*" (LOZIOF). Even children who used a relatively limited set of letters to represent their spellings consistently used a different letter order for each different word.

Word	Joe	Nash	Monali	Zeena
Rag	EID	GnIRS	ICLV	RNCRO
Nice	LTOJE	SIRN	2zro	tCt
Game	Joe	Nsi	B-P	OyrCiCW
Yellow	JOET	ISTR	ns	(No attempt)
Lid	ETEQ	CRN	V	SprCO

Although there appeared to be no obvious relationship between most of their marks and either the look or the sound of the conventional spellings, the children did understand that print carried a message that could be comprehended by somebody else. This central notion of writing as a means for conveying meaning seems to be established very early. Allan demonstrated this when he said, "I'll write you a story," quickly produced two pages of cursive-writing-like lines, and, with the words "I'm done," handed the pages over, confident that his story could be read.

Similarly, in November of grade 1, Joe was writing a story that consisted mainly of drawings accompanied by simple messages using words that he copied from around the room, including a list of children's names. At one point he asked Margaret a question about one of his spellings.

JOE: What does this word say?
MARGARET: It says "Eric." Is that what you wanted it to say?
JOE: Yes.

Each day during kindergarten, the children were being read to regularly and had opportunities to "read" books themselves and to write their stories. They were able to tell the stories of the books they were looking at by using their memories of previous readings, the pictures, and their understanding of story forms as the basis for their tellings. In their writing, many children used pictures to tell stories. Others attempted to put their stories into words, either by inventing the spellings, by copying sentences that they had dictated to their teacher, or by copying words from books they found in the classroom. Even the pre-sound spellers had a good knowledge of the layout of books, and almost all knew the directional orientation of print on a page. All had a concept of letter (Clay 1979): they could point out a letter on a page in a story; they knew most letters, especially in their uppercase form, by name; and they could even provide many letter sounds. For example, at the beginning of grade 1, Joe, whose spellings were all pre-sound, knew twenty-two uppercase and seventeen lowercase letters by name and sixteen letters by sound. Many children, even at this early stage of spelling development, appeared to be making rudimentary attempts at phonemic segmentation, which suggested that they were beginning to understand that print was related in some fashion to the way language sounds. The following dialogue with Joe illustrates this development:

MARGARET: How will you write *kiss*?
JOE: Ka—ka—ka—
MARGARET: What *is* that letter?
JOE [*muttering*]: Ka [*writes* Y].
MARGARET: What's that letter after *ka*? Kiss [*stressing the "ss"*].
JOE: It must be a *b*. [*Joe writes* B, *then adds to his Y to form a figure:*]

Beginning to Represent Sound

The children made a major leap forward when they began to use their writing to represent sound, using whatever they knew about letter names and sounds. Most of the children had discovered the connection between letters and sounds before our study began, in their kindergarten year, or they made it during the course of their kindergarten year. In fact, by early in grade 1, only four children, one in Hampton Park and three in Fulham, were still pre-sound spellers.

Typically, when we asked the children who were beginning to use sound how they did their spellings, they would say, "I sounded it out." For example, Jeff had just completed a set of one- and two-letter spellings: R for *rag*, B for *buzz*, LO for *lid*, KS for *kiss*, NS for *nice*, and CS for *six*.

MARGARET: Tell me, how do you do those? How do you decide what to write down?

JEFF: I sound it out. Sometimes there are two letters; and there's more to *rag* [*he had written* R], but I forget what it is.

When children made the move toward sound, they usually began by representing an initial or final consonant sound (though sometimes they would represent a dominant vowel sound, such as O for *yellow*), and would then move on to represent two or more phonemes. Zane, for example, in June of his kindergarten year, was often able to identify a consonant that represented either the initial or final sound of the word; then, demonstrating another generalization about how words work, he would add a vowel, usually an A, and a final consonant that was unrelated to the sound of the word. This strategy produced VAC for *view*, BAG for *buzz*, and LAN for *yellow*. By November of grade 1, he was consistently representing two phonemes, usually the first and last sounds in each word, producing BZ for *buzz*, NS for *nice*, LD for *lid*, and CS for *kiss*.

For us, the important feature of this shift in thinking is not the degree of accuracy the children manage to attain in representing sound, but their realization that there is an underlying system to these marks on the paper and their attempt to search for that system through the use of sound. Sometimes children were able to recognize a sound and attach it to the correct letter, but weren't sure how to print that letter. Joe, for example, when spelling *buzz* early in grade 1, said, "Buzz—Buzz, I can't do very good *z*'s. I can't do *z*'s very good," and wrote]]]].

These early sound spellings demonstrate that the children had at least some basic understanding not only of the names of letters, but also of their sounds. In fact, the amount of letter-sound knowledge most children had was remarkable even in kindergarten, when direct instruction on letter-sound correspondences had barely begun. Zane's knowledge was typical of spellers who were beginning to use sound. By early in grade 1 he knew all the uppercase letters by name and twenty-one by sound, and made only four common mistakes in lowercase letters: presented with letters out of context, he mistook *q* for *p*, *t* for *j*, *d* for *b*, and *g* for *e*.

Interestingly, although letter-sound knowledge appeared to be essential for children's representing sound in writing, it was not the sole key.

Several children moved to a use of sound in spelling when they had less knowledge of letter names and sounds than children who were still pre-sound spellers. David, for example, began to use sound in his spelling early in grade 1 when he knew only sixteen uppercase names, nine low-ercase names, and twelve sounds; whereas Joe, who knew more letters and sounds than David, remained a pre-sound speller. It seems more important that children be confident of their ability to harness letter-sound knowledge in their spelling. It also seems important that children be will-ing to risk using the letter knowledge they have to get messages into print. We noticed a marked difference between the children in the two schools in this respect. In Hampton Park only Soo, who spoke very little English, was unwilling during kindergarten to attempt to spell dictated words, while in Fulham, six children attempted fewer than three words. They all had sufficient letter knowledge to make attempts, but chose not to.

The move to using sound to generate spellings appeared in tandem with the children's beginning to develop a concept of word in print (Clay 1979). The children who showed signs in kindergarten that they were on the verge of moving from pre-sound to early sound spellings (that is, were representing one or two sounds in each spelling), and in fact made the move by early in grade 1, were increasingly able to generate words begin-ning with a particular sound, were beginning to isolate a word on a page of text, were able to identify the beginning and end of a word, and were even able to find a matching word.

Clearly, children's developing concept of word evolved from their ongoing interaction with text. They began to see that writing is not a ran-dom set of marks on a page, but that there is a system, and that it is a sys-tem they can control. This understanding made them willing to try to use their knowledge of letters to communicate, still through simple story-labels that accompanied their pictures. As can be seen in Figures 3.1 and 3.2, at this time the children did not consistently use spaces to differenti-ate their words. Perhaps this reflected an emerging, but not yet stable, concept of word.

The fact that the children's concept of word was at this point emerg-ing rather than stable may explain another phenomenon we observed. We frequently heard children at this stage vocalizing or subvocalizing all the sounds in a word as they worked on a given spelling, and we were at first surprised to find that only one or two of these sounds were ultimately rep-resented on the page. Mitch, for example, sounded out *nice* "nn-ice-I-ss," but only wrote S. In the same way he sounded out each phoneme in *rag*, *six*, *kiss*, *yellow*, *view*, and *game*, but wrote just R, S, K, EO, U, and M to represent these words. Without a stable concept of print it is difficult for children to deal with the complex demands of remembering what word they are spelling while phonemically segmenting it, linking each sound to the appropriate letter, remembering what each letter looks like, and per-forming the mechanical task of producing it on paper. Trevor provides an

Figure 3.1 Paul, Grade 1: *"An alien was dancing on the moon"*

example of this challenge as he attempts to spell *buzz* in November of grade 1.

MARGARET: What about *buzz*? *Buzz*. What do you think *buzz* starts with?
TREVOR: Ba, ba...*B*.
MARGARET: Good.
TREVOR: I don't know what a *b* looks like.
MARGARET: What do you *think* it looks like?

Figure 3.2 Vikram, Grade 1: *"Yesterday I went to the aquarium"*

TREVOR: [*Looks on the table at something printed.*] Is there a *b* on there? Yes, *there's a B.* [*Writes* P.]

MARGARET: Now can you hear any other sound in *buzz*?

TREVOR: Doesn't it look as if it's snowing out?

MARGARET: Yes, it does. What about *buzz*? Can you hear anything else at the *end* of *buzz*?

TREVOR: [*Shakes his head no.*]

Even though Trevor claimed not to hear another sound, he did indicate during the same interview that he knows that "*zebra* starts with *z.*" Even a year later, when Trevor was able to represent successfully two sounds in most spellings (for example, BZZ, GM, and NS), he would frequently get lost in the middle of his spellings and ask, "What was that word again?"

Matching Letters to Sounds

Typically, children who are involved in a range of early literacy activities quickly move beyond representing one or two sounds in a word to representing increasingly more of the sounds in words in the correct order—in other words, moving to what has been called *phonemic spelling* (Gentry 1982). By the spring of grade 1, almost all the children in our study had reached this stage; in retrospect, we see that the small group of children who had not moved by then became poor spellers who consistently and increasingly lagged behind their classmates.

In the early stages of letter-sound matching, children would frequently represent all the sounds in one-syllable words while capturing maybe only four sounds in two-syllable words. We also noticed many instances of substitutions for the correct forms of both vowels and consonants—for example, SECS for *six*, ULO for *yellow*, CES for *kiss*, DADR for *doctor*, and NAS for *nice*. Zeena, for example, had written DOTR for *doctor*, yet in her explanation to our research assistant, John, we can tell that she is aware of all the sounds in the word.

JOHN: You look in the dictionary?
ZEENA: Or I try to sound out the word.
JOHN: Sound it out.
ZEENA: That's what I did with these.
JOHN: How do you sound words out? How do you do that?
ZEENA: You know the letter. It's like you try and make the sound.
JOHN: Oh. Let's do one together. Let's say the word is *doctor*. O.K.? How do you sound out *doctor*?
ZEENA. Duh-ha-kuh-ta-er.
JOHN: O.K., once we've done that, what do we do with the sound? What can we do with that?
ZEENA: Try and make it, if it's the right kind of word.
JOHN: Like what?
ZEENA: *Doctor*. The sound "duh," "duh" says *d*. "Ock," I think it's an *o*.
JOHN: I see, and that's how you did it.

The children tended to use their knowledge of letter names and sometimes made analogies to sounds from other words they knew. For example, we noticed that many children substituted a *c*, probably from an already known word like *cat*, when the letter name would have suggested *k* (see, for example, the spellings of *six* and *kiss* above). Increasingly, though, children would account for all the sounds in both one- and two-syllable words in their spellings, still frequently by common letter-name substitutions, but increasingly by the correct forms, as in SIKS, YELO, KIS, DOKTR, and NIS.

Growth at this stage seemed to depend on children reaching what Morris (1983) calls a *functional concept of word,* indicated in our study by children's ability to point accurately to words as they read previously memorized text (in other words, a stable voice-print match). None of the children moved to consistent letter-sound matching before demonstrating this degree of understanding of word. It would seem that children with a functional concept of word are able to "hold on" to parts of a word as they generate it—that is, they can identify an opening sound and keep it in mind as they move to identify the next sound, then hold onto that and move on to identify succeeding sounds. It was necessary to assist some children with this process, as in the following conversation between Joe and Margaret.

JOE: *Game.* G. I know that, sort of, because...[*writes* A]...Ga-AAA-aim. Four words [*meaning letters*] in it. [*Appears to be stuck.*]
MARGARET: *Game* [*emphasizing the "m" sound*]. What's that?
JOE: M. Ga-A-M-aim.
MARGARET: Have you finished with *game?* [*Now* GAM.]
JOE: No, one more. [*Meaning one more letter, but he couldn't figure out which.*]

John, our research assistant, asked Parviz whether there were any of his spellings he wasn't quite sure about, and Parviz, who had written RAC for *rag,* BAZ for *buzz,* and LAD for *lid,* replied:

PARVIZ: There's only one word. [*Indicates* XE *for "six."*]
JOHN: How would you change it?
PARVIZ: I'd sound it out *good.*
JOHN: Well, don't erase it, sound it over here.
PARVIZ: Sik, ka, *K.* Ss, ss, ka, six, si-ka-six. [*Writes* XKC.]

It is evident from this example why the ability to work with the complete word is vital as children develop. Parviz's solution is unconventional, but he demonstrates his ability to pay attention to all the sounds in the word and recognizes that he should account for them in his spelling.

Although the children were focussing on sound, they demonstrated a steady growth in their mastery of conventional spellings, especially of the most commonly written words and words memorable for some reason to a particular child. Carol Chomsky (1972) demonstrated that children can write before they learn to read. We certainly saw evidence of that. In fact, we were surprised to find that children who were not yet independent readers could create text that, at least to a reader familiar with children's invented spellings, was readable. Kareem's piece about a brontosaurus (Figure 3.3) is a good demonstration of this. When Kareem wrote this piece in the spring of grade 1, he was still far from being an independent

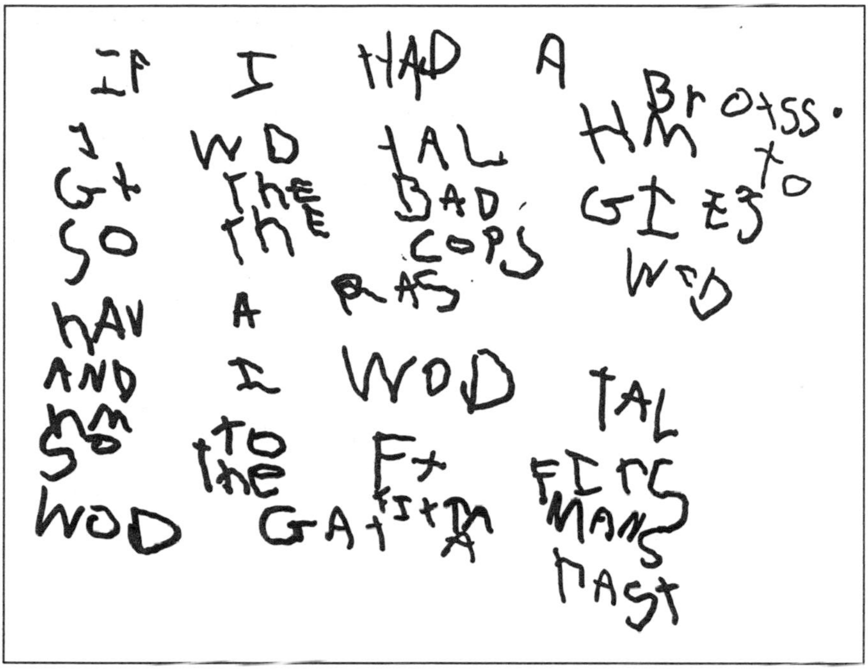

Figure 3.3 Kareem, Grade 1

reader, but he was a solid sound speller. His story demonstrates a range of two-sound and multisound spellings, as well as correct spellings. (For those out of practice reading young children's writing, Kareem wrote, "If I had a brontosaurus I would tell him to get the bad guys so the cops would have a rest. And I would tell him to fix fires so the firemen would get a rest.")

With exposure to print through writing and learning to read, children gained control over word spacing, moving from recognizing words in text to *producing* them with separate spaces in continuous text. As children gained control over the various activities involved in writing stories, we noticed that the overall quality of their spelling in stories tended to lag behind the quality of their spelling of dictated words. Perhaps when responding to dictated words, the children were able to focus entirely on their knowledge of spelling, but in composing their attention was necessarily more diffused. At this stage, at any rate, we believe that we got the most insight into how far the children's knowledge of spelling had advanced from their responses to dictated words. But their writing showed us their ability to *use* their knowledge of spelling to generate text.

An important factor that governs growth in spelling ability at this point is the development of fluent, independent reading. Clearly, ongoing experiences in learning to read contribute to children's ability to represent sound accurately. After all, it is impossible for teachers to demonstrate the range of ways to represent sound that children encounter as they read and write, or to make them aware of all the options used in conventional spelling. Exposure to print provides much of this information. In fact, our observations suggest that, without the experience with print gained by being active, independent readers, children do not progress beyond the ability to represent sound in a readable, but unconventional, way. Reading introduces children to those features in the system that are not directly related to sound. It opens the way for them to begin to incorporate these features into their own spelling and to become conventional spellers.

"If It's Not Sound..."

Early in grade 1, when talking about how she spelled words, Alice told us, "I sound them out unless I know the word [e.g., the]...Whenever I do a story, I just do what I think, [but] sometimes they aren't exactly right [because] words can have very tricky sounds...When I'm stuck on something...I ask a grade 2.

By February of grade 2, Alice was telling us, "It just doesn't look right. I can look at words and I know if they don't look right."

By May of the same year she was saying, "I know most of the words, but if I get stuck on one there are these little scraps of paper on our table and I just write on them on the back of a rough copy or something." Alice went on to demonstrate how she tested alternative hypotheses in her correct spelling of nature. *"I went n-a-t, and then I thought at first it could be s-h-u-r, nature, but then I decided that I can use a couple of words, because I can just see that word in my head and it didn't look right, so that I was flipping through a couple of words [i.e., alternatives]. Does this look right? No. Does this look right? No."*

The next major development in spelling, captured clearly in Alice's explanations, occurred when the children moved from perceiving spelling as based solely on sound to recognizing that there are features in the spelling of words that cannot be explained entirely by sound. In time they came to understand that, while sound is important, it is only one of several interacting logics that form the basis of written English. This development requires a definite shift in the way children think about how written language works—a shift we found to be essential to their eventual success as spellers. To continue to develop, children must recognize and learn to control sound within a variety of other features of language.

Moving Beyond the Logic of Sound

This point in children's development has been referred to as the *transitional stage* (see, for example, Gentry 1982) because it marks a transition from letter-sound matching to correct spelling. Although the term "transitional" is convenient, it is somewhat misleading, because this period of development is more complex and long-lasting than the term "transitional" might suggest. It took almost all the children in our study a long time to move from their first tacit use of nonsound features to a state where they might be described as correct spellers. We would characterize this period as a time when children work consciously to understand, master, and integrate the various logics that together constitute English: sound, look, and syntactic and semantic meaning. We cannot overemphasize the importance of this change in thinking about spelling to the long-term development of spelling ability. As you will see, children in our study who hung onto sound as the overriding logic for their spelling cut themselves off from other knowledge that would help them to develop. In a sense, prior to this point, when the children were spelling by matching sounds to letters, the problem of creating spellings was relatively simple and free from conflict. Although there clearly was a logic underlying the children's spellings, it was one-dimensional: if the word you are spelling isn't one you already know how to spell, you just "sound it out." In addition, expectations, both internal and external, to produce correct spellings were usually quite low during kindergarten and first grade. But as soon as children became aware that their "sounding-out" strategies did not necessarily produce correct spellings (a realization that was inevitable when they became readers and experienced on a daily basis what words actually look like), spelling became more complex and more prone to conflict. Children then had to deal with the overlapping and often conflicting logics of English spelling; and, at the same time, they experienced greater pressure, possibly from within themselves and certainly from others at school and home, for their spellings to be correct.

In spite of its obvious importance, this stage in spelling development has been less fully described then has earlier development. We think there's a very good reason for that. Although there are individual differences in children's earlier development, there are many similarities, which makes it relatively easy to generalize across children and to chart development. In fact, as you can see from earlier examples, many words were misspelled in exactly the same way by a great number of the children. This was less likely to be the case when the children began to negotiate the multidimensional complexities of English spelling. At this point there is much more potential for diversity—which we saw demonstrated again and again in individual spelling profiles. How children actually made sense of the system was personal in that it depended, among other things, on the constructions about spelling each child formed from experiences with reading, writing, and instruction, both in school and home. In many instances children who appeared to have similar instructional experiences understood and applied that instruction quite differently. There were also children who were early, fluent readers and who continued to read frequently (like Elly, who loved to read above all else) and yet had very different spelling profiles from each other. We did not find that specific spelling features, whether sound, look, or meaning-based, occurred at the same time or even in the same order in the children's spellings.

Nevertheless, we did observe some broad patterns, particularly in how children problem-solved as they made sense of specific logics within the system and in what they told us about their understandings. Our description of some of these patterns is necessarily based on what we learned from the more proficient spellers we observed, because while all the children in the study moved away from solely letter-sound matching, albeit on different time lines, many children had not emerged as correct spellers when we completed our observations at the end of grade 6. Therefore, we cannot suggest that all children would fit conveniently into these patterns of development, and we must emphasize that the children who did reach correct spelling did so in different ways.

Looking back at what was happening around this time in children's spelling development, we noticed that there were precursors of change. Before any actual change in thinking happened, there was usually a period when a few instances of new features appeared in the children's spellings, such as a double s in KESS, or a double l in HLL. These features, however, were not generalized across words or used in any consistent way. We found when we talked with the children that the governing principle that they were using to generate and justify their spellings was still sound. When pressed about how they generated a spelling, children would typically respond that they "sounded it out"; when confronted about this, they would invent all sorts of rationales to demonstrate that they still used sound alone.

At the beginning of grade 2, for example, when Monali was still spelling by letter-sound matching (for example, GAM, DATR, CAP for *camp*), she spelled *view* as VUAW. Margaret asked her how she had spelled her words.

MONALI: Well, like, sounding them out.
MARGARET: When you sounded out *view*, I wondered how you knew there was [*Monali began whispering "view" repeatedly*] that *w* on the end?

MONALI: Because "wa"—the "wa" sound makes *w*, and so does a *y*.
MARGARET: Oh, so show me how you did that one.
MONALI: Va-ya-oo.
MARGARET: And where's the *w*?
MONALI [*whispering*]: Wa...[*pause*].
MARGARET: Well, there *is* a *w* on the end, but I didn't know how you *knew* that.
MONALI: Because there's more than two or three words [letters], there's more than two in every word...There's more than what you *think* it is.
MARGARET: Well, how do you decide—
MONALI [*interrupting*]: Well, just the *sounding*, 'cause I know, like, what the words *sound* like.

Similarly, though most of his spellings were typical letter-sound matchings using letter names (FIV, GAM, KIS, TAC, ELO), Parviz also wrote BUZZZZ, DOCKTR, and CKWIC, and gave John the following explanation.

JOHN: When you spelled *doctor*, how did you know there was a *c* and a *k*?
PARVIZ: Because it sounded like a *c* and a *k*.
JOHN: Say the word for me so I can see how you get them.
PARVIZ: Do*ck*-ter.
JOHN: Now, when you started *buzz*, you put down *b-u-z-z* and then you said, "Oh no, no, no, there are two more *z*'s." How did you know there were four *z*'s in *buzz*?
PARVIZ: I just said, "It doesn't go 'bizz,' it doesn't go 'buzz,' it goes 'buzzzz.'"

The end of the children's use of sound as the overwhelming determinant of spelling was usually indicated first by their use of increasingly correct consonant and short vowel forms and a marked increase in such features as consonant doubling (*ck* where only a *c* or a *k* had been used before) and the use of the silent *e* to mark long vowel sounds. These features were not just in the children's rapidly growing set of known words, but in their misspellings and overgeneralizations as well. For example, in February of grade 2, when many children were making this move, Paul's dictated spellings included GAME, NIS, FIVE, WIF, HEROE, YELLOE, QUCK, DOCKTR, PICKL. Paul used the silent *e* correctly in *game* and *five*, overgeneralized that feature in *yellow* and *hero*, and did not generalize to *nice* and *wife*. Similarly, he used *ck* correctly in *pickle* and *quick* and overgeneralized in *doctor*.

The children also began to show obvious dissatisfaction with many of the spellings they produced using their old sounding-out strategies, which, in many cases, they had previously regarded as correct. They signalled their ambivalence by frequent references to spellings not "looking right." Paul told us, "I can look at *hero* [HEROE] and I can see that's not right."

Clearly reading is a major source of information about the way words look, so it was no accident that none of the children reached this point until sometime after they had become independent readers.

Just as reading is vital to producing this change in spelling behaviour, so also is writing. Reading alone cannot provide sufficient information to create expert spellers. After all, the purpose of reading is not to pay attention to the spelling of words, but to attend to the meaning of text. Inevitably, though, as they read, children see more words and letter patterns and develop a better understanding of how words work. It appears, however, that if they are to develop as spellers, children require ongoing experience with word generation. For most of the successful spellers in our study, this experience came through their involvement as committed writers. A writer cannot avoid spelling. Writing requires one to make choices about which letters to put down when constructing words. It is this need to make choices, we believe, that can make children aware of their own tacit knowledge about spelling and can make the system visible to them, so that they can learn to control it. The children who moved forward at this point were those who were involved in extensive writing for personally relevant reasons. Opportunities to write were important, but so was the commitment. Engagement in what they wanted to say made them concerned about the role of spelling in helping readers to understand them. They were more thoughtful in their choice of words, choosing words that best expressed what they wanted to say, whether or not they already knew how to spell them; but their strong sense of audience made them want to spell correctly.

When faced with conflicting information about spelling gained either from personal experience with print or from direct spelling instruction, most children first tried to accommodate new information in terms of their "old" spelling logic based on letter-sound matching. This was very evident when the children first faced a conflict between the sound and the look of words. Initially, most children tried to resolve the conflict by justifying their spellings by a logic based on sound.

As mentioned earlier, many children held onto their sound-based explanations well beyond the point when such rationales could account for many of their spellings. We believe that what the children were doing was justifying after the fact what they had produced rather than explaining what they had been thinking during actual generation of a spelling. Naturally, in such justifications, they fell back upon what had been to that point their spelling logic: sounding out. For example, Parviz was still giving sound-based explanations in the fall of grade 2, when he had many correct dictated spellings, including the use of *ck* (BACK, TACK, PICKLE, and SHOCK) and the silent *e* (FIVE, GAME, WIFE, LATE, SHOVE), and overgeneralizations of both features in his spellings of *quick* (KUICKE) and *doctor* (DOCKTORE). When pressed, Parviz referred to "knowing" some of the words.

MARGARET: How do you *do* your spelling now?

PARVIZ: I just, like, all I did was I sounded out. *Some* of the words I already knew. [*Parviz indicated some of the spellings he "knew," which didn't include "tack" or "five."*]

MARGARET: I don't understand, if you only sounded these out, how you knew about the *ck* at the end of *tack*.

PARVIZ: Because—you see—tack-ka. [*Then he said he just knew that one.*]

MARGARET: I don't see how you can *hear* an *e* on the end of *five*.

PARVIZ: Yes, you *can*! Five-*va*. E is "a"—five-*va*.

Even when probed about whether he used any other strategies, Parviz showed unwavering confidence in the use of sound, even for spellings he already knew.

MARGARET: Do you do anything else, besides sounding it out? When you're writing your stories, do you *always* just sound out every word?

PARVIZ: When I'm writing my stories? Of *course*! I want it to be *nice*.

MARGARET: Oh, you *always* sound out every one, do you?

PARVIZ: *Yeah*, even if I *know* [them].

At a similar stage, also in grade 2, Najali demonstrated ambivalence about sound and look in the following explanation of why she changed her spelling of PICL to PICKL. (She had spelled *pack* and *tack* correctly.)

NAJALI: Well it sounds like a "ka"...*K* has to get in there.

MARGARET: Oh, I see...How can you tell? Why couldn't it be just a *c* or just a *k*?

NAJALI: I don't know. It didn't sound right to me.

MARGARET: Do you think *quick* [QWIC] has a *k* at the end?

NAJALI: Kooohh-wa-ii. No. It doesn't look—Oh! Yes, yes, yes.

MARGARET: You think it does?

NAJALI: It sounds like it. [*Adds "k": QWICK.*]

For other children the shift in thinking was apparent in both the spellings and their explanations. Saul illustrates this change in thinking about spelling over time. In February of grade 2, his spellings were still mainly sound-based (as in NIS and DICDR) and so were his explanations.

JOHN: How did you know there were two *l*'s in *yellow* [YELLO]?

SAUL: I sounded out how long the *l* is.

JOHN: And how did you know there were two *s*'s in *kiss* [KISS]?

SAUL: 'Cause of how long the "sss" is [*makes a long "s" sound*].

By the following year, when asked about the high number of *e*'s at the end of his dictated spellings (as in NISE, GAME, VUOE, YELLOE, HEROW,

KISE, and SHOCE), Saul demonstrated that his thinking was beginning to change.

SAUL: Otherwise it wouldn't look proper, and all the words need a vowel in them.

MARGARET: Oh, do they? But *kiss* already has a vowel in it. It has an *i* here. Why would it need an *e* at the end?

SAUL: Well...[*Pause. Saul looks troubled.*]

MARGARET: You didn't used to put an *e* at the end of lots of words, and I'm just wondering how you figured it out.

SAUL: I guess because I see other people's writing. [*He goes on to explain how he saw words in books, and...*] all sorts of things.

It wasn't that Saul had stopped referring to sound in explaining his spellings. In fact, he told us that he "sounded out," especially "when it's a word I know, but I can't write with just knowing how." The difference at this point was that his hypotheses about spellings included other considerations, such as "All words need a vowel in them" and the "look" of words remembered from his reading. Saul, like other children at this time in their spelling development, used sound as only one of his sources of information.

Finding a Logic in the Look of Words

For a few of the children, like Joe and Vikram, visual features had always been a major part of their spelling, and all of the children demonstrated their visual memory of words when they produced known correct spellings in their writing and during their conversations with us. Also, all the children showed us that they were at least tacitly aware of visual aspects of words when they occasionally included, among their phonemic spellings, features that could not be explained solely by sound, such as a double *s* in KESS or a double *l* in HLL. But now we observed a marked growth in the children's understanding of the visual logic of spelling, both when they used visual information to generate spellings and when they used their sense of the look of words to check their completed spellings.

When they moved to using visual knowledge consciously to generate their spellings, we heard frequent references to spellings not looking "long enough" or "needing more letters." Joe was one of the first children to mention word length. In the following discussion of his spelling of *view*, he still confuses the terms "word" and "letter," but shows his awareness of word length.

MARGARET: *View.*

JOE: *V?* [*Writes* VEU.] I know there are four words.

MARGARET: How did you know that? You've seen it, have you?

JOE: Uh-huh, yeah, before.

MARGARET: So there's something else, and it's before that *u*, is it?

JOE: Yeah.

MARGARET: What could it be?

JOE: *A*?

MARGARET: Try it. What do you think?

JOE: [*Writes in the "a"*: VEAU.] Um, yes.

Similarly, Saul showed an early awareness of the length of words. He told us he had "sounded out" *view* (VUOE), and when asked why it wouldn't just be *v-u* he replied, "But that wouldn't be long enough." Asked if it should be longer, he explained, "Yeah, it doesn't sound long enough."

For a child like Alice, visual imaging of words became a major strategy once she left behind simple sounding out. Early in grade 3, Margaret noticed that Alice seemed to use visual knowledge and talked to her about it.

MARGARET: I was very interested when you were doing one of those words, you said, "I can look back and see how I think it looks."

ALICE: *Special.*

MARGARET: Yes, and you sort of scrunched up your eyes, and sort of looked out in the distance. What are you doing when you do that?

ALICE: Well, I just, when I'm reading and stuff, like, I can read it but I'll remember what it *looks* like, so sometimes I get it a bit wrong but a lot of the time I get it right.

MARGARET: Yes, and when you look back like that, what do you see? Do you see the word spelled? Do you see the page it was on? Do you see the story? What do you see?

ALICE: No, I sort of—well, I don't exactly *see* it, but when I close my eyes and sort of remember where I've seen it and everything, I can sort of *think* what I think it is and stuff.

A year later Alice is even more explicit about this process.

MARGARET: O.K., so when you have to do a spelling list, do you have any spelling lists to learn?

ALICE: Well, yeah, when we have them, I'll write...we have to write it over and over again, but I'm just—I can just, by looking at it a lot, for a while, just seeing it every day, when I look up or something...

MARGARET: You can get it, you can remember it?

ALICE: I can just remember it. It's sort of—the page sticks there.

MARGARET: Well, how did you realize—Do you, do you picture the word up there, or what do you do?

ALICE: Yeah, yeah, I can picture it. I can see it.

MARGARET: I see. But do you think about the situation in which you saw it? Is that what you do? You sort of think back to sitting at your desk and looking at it, or what?

ALICE: Yeah.

MARGARET: Is that what happens?

ALICE: And I can also, when, since I read a lot and usually like *happily* or *watching* or *knocked* or *everybody* or *exciting* or, like, *excellent*...a lot of times shows up in a book.

MARGARET: Yes.

ALICE: Things like that.

MARGARET: Um-hmm.

ALICE: And so, just, I read over and over again in different books and in the same book and everything. And then, when I write it down, like, if I write it down, I would look at it and remember if it's the same spelling I saw in a book I read.

The children showed a growing awareness of letter order possibilities. Asked why she was considering putting a *c* into her spelling EXELL, Lorna answered, "There might be a *c* in there." When asked why, she said, "Well, because there are other words." Later in the conversation, she added, "There's another word and I always spelled it *e-x*, and there was a *c* in there, and I kept missing it." Often the children would know that a particular letter belonged somewhere within a word, even though they weren't sure exactly where. As Najali considered how to put an *a* into her YER (for *year*), at first she thought the *a* would follow the *y*, but rejected that, saying, "I mean—nothing goes between those two," and wrote the word correctly. We also saw more examples of letter transpositions, in which a spelling had all the correct letters but in the wrong order. A few children, like Dhara, made some letter transpositions even when her spelling was mostly letter-sound matching (for example, SXI and FVIE in kindergarten and LAET in grade 1), but we noticed that more children had such spellings soon after they left that stage. For example, several children wrote SING for *sign*, ONEC for *once*, and YAER for *year* just before they spelled these words correctly.

The first conflicts for all children came when their reading and other experience with print caused dissonance because, while all the sounds were accounted for, the spelling didn't *look* right. Initially, most children tended to refer to the look of a word in a global way. Paul told us, "It doesn't look right," but in the following conversation he, like others, proved unable to indicate the problem areas within the word.

PAUL: I'm not sure of the *yellow* [YELLO].

MARGARET: What part of that aren't you sure about?

PAUL: The whole thing.

MARGARET: Oh, because most of that's right.

PAUL: I know *y-e-l-l*, but I'm not sure *o* is right.
MARGARET: *Yellow*. What else could it be?
PAUL: I don't know.

In order to make progress, children needed to become able to pinpoint where exactly a word didn't "look right" and to generate a workable alternative. Sometimes, as with Alice, the test for correctness was comparison with a visual memory of the word if it had been seen before, but sometimes an alternative was tested against the child's knowledge of letter order. Lorna, for example, dismissed her attempt to put a *c* between the *e* and *x*, saying, "Well, there aren't many words that begin *e-c-x*."

As Hana showed us, if the first alternative didn't work out, another and another might be tried. She would keep comparing alternative spellings until she was satisfied that she had the correct one, or at least had come as close as she was able at that point. In one instance, trying to spell *geese*, Hana had generated three spellings: GESE, GEISE, and GIESE. During the following conversation she went on to try GUESE and GEESE.

MARGARET: Now, *geese*, you've now tried three versions and crossed them out. You said you know it's a five-letter word. It seems to be that *i* that's troubling you. How do you know it's a five-letter word?
HANA: Well, there's Cherry Beach down there, and there's lots of geese and it says, "Don't Feed the Geese."
MARGARET: So you know it has five letters, and you have to work out that letter. Do you know it ends with an *e*?
HANA: I know it's *e-s-e*.
MARGARET: O.K. So what else could it be?
[*Hana goes on to try a "u" and then an "e" in the spot she knows she needs something. She is not entirely happy with the final, and correct, version, and labels it a word she is not "dead sure about."*]

Hana demonstrates excellent recognition of what she needed to correct in the word as well as a desire to explore alternate possibilities. We noticed that the better spellers rapidly moved to this process of testing alternatives, and not only generated good alternatives, but spontaneously tested them by rewriting a spelling rather than being prodded to do so.

Complex Ways to Represent Sound

Even as the children were starting to incorporate visual features and use the look of words to monitor their spelling, they continued to increase and refine their knowledge of how sound works in English. For a while, the children usually continued to work at a single sound level, generating more conventional ways to represent a phoneme. Consonants and short vowels were increasingly correct, as were digraphs such as *th, ch, sh,* and *ck,* which had previously been represented by a single letter: SED became SHED; CEK became CHICK. Unstressed syllables began to be marked, at first not necessarily correctly (we saw a lot of spellings such as MUFEN, DOCTER, and PICKEL), but then gradually in conventional forms. We observed early knowledge of the silent *e* pattern, and through their reading and instruction, the children came to learn other ways to mark long vowels. For example, from September of grade 2 Louisa tried GEES, GISE, GEAS, GEYS, and GEES again, before spelling GEESE in March of grade 4. Shauna wrote GEIS (February of grade 2), GEICE, GECSE, GESS, and GEECE; and Kareem wrote GESS (October of grade 3), GESSE, GEASS, GESSE, GEASE, and GESCE before they both had the correct form early in grade 5.

When the children first began to use more complex ways to represent sound, many referred to "rules." The following example with Catrina in February of grade 2 illustrates this point.

MARGARET: I was interested that you put two *t*'s in *batter* [BATTER]. How did you know there were two *t*'s?

CATRINA: Because when you put an *e-r,* or an *e-d,* or an *i-n-g,* or something like that and you have—what is it called?—*vowels,* and you have another letter that is not a vowel, you have to double that letter.

In February of grade 3, Thomas explained his spellings of *pickle, quick, chick,* and *tack* (PICKUL, QICK, CHICK and TACK).

MARGARET: How did you know about that *c-k?*

THOMAS: I guess I just *learned* it...because when I was doing some spelling and stuff at home, my mum just corrected me that they were c-*k*'s, and I just learned that in most words it was *c-k.*

In October of grade 3, Braden explained his use of silent *e* in his spellings.

MARGARET: I want to know how you knew about this *e.* You put an *e* on *game* [GAME] and *nice* [NICE].

BRADEN: This [*indicating the "a" in "game"*] is supposed to say its own name.

MARGARET: How did you *know* that?

BRADEN: Well, the *a* and there's an *e* at the edge of it, so it says "a."

MARGARET: What about *hero* [HEROE]? Why is there an *e* on *hero?*

BRADEN: Because o—"here-o."

Most children progressed fairly rapidly from single phoneme sounding out to sounding out by syllables. A new problem to solve was whether to double consonants at syllable boundaries. This was a challenge for most children, initially in such two-syllable words as *muffin, butter, batter*, and so on. We often observed the kinds of inconsistencies illustrated in the following conversation with Julian in early grade 5. Julian had written BUT-TEN, BOTOM, BUTTER, and MUFFIN, then changed his two correct spellings to BUTER and MUFIN.

MARGARET: Now, only in *button* did you put two *t*'s. In *muffin* you did put two *f*'s, but you crossed one out and said, "Oh no, it's only one *f*." How do you decide whether it's doubled up or not? Why would it be doubled up in *button* but not in *butter*? In fact, you *did* have it doubled in *butter*, didn't you? You crossed one off. And in *bottom* you've gone to one *t*. How do you decide that?

JULIAN: I don't know. I take a wild guess.

MARGARET: Can you tell by looking at it?

JULIAN: Not usually.

MARGARET: Well, you looked at *muffin* again after you'd taken the *f* out. Were you happy with it without the *f*, or not?

JULIAN: Yeah.

MARGARET: It looks right now, does it? [*Julian nods.*] O.K. Is that how you decide?

JULIAN: Usually…[*mumbles*]…I just do whatever…I don't really *have* one way of spelling.

Similarly, in grade 3, Parviz explained his choice of doubling consonants based on reasons of sound.

MARGARET: In *butter*, you put two *t*'s [BUTTER] and in *batter* you put one *t* [BATER]. Now how did you decide *that*?

PARVIZ: Because I know *bat* and then I put *e-r*…Because I already *knew* butter, and I already know *batter*, too.

MARGARET: Well, is it *possible* that there could be two *t*'s in *batter*?

PARVIZ: *No!* Can't be [*very sure*]. Can't be.

MARGARET: Why *not*?

PARVIZ: Because it would be "batt-er" [*pronounced with exaggerated "t" sound and extended last syllable*].

MARGARET: Oh, I see. With two *t*'s, you'd have to put more sound in it, would you?

PARVIZ: Yeah. Because *one t* is "bader" [*pronouncing the "t" almost like a soft "d"*], not "batt-er."

For almost all the children, problem-solving around doubling consonants reared its head again later, when they were trying to spell words such as *attractive, appearance, connection*, and *immediately*. For example, in March of grade 4, Alice wrote OPPOSITION correctly but then APOSE for *oppose*, after which she tried APPOSE but rejected it. At the same time, she wrote CONNECTION but also ATRACTION and ACOUNT. A year later we saw similar inconsistency in her spellings. She had spelled *appearance*, *surround*, and *approachable* correctly, but wrote APOSE, ATRACT, ATRAC-TION, and ACOUNT (but ACCOUNTANT!). At that point, Alice made it clear that she was using only "look" to decide. Even for a good speller like Alice, this consonant doubling feature didn't become consistent until the end of grade 6.

A positive side to sounding out words in syllables appeared to be that the children were reminded of words they knew that sounded like one or more of the syllables they were sounding out or saying. We saw early evidence of this common strategy in the children's spellings. The children demonstrated their use of word analogy in such misspellings as RE*JOYCE*, RE*JOYS*, *GROSSERY*, *GROW*SERY, S*O*ROUND, *ONECE*, *ONES*, *HE-ROW*, *HEARO*, *STAYED*, *YELLOW*, *A*TRACK*TION*, EX*QUSE*, ECS*QUSE*, EX*USE*, EXSQ*YOUS*, and EXS*CUSE*. The following explanation by Chan in October of grade 3 illustrates children's use of word analogy when spelling.

MARGARET: Tell me how you worked out *rejoice*.
CHAN: 'Cause...I just needed to put "re" and then my sister's name, Joyce.

Similarly, Julian explains his spelling of the word *once*. He was convinced that *one* was in the spelling of *once*, but he couldn't work out how to represent the *s* sound at the end.

MARGARET: What about *once*, is *that* right? [ONECE.]
JULIAN: No.
MARGARET: So what do you think it is, if it isn't that? [*Julian scribbled out his final "e," leaving ONEC, but he didn't seem happy with that version either.*]
JULIAN: [*He rewrites ONE.*] I know *one*, but then...[*he tries ONECS, then ONECSE*]. *This* means nothing!
MARGARET: That's not right either, is it? Well, how do you know when you look at it that it isn't right?
JULIAN: 'Cause it doesn't *look* right.

Julian's reasoning here illustrates the way he uses both sound and look in his spelling, as do the following conversations with Elly and Kareem, who used analogy to sounds in subtle ways, together with their growing visual knowledge of letter patterns. In October of grade 5, Elly described how she worked out her spelling of the word *rejoice*.

MARGARET: How did you work that out? [REGOISE.]
ELLY: I thought about the way it sounded. I knew it would be a fairly long word.

MARGARET: Yes. And are you pretty happy with that or not?

ELLY: No, but I don't know how to spell it differently.

MARGARET: Well, what else *could* it be? What parts of it are you not sure about?

ELLY: The *i-s-e*.

MARGARET: Oh, so you're pretty sure about the *g*, are you?

ELLY: Uh—um—I'm pretty sure it's not a *j*. I'll try it with a *j* [*she writes* REJOISE].

MARGARET: What do you think?

ELLY: I need to see them close together…

MARGARET: So you're not sure whether it's a *g* or a *j*, but the rest's O.K., is it?

ELLY: Yeah.

MARGARET: So, how did you work out the *o-i* part—that's quite a difficult part—how did you know about *that*?

ELLY: I don't know.

MARGARET: Have you seen it or written it before?

ELLY: No.

MARGARET: So how did you know it was either a *j* or a *g*, then?

ELLY: Well, I thought about the way it sounded.

MARGARET: Does it sound like anything else you know?

ELLY: Well [*pause*] *rejoin*. That's spelled with a *j*.

In May of grade 5, Kareem explained his spelling of the word *sign* (SHIGHN, corrected to SIGHN) with reference to a similar-sounding word.

MARGARET: Now, how did you know the second *h* was there?

KAREEM: Well, that, umm, oops [*rewrites*].

MARGARET [*laughing*]: It's the *s* you need to put back…Let me just write what you had before. You had it *s-h-i-g-h-n*. What were you thinking? How did you figure it out? You can't *hear* that *h*, can you?

KAREEM: No, but it's—you know, it's something like how you put in *right*—*g-h-t*?

MARGARET: Yes.

KAREEM: Well, I sort of figured that in *sign*, it's *almost* the same because I know that you have the *g* in *sign* and then, I just took a chance and put *h*, and instead of *t*, *n*. [SIGHN.]

MARGARET: Oh, so you were thinking of *right* when you wrote that.

KAREEM: Yeah.

MARGARET: You sometimes do that, do you—think of a word that *sounds* like it?

KAREEM: Mostly I do that.

As the children developed, their word analogy strategy was extended to larger chunks of words, as Najali did when spelling *condemnation*: "I sound it out 'con-dem-*nation.*'" Increasingly, analogies were made to words that had the same meaning connection (as, for example, when Parviz wrote INTER-*NATION*-AL), though the children did *not* think of meaning. Instead, like Parviz with *nation*, they saw the words as *sound units* within another word.

Perhaps because an awareness of the look of words grew out of their experience as readers, most children eventually came to use information associated with the visual features of the language and also developed more complex ways to represent sounds. As will be seen in the next chapter, however, they were about to face another major challenge to their understanding of spelling.

Integrating and Monitoring

In October of sixth grade, Naveen was explaining why his spellings of com-pete [COMPETE] *and competition* [COMPATISHION] *were different in that one had an* e *and the other an* a *after the* p, *even though, as he knew, they were related in meaning.*

NAVEEN: *It* does *mean something similar, but that doesn't mean it has to spell the* same *thing.*
MARGARET: *Doesn't it?*
NAVEEN: *No.*
MARGARET: *Oh, so does meaning help your spelling then?*
NAVEEN: *No. Like* cat *and* feline, *they both of them mean the same thing— like a cat is a feline, but they're not* spelled *the same.*
MARGARET: *No, but* compete *and* competition *do sound a bit alike, don't they?*
NAVEEN: *Yes, only the* c-o-m-p—*"comp"—but here it's "*comp*atition," here it's "*comp*ete"* [emphasizing the difference].

As this conversation with Naveen illustrates, the greatest challenge for all the children occurred when the sound logic contradicted the meaning logic of English spelling. Understanding how meaning might be connected to spelling took a very long time for all the children to grasp, including the very best spellers. During this period, however, there was a general progression in the children's understanding of factors relating to the logic of meaning.

Early Understanding of Meaning: Homonyms, Compounds, and Root Words

We usually saw the first breakthroughs in understanding of meaning links in spelling when the children distinguished homonyms. Early in grade 2, Vikram used his understanding of homonyms to justify why *know* would be spelled with a *k* (KNOW) while *knife* (NIFE) and *knock* (NOCK) did not need *k*'s.

MARGARET: I wondered how you knew how to spell *know*—that's a difficult one.

VIKRAM: *Know?*

MARGARET: Yes, how did you know how to spell that?

VIKRAM: Well...I saw it in a place...in *The Sun* [a newspaper].

MARGARET: Oh, did you. You *saw* it. So is that how you knew it? You didn't sound it out, then?

VIKRAM: No.

MARGARET: I wondered how you knew about that *k* at the beginning, 'cause you can't hear that *k*, can you? [*Vikram shakes his head.*] So, would there be a *k* in any of these, then? In *knock* or *knife?*

VIKRAM: No.

MARGARET: Oh, so do you think it's possible that they *might* have a *k* there at the beginning—in front of them? I wondered how you knew when to put a *k* and when *not* to put a *k?*

VIKRAM [*after a pause*]: I think it's because, um, if the thing's more different—if the word has two meanings, and one word's more different, you spell it a different way.

MARGARET: I see. Good thinking. That's a good reason to have it a different way.

Clearly, Vikram had an early concept of homophones and saw that spelling would be a good way to distinguish different meanings.

Alice showed how she was coming to understand homophones in grade 3 when she was asked to spell *knew* and wrote NEW.

MARGARET: Did you know that there are two ways to spell that?

ALICE: *New?* Um. No. I know two ways to spell *know*, though.

MARGARET: Oh? What are they? [*Alice wrote* KNOW *and* NO.] Aha, so which one are we talking about here? Which one is more like the one we are doing here? Of the two ways, which one is more like the one we're doing here? [*Pause while Alice looks and tries to make sense of the question.*] "I *know* you can spell." "I *knew* you could spell." [*Pause.*] Which of the two you wrote would be, "I *know* you can spell." [*Alice selects the correct version.*] Now what if I said not that "I *know* you can spell," but that "I *knew* you could spell"?

ALICE: I don't know two ways to spell this [*i.e., "knew" and "new"*].

MARGARET: Oh, you don't? Well, I'll leave you with that little problem. [*Both laugh.*]

Later in the conversation, Alice suddenly said that she knew "how to spell it."

MARGARET: *What* do you know how to spell?

ALICE: *Knew* [*writes it correctly*].

MARGARET: Ah, very clever. How did you work that out?

ALICE: 'Cause *know* is like *this*, then there's "I *knew*" [*laughs*]. You see, I know if I just added on it would be "I *knew*."

Sometimes an understanding of homonyms can lead to confusion about the role of meaning in spelling, as Monali showed us at the end of grade 5. Monali believed that the very fact that there were homonyms confirmed that meaning was *not* relevant to spelling! She had just corrected ACGNOLADGE to ACKNOWLEDGE, which she said she had done by sounding out into syllables:

MARGARET: If words *mean* something similar, should they be *spelled* similarly? I mean is that why *know* is in *knowledge*?

MONALI: If, like, *wood* and *would*, like, "I chop the *wood*" and "I *would* go"—just because they have the same *meaning* or *sound* the same, it doesn't mean they have to be *spelled* the same.

MARGARET: No, but with *wood* and *would*, they *sound* the same, but they have very *different* meanings. But with *know* and *knowledge*, they sound a little bit *different*, but they *mean* something similar. And I wondered whether you'd go more on the *sound* or more on the *meaning*. Which is more important in spelling—the way it *sounds* or the way it *means*?

MONALI: The *sound* [*very sure*].

MARGARET: It is? Why's that?

MONALI: Because in the English language, there are lots of silent vowels and consonants, and you can't always depend on the *meaning* [*said very confidently*].

No one ever said teaching was easy!

The meaning in compound words was understood relatively early, probably because the sound of each word remained intact and the meaning of the whole was explicitly related to the meaning of the two words that formed the compound. Unfortunately, most children understood meaning roots in terms of compound words only, as the following conversations with Vikram illustrates.

MARGARET: What do you know about root words?
VIKRAM: Um. I think they're words with, um, two words in them.
MARGARET: Are they? What about a family of words? Do you know anything about families of words? You know—have any of your teachers talked about word families?
VIKRAM: No.
MARGARET: Or root words?
VIKRAM: Yeah. Um. They told us about root words, but I keep forgetting what they are.
MARGARET: You don't know if there are any root words...What did you *think* it was?
VIKRAM: Um, when a word has two...
MARGARET: Two parts?
VIKRAM: Yeah.
MARGARET: Can you think of any?
VIKRAM: *Nighttime.*
MARGARET: So, it would be *night* and *time*?
VIKRAM: Yeah.
MARGARET: Those would be root words of *nighttime*, would they?
VIKRAM: Yeah.

Saul demonstrated a similar concept of root words when he described them in terms of combining the two words *tree* and *house*.

MARGARET: Now, tell me about root words. When did you learn about root words?
SAUL: At school.
MARGARET: Last year?
SAUL: I don't know. I just *know* about them.
MARGARET: And do you use them a lot when you're trying to work out spellings?
SAUL: *Now* I do. Like, the past years I haven't been doing it, but now I, like, say—to spell, for example, *tree house*. So you think, "*Tree house: tree*'s spelled *t-r-e-e*, and *house h-o-u-s-e*." Or, like *trees—tree* is *t-r-e-e* and *trees*, you just add a *s*.
MARGARET: So you use it quite a bit?
SAUL: Um-hmm.

One obstacle children encountered in coming to understand how root words could be used to generate spellings was their insistence that the root of a word had always to be a *complete* word, a misconception perhaps arising from their equating root words with compound words. Margaret pressed Vikram on his understanding of root words in the following exchange.

MARGARET: What is the root word in *invitation*? Is there one?
VIKRAM [*after a pause*]: Mm...no.
MARGARET: There isn't one. O.K. Spell for me *invite* [*he writes* INVITE].
    Now could it be that *invite* is the root word of *invitation*? Or not?
VIKRAM: No.
MARGARET: Why not?
VIKRAM: *Invite* has an *e* at the end, and "invit" [*i.e.,* "invit*ation*"] doesn't.
MARGARET: Oh, so to be a root word, you have to have every single bit of
    it, do you?
VIKRAM: Hum?
MARGARET: You have to have exactly the same letters? I'm trying to figure
    out what a root word is.
VIKRAM: Yeah.

Jamal shared Vikram's understanding of root words.

MARGARET: And is the whole word usually in the root word, or can it not
    be? Can you have a root word without all the bits of the words?
JAMAL: I don't think so. I think it has to have the whole word in it.

This tendency to consider root words as whole words may have led children away from considering derivational meaning relationships in spelling. Almost five months later, Vikram was still trying to make some sense out of the idea of root words and seemed at that point to be seeing roots as merely small whole words within the larger whole word, without their necessarily having any relationship to meaning.

MARGARET: O.K., how do you work out what's a root word?
VIKRAM: Um, I just sound out the word, and it has a word in it. And I just
    know.
MARGARET: You mean, if you can just see a word in there? For example, in
    attractive [ATTRACKTIVE], there's the word *rack*. Now does that make
    that a root word? [*Vikram nods.*] It's a root word, is it? If it's in there?
VIKRAM: Um-hmm.
MARGARET: Even if it doesn't have anything to do with the meaning of the
    word. [*Vikram nods agreement.*] So root words don't have anything to
    do with meaning, then?
VIKRAM: Um-hmm...

MARGARET: Do they? [*Pause.*] I'm just wondering what words are really...What do you think a root word is?

VIKRAM: Um—a root word is one word in a word.

Saul demonstrates that this kind of "word in a word" concept isn't very helpful and, with some help, learns how root words can help generate spellings.

MARGARET: You're not happy with that [EXCELL/*excel*]. What part aren't you happy with?

SAUL: The *c*.

MARGARET: Ah-ha! Well, how did you work it out? Tell me that first, before you change anything.

SAUL: O.K. First, all the "ex" words are *e-x*.

MARGARET: Yes.

SAUL: So, then I said, "sell," it's sometimes *s-e-l-l*, and so I was just thinking, but...

MARGARET: So it could be an *s* you mean, not a *c*?

SAUL: Yeah.

MARGARET: All right. Is this a root word for anything?

SAUL: Yeah. It's not really supposed to be a root word, but there's another word in it.

MARGARET: Yes, there's *sell* or *cell*. But what if I said that this is a root word for another word you know?

SAUL: *Excellent!*

MARGARET: O.K. So, does this give you any help? If this is the root word...?

SAUL: Yes, it does.

MARGARET: And what does it tell you?

SAUL: That if I spell *excellent* that I'll be able to spell it *excel* because *excel* is the root word of *excellent*.

MARGARET: O.K., so what does that tell you? Is it a *c* or an *s*?

SAUL: *C*.

MARGARET: Great!

Saul obviously had enough knowledge to use the root word, but his overall understanding made it difficult for him to use the concept without help. This might explain why several children reached a similar point of understanding, but still claimed that they did not use root words. Kareem, in the following example, understood root words, but did not really see any value in his knowledge.

KAREEM: So you take, like, a big word, and the main thing is it, it's like, the main word in it.

MARGARET: And when you say the main word in it, is it to do with the meaning of the word or not?

KAREEM: Uh...

MARGARET: Are the root words anything to do with meaning, or are they to do with something else?

KAREEM: Yeah. 'Cause a root word is like, it's like a whole word, but, except that it's, like, there's a little word inside, like gives a whole meaning to the big word.

[*Later in the interview.*]

MARGARET: Now, do you ever use that, you know, about root words, do you ever think about root words when you're trying to figure out a word?

KAREEM: The root word? Not really...Maybe sometimes.

MARGARET: You know about it but you don't really use it?

KAREEM: Well, maybe, like, I use it sometimes, but only when I'm really, really, really, having a hard time—if I can't see, if my eyes won't tell me the answer, or my ears, then I sort of, you know...

In grade 5, Sarita was even more adamant about her refusal to use root words, telling us, "I never use the root word. I didn't even learn about that until last year."

Coming to an understanding of the spelling relationship was more complicated if the children didn't know the two words were related in meaning. For example, in grade 3, Najali spelled *nature* NACHER and *natural* NACHREL, and we thought that this was perhaps based on her understanding of the meaning connection. The following conversation quickly proved us wrong.

MARGARET: You know, with *nature* and *natural*, they look—you've got those spelled quite similarly. Why's that? Are they *supposed* to be similar?

NAJALI: Well, not *really*.

MARGARET: Why?

NAJALI: Because *natural* is, like—well, there's *nature*—*nature* and *natural* are *not*—means the *same*.

MARGARET: Aren't they?

NAJALI: *No*, because *natural* means, like, a natural *food* or something.

MARGARET: Yeah?

NAJALI: And *nature* tells you about the *insects* and all that.

MARGARET: So is it just an *accident* that they *look* like each other, then?

NAJALI: No, it's just that the *first*, the *first* part of both words *do* sound the same. Just *n-a-c-h*.

MARGARET: Uh-huh.

NAJALI: *E-r*. No! *E* is *here* and the *r* is not there, and there's "rel" in *that* one.

We had an almost identical conversation with Sarita during the same period, when she spelled *nature* NACHER and *natural* NACHARELE. While acknowledging that "they both *start* the same," Sarita insisted that this was only because "it *sounds* similar."

Syntactic Meaning Features: Prefixes, Suffixes, and Inflections

Even though it was a challenge that took most children at least to the end of the study to fully work out, they did manage to grasp more easily meaning relationships that involved adding parts (such as prefixes, suffixes, and inflections) to a word. The difficulty here was not in remembering how to spell the added part, but in knowing how to link that part to the root word. For example, the difficulty in adding *ing* was in knowing whether to double a final consonant or to drop a final *e*. Dropping or keeping a final *e* was also an issue when the children were required to add other suffixes, such as *ly*, *able*, or *ment*, but by that point the children had begun to apply rules to guide their spelling, as shown in the following conversations with Alice in the grade 5 and Vikram in grade 6.

In attempting to spell *immediately*, Alice had written IMMEDIATLY, then IMMEDIATLLY, then IMMEDIATE (having gone back to insert the second *m*), and then IMMEDIATELY.

MARGARET: Do you think there's something missing in this part [the TLY]? Is that the problem? [*Pause.*] Why did you write it again?
ALICE: No, I just think it might have two *l*'s, but…I think…
MARGARET: It has one?
ALICE: One.
MARGARET: There *is* something wrong with that part. [*Short interruption.*] Did you know that you needed the *e* in IMMEDIATE?
ALICE: Yeah.
MARGARET: Or did you think you dropped it when you added the *l-y*?
ALICE: Well, up there [*her first two attempts at "immediately"*] I thought you dropped it, but when I got down here, and I did IMMEDIATE—
MARGARET: Uh-huh…
ALICE: I knew that, when you said, you know, about the *e*, I had to put the *e* in, in *immediately*.
MARGARET: You rarely do drop the *e*, you know.
ALICE: You do?
MARGARET: You *rarely* do.

Later in the same conversation, Alice remembered the "rule."

MARGARET: How did you know that you didn't drop the *e* [*in* ATTRAC-TIVELY]?

ALICE: 'Cause you said, er, that you don't usually drop the *e* when it's at the end.
MARGARET: And does it look right to you?
ALICE: Uh-huh.

Vikram is also able to quote a spelling rule to explain how he changed FETURE (*feature*) to FETURING (*featuring*).

MARGARET: Now, how did you know to drop the *e* when you changed *feature* to *featuring*?
VIKRAM: Because we learned in class whenever you put *ing* with something with an *e*, you always drop the *e*.
MARGARET: Oh. So you drop the *e*? Are there times when you don't drop the *e*? When you add *i-n-g*? Is it always like that?
VIKRAM: Yeah.

For most of the children, adding *ly* to words ending with *l*, as in SPECIALY, or adding *ir* to words beginning with *r*, such as IRESPONSABLE, was a problem to the end of the study, because the sound was already accounted for by the single letter, and the children still appeared to think of prefixes and suffixes as sound patterns more than as meaning features.

All the children encountered the past tense inflection *ed* early, at a time when they were still influenced mostly by sound, so it wasn't surprising that they all initially dealt with *ed* as a sound pattern. For many it continued to be a sound or visual feature rather than something that marked a change in meaning. Although no two children followed exactly the same pattern in moving from treating the *ed* as sound to treating it as a unit of meaning, Najali is the closest to being a "textbook example" in that she clearly showed changes in her understanding of how to integrate a syntactic feature into her spelling. Midway through grade 2 she wrote JOPT for *jumped*, SRPT for *chirped*, LERND for *learned*, and TRAND for *trained*. These spellings showed that she differentiated the sounds she heard at the end of the words, and in conversation she substantiated our view that she was using sound.

MARGARET: So, tell me how you do your spelling. How do you spell these words, all of them?
NAJALI: Oh, well, I just sounded them out, really.

By the end of grade 2, she wrote JUMPT, CHARPT, LEAND, and TRANDE, and provided detailed insight into her spellings. The visual feature in her spelling of *trained* was still an attempt to represent sound, as she told our research assistant, Nancy.

NANCY: Now, how about *jumped*? How did you know that was a *t* at the end of *jumped*?

NAJALI: 'Cause *t* makes the sound of a "ta" and it sounds like "jump-ta—jumpt."

[*Later in the conversation.*]

NANCY: *Chirped*—you've got *p* and *t*. How did you know that?

NAJALI: Um. *P* makes a "pa" sound and *t* makes a "ta" sound.

NANCY: So you sounded that out?

NAJALI: Uh-huh.

NANCY: *Trained*—how did you know that there was an *e* at the end of *trained*?

NAJALI: Because *a* sounds out with *e* [i.e., the *e* makes the *a* long—the silent *e* rule].

Over the next two years, Najali moved very slowly away from such sound-based decisions. At the end of grade 3, for example, she still wrote JUPMT for *jumped*, but seemed to be moving to a correct use of *ed*, including it in CHIRPED, TRAINED, and STAYNED (*stained*), but not in LEARND (*learned*). In February of grade 4, she changed her spelling of *jumped* to the correct spelling and repeated that spelling again in the spring. By then, Najali was fairly consistent in her use of the *ed* marker, although, as the following conversation shows, she still has trouble explaining her practice without reference to sound.

MARGARET: See what you did, you put an *e-d* on *chirped* [CHURPED], right? You're sure about that, aren't you? Good. Now, why wasn't there an *e-d* on *jumped* [JUMPT], because it sounds absolutely the same to me: *chirped* and *jumped*.

NAJALI: Because "jumpta" and "jumped"

MARGARET: Yeah.

NAJALI: Sorry, do you want *jumped* or *jump*?

MARGARET: Well, which one do *you* want?

NAJALI: I don't know which one you meant. I thought you meant *jumped* [*pronounced "jumpt"*].

MARGARET: Oh, well, are they different words then, *jumpt* and *jumped*? Does it mean something different when it's *t* and *e-d*? Are they two different words, one with a *t* and one with an *e-d*?

NAJALI: I *jumped*, yeah.

When probed further about the difference, Najali went on to explain that *jumped* meant "I jump, like, a few minutes ago," but she couldn't generate a sentence for JUMPT, "so that makes me think now that they are not two words—they just mean the same thing, just spelled differently." Najali was determined to hold onto her spelling JUMPT!

Najali was not the only child to make subtle distinctions about the role of sound in these words. There was considerable confusion on this point.

Many children made the change to *ed* in *jumped* and *chirped before* they made the change from a *d* to *ed* in *learned* or *trained*. For those children it seemed easier to move to the correct tense marker in situations in which sound obviously had to be abandoned than it was in situations where the *d* alone could account for the *ed* sound. By the fall of grade 5, Najali used the *ed* marker consistently. She still, however, was not able to justify this on the basis of its being a syntactic meaning marker, but was confident because of "the way it *looks* to me now."

Derivational Meaning Relationships

All the children had the most difficulty in understanding more derivational relationships when the meaning links were hidden by modifications in sound. For example, it was much easier for the children to understand the notion of adding *ing* to *excite* in order to make *exciting* than it was for them to understand the meaning connections between *sign* and *signal* and to use that understanding to help them spell correctly. That is, they had difficulty modifying their spelling logic based on sound to allow for the influence of meaning in such cases. In fact, when we first inquired about the role of meaning in spelling, all the children were adamant that meaning had nothing to do with spelling, and many had trouble recognizing meaning connections between words. Even Lorna, the best speller in the study, when asked whether meaning is part of the logic of spelling, answered, "No, it's not part of spelling." When children started to understand the meaning relationship between words, a necessary step on the way to using the logic of meaning in their spelling, they were still convinced that it had nothing to do with spelling. By the beginning of grade 3, Najali was making great strides toward becoming a good speller and recognized certain meaning links, but was totally convinced that meaning had nothing to do with spelling and that it would not help her to generate a spelling.

MARGARET: Well, tell me something. Is *sign* [SIEN] anything like *signal* [SIGNEL]? Do they mean similar things?

NAJALI: Well, *sign* is sort of like *signal*.

MARGARET: In what way?

NAJALI: *Sign* is like, *signal* tells you, like, do something.

MARGARET: Uh-huh.

NAJALI: Sort of stop, sort of *sign*.

MARGARET: So if they mean similar things, would that mean that they would be spelled the same way?

NAJALI: No. [*A fast and firm reply.*]

MARGARET: Oh, I see.

NAJALI: Because, like, they sound different and they are pronounced different.

MARGARET: I see. So sound is more important, is it, than the fact that they mean similar—

NAJALI: Well, sort of [not so sure now].

MARGARET: Um-hmm?

NAJALI: Not really important, but...

MARGARET: That's how you tell, though, is it?

NAJALI: Uhm.

MARGARET: So meaning a similar thing doesn't really tell you how to spell it, then?

NAJALI: *No*!

At the end of grade 4, when Najali spelled *surround* [SOROUND] and knew that the meaning was related to *around*, she still insisted that it was "a coincidence" that the word *round* was in her spelling of *surround*!

Similarly, Lorna told us that "a sign sometimes is a signal to do something or not do something," but when asked whether that connection would have anything to do with the spelling, answered, "I don't think so." This was especially interesting, because Lorna had just admitted to having difficulty learning to spell *sign* because she wanted to include an *h* after the *g*, because the *g* "looks so abrupt."

By the end of the study, Lorna, Najali, and a very few others got to the point of admitting that there was a relationship between spelling and meaning. At the same time, however, they were steadfast in their insistence that they didn't use it. For example, Margaret probed Najali's spelling of KNOW and KNOWLAGE to see whether she used a logic connected to meaning.

MARGARET: And did you think something about the meaning when you were actually doing it, or did you think more about the way it sounded?

NAJALI: More about the way it sounded.

MARGARET: Do you ever think about the meaning first, as the most—trying to work out a word?

NAJALI: Sometimes, but hardly ever.

Margaret pointed out to Lorna an instance where she seemed to use her knowledge of the word *prepare* to spell PREPARATION.

MARGARET: Now, you told me you didn't think meaning had anything too much to do with it, and yet there's an example where you seemed to have used what you knew about another word.

LORNA: Uh-huh.

MARGARET: Do you think that happens very often or not very often?

LORNA: No.

MARGARET: It doesn't happen very often, eh? You mean it doesn't happen in spelling, or it doesn't happen in the way you do spelling?

LORNA: Not in the way I do spelling.

MARGARET: O.K., so you think it happens a lot in spelling in general?

LORNA: Umm, maybe, but there are just some times when it doesn't.

Lorna is very specific about how she goes about spelling and, in response to Margaret's questions, tries to show that the logic of meaning is not necessary as they talk about spelling *condemn* and *condemnation*.

LORNA: I think that if you don't know how to spell *condemn*, you could still spell *condemnation*.

MARGARET: But if you knew how to spell *condemnation*, would you know how to spell *condemn*? Because that's the difficult one, isn't it, the one with the silent *n*? This one isn't so difficult because all the sounds are there.

LORNA: I don't think that if you knew how to spell this, you'd automatically know how to spell that.

MARGARET: Why not?

LORNA: Because you'd think that *n* was part of *nation*.

MARGARET: Yeah, but that's only if you were thinking about sound. What if you were thinking about meaning?

LORNA: I don't think you could either way. I just think you'd put the *condem*[n] with the ending at the *m*.

We are reasonably sure that in spellings like PREPARE and PREPARATION, and COMBINE and COMBINATION, Lorna was using a tacit understanding of meaning to make good choices. However, clearly this logic was not used explicitly by the children.

Correct Spelling

As the children were working through their understanding of spelling they were also greatly expanding their experience with text. The best spellers especially were reading for an increasing variety of purposes, which caused them to read in a variety of topics in several genres in both fiction and nonfiction. Writing demands expanded to include report writing on a variety of subjects and personal attempts to experiment with the forms of fiction they encountered in their reading. Increasingly, the children had expectations for personal editing and proofreading of their own writing and that of their peers. These activities provided still more experience with the various demands of text and opportunities to understand the spelling system—a vital basis for developing correct spelling.

It seems that it should be an easy task to identify and define what we mean by a "correct" speller, but if you try it for yourself, you'll see how hard it is. Does a person have to be correct all the time? If not, how many errors, or what kind of errors, are acceptable? Is "correct" relative to age level? Is a person who uses a dictionary and a spell-checker to produce correctly spelled essays, but who makes several errors in draft writing, a correct speller? Does being a correct speller involve knowledge, attitude, or performance? What would a person have to be able to articulate about the spelling system in order to be considered a correct speller? Correct spelling seems to be a lot like love or comedy: you can't define it, but you're sure you'd recognize it when you see it.

Perhaps part of the problem is that no change in thinking distinguishes a developing from a correct speller. In fact, we all continue to develop in our ability to apply what we know to generate new spellings and to learn about the ways spelling works. Once we recognize that spelling is controlled by various competing and overlapping logics, and that we can understand and control those factors, what remains is to work out the detail. At some point, learners become strong enough in their ability to control the system that they are considered correct spellers. At what point do we consider this to have happened? Maybe the best place to start answering this complex question is to examine the behaviour of correct spellers.

The following description by Chan of her spelling strategies in grade 6 reflects the kind of flexibility and integration of multiple logics that we observed among correct spellers.

MARGARET: How do you do your spellings now?

CHAN: Well, I guess, *most* words I remember from books. And the rest, I just try to figure them out by the sound and what it looks like... because if it's a word like *ambidextrous*, then I wouldn't know what the root word would be, because I really don't *use* that word a lot. [*Chan then wrote* AMBIDEXTROUS.]

MARGARET: *Is* there a root word there, do you think?

CHAN: *Extra*, maybe? No! *Dexterity?*

MARGARET: So how did you actually *do* that spelling?

CHAN: Well, I just kind of sound it out.

MARGARET: Show me.

CHAN: "Am-bi-" and then "dextrous" [*saying this as she rewrites the word.*] Like, I do it in little parts and then I put it into bigger parts. Like, once on the piano...I take it bar by bar, and then I put these bars together.

MARGARET: And that's how you do your spellings as well, is it?

CHAN: Yeah, only with a really *hard* word.

[*Later, in the same conversation.*]

MARGARET: So, how did you figure out *tyrannical* [TYRANNICAL]?

CHAN: I just thought of *tyranny* without the *y*.

Chan showed us how she interweaves her sophisticated knowledge about sound, about the way words look, and about meaning to produce her spellings. This conversation also demonstrates the level of complexity in

Chan's writing vocabulary and her ability to talk about her spelling processes, two features that characterized correct spellers.

Children who were correct spellers saw themselves as correct spellers and were motivated to actively engage in problem-solving about their spelling. Like Lorna in the following example, they approached their spellings in ways that showed confidence that there was an orderliness to the system that they could control. In this instance, Lorna was puzzling about whether it was an *e* or an *a* in the second syllable of the word *preparation*.

LORNA: *P-r-e-p-a-r*—or it could be an *e*.
MARGARET: What do you think it is—an *a* or an *e*?
LORNA: An *a*.
MARGARET: O.K. Why is it an *a*?
LORNA: Because of *prepare*.
MARGARET: And why is that?
LORNA: Because *prepare*. In preparation time, you prepare.

Correct spellers had a large body of known words and words they had seen before, mostly in their reading, to draw upon when making their spelling decisions. What is more, they chose to use their wide vocabulary in their writing. On the whole, they spelled correctly in their writing drafts even though they tended not to restrict themselves to known spellings. In both composing and dictated spelling situations, they could usually recognize their correct spellings and had effective strategies for correcting misspellings.

All of the correct spellers in our study were excellent and avid readers at home and at school. Most of them were also active, committed writers who wrote at home for their own pleasure or, as will be seen, were simply fascinated by spelling and had a personal interest in exploring words and how they are spelled.

In this chapter we described what happens as children learn about the spelling system and move to become correct spellers. In later chapters we will consider the instructional implications of this learning process and consider ways teachers can help children proceed. However, one instructional observation must be made here, and it cannot be overemphasized. Our research was concerned with spelling development within the context of literacy development. Reading and writing play a key role in children's learning about spelling. We believe it would be impossible to learn about a system as complex as English spelling without opportunities to explore that system through reading and writing. *After watching children learn to spell throughout the elementary school years we can say unequivocally that, if children do not have a strong programme of literacy development that includes spelling within a context of the development of reading and writing, then they do not have a spelling programme.*

Good Spellers and Poor Spellers

VIKRAM: A good speller isn't necessarily a person who can spell words right, but, um, has knowledge of word structure.

MARGARET: ...Tell me again—how do you become a good speller?

VIKRAM: Mostly to use what you know. Use what you know and find your strengths to spell words.

In our naïveté, when we began our study, we hoped that by the end of it we would be able to look at the levels achieved by the children, identify good and poor spellers, and then look back at the nature of their learning to determine where things went wrong for the poor spellers and what early signs might indicate that a child was not progressing. We used a "journey" metaphor and wondered whether there was only one route to becoming a successful speller. Perhaps poor spellers were just slower travellers—they had not reached the end of the journey by the time the study ended, but were moving slowly in the right direction. Alternatively, perhaps they had taken a different route, and were stuck on a dead-end road that doomed them to poor spelling for life. In the preceding chapters, we outlined the kinds of understandings and attitudes that would seem to chart the route that led to successful spelling. What we want to look at now is how different children negotiated that journey.

Once more the problem of terminology rears its head. "Good speller" and "poor speller" are commonsense terms that are commonly used among teachers, in teacher-parent conferences, and in popular criticisms of schools. Everyone is confident that good or poor spellers can be recognized from even limited samples of writing. Indeed, we had little difficulty in recognizing the best and poorest spellers in our study, but we *did* find ourselves with a problem of where exactly to draw a line between good spellers on one side and poor spellers on the other. By the end of the study all the children were aware of the importance of correct spelling, used a variety of strategies to generate their spellings, and could identify and correct at least some of their misspellings. In the interviews all the children consistently drew on features other than sound for their spellings. A review of their writing in grade 6 showed that even the worst spellers wrote approximately 65 percent of their words correctly in their drafts, although it must be said that the poor spellers used very simple, basic vocabulary. What criterion, then, should we use to declare somebody a good speller or, more worrying, a poor speller? Correctness in initial drafts? Final drafts? Spelling tests on pre-learned words? Tests based on age-appropriate vocabulary? The ability to articulate an understanding of the spelling system? Or some combination of all these measures? In the end, we decided that it was more useful, especially from an instructional point of view, to describe the development and achievement in spelling and literacy of groups of children we identified as sharing common characteristics, and to let you decide where to draw the line between successful and unsuccessful spelling.

For all the idiosyncratic differences, we found that there were discernible patterns in the way the children negotiated their spelling journey. By the time the study was completed, we could easily identify a group of good spellers. These children had a sense of system in spelling and were able to integrate multiple logics and effectively solve problems as they generated and monitored their spellings—qualities that we described in Chapter 5 as some of the characteristics of correct spellers. To use our journey metaphor, these children might be seen as having reached one destination: they now had the kinds of attitudes towards their spelling and an understanding of the system that would enable them to engage in further exploration of spelling as their literacy interests and needs continued to grow. We could also easily identify a group of poor spellers. Their general literacy development was slow, they had difficulty in reading throughout the study, they moved beyond letter-sound matching late, and they seemed almost immediately to have hit a thick fog of confusion about spelling that appeared to be so impenetrable that they gave up and pulled off the road.

The rest of the children were strung between these two groups at various points along the journey. Some were very close to the good spellers, others were closer to the poor spellers, some were moving slowly but surely towards correct spelling, while others seemed to be stalled, or to have pulled off the road into a rest area. It was interesting to us that one group of children, who early in the study looked as if they would become good spellers (that is, had early literacy profiles similar to the good spellers) did not fulfill their promise, while another group of children, whose early literacy profiles were similar to those of the poor spellers, managed to move steadily on in their spelling development once they had reading under control.

In this chapter and the next we look more closely at the characteristics of these groups. We hope to do this by describing the patterns of spelling behaviours and attitudes that led us to place children in a particular group, but without losing the sense of uniqueness in each child's development as a speller. We had to choose what order to present the different groups of spellers, each alternative having its own advantages and disadvantages. In the end, we decided to begin with the group of children who were the best spellers—the "good" spellers—and then describe the group of children who were not only the poorest spellers, but whose literacy development generally was slow. In Chapter 7, we describe three groups of children who were stalled at some point, some of whom remained stalled on the journey to correct spelling.

Good Spellers

There were nine children who generally demonstrated the behaviour we associated with correct spelling; you have already heard many of their voices in Chapter 5. This group included three girls from Hampton Park (Lorna, Alice, and Hana), and four girls (Chan, Najali, Zeena, and Sarita) and two boys (Saul and Jamal) from the original Fulham group. We had to work hard to keep in touch with this group through the study. By the end of grade 4, Chan and Jamal had left Fulham, Chan for a full-time gifted programme and Jamal for a school closer to his home. In addition, Lorna left Hampton Park at the end of grade 3 for a full-time gifted programme. Fortunately, we were able to maintain contact with these children, Jamal and Chan to the end of the study and Lorna until the middle of grade 5. Hana, Chan, and Sarita were from homes in which English was a second language. Hana and Alice were selected for their school district's half-day withdrawal programme for gifted children.

It takes a long time to become a good speller. Most of these children did not demonstrate the characteristics of correct spellers until the end of the grade 6. Even then, it was clear that they were continuing to learn. For example, many of these good spellers, although open to the possibility that meaning could be a basis for spelling, still did not fully understand how the more subtle aspects of meaning (for example, some derivational relationships) worked in spelling. The following examples from dictated lists at the end of the study show both the level of success and the areas of difficulty for this group of children.

Child	Correct	Incorrect
Lorna (mid grade 5)	AMNESIA FICTITIOUS PREREQUISITE	NEMONIC CONCIENCE SOLOMNETY
Alice	PLEASURABLE FEATURING CONFIDENTIALLY	FACILUTATE IMMEDIATLY CONCIOUS
Hana	INSIGNIFICANT CONSCIENCE FACILITATE	CLINITION CONSCIENSIOS MISCHEVIOUS
Chan	AMBIDEXTROUS PSYCHOLOGY DISSIPATE	TYRANICAL TEMPERMENTAL CONSCIENCIOUS
Najali	PATIENT CONSEQUENCE RESPONSIBILITY	IMMEDIATLY CORASPONDANCE DECLORATION
Zeena	ESPECIALLY CONDEMN ACKNOWLEDGEMENT	PROSPARITY REMEMBERENCE PACIENT
Sarita	CONSCIENTIOUS SOLEMN MECHANIC	CORASPONDANCE BUSSINESS INSEPERABLE
Saul	CONSCIENCE PATIENT KNOWLEDGEABLE	EXCELL SEPERATELY CONSCIENCIOUS
Jamal	MISCHIEVOUS PATIENT CORRESPONDENCE	IRRESPONDSIBLE CONSCIENCOUS SOLUMN

In looking back at the development of these children, we noticed that they had all moved quickly through the early phases of literacy, including spelling. Hana, Lorna, and Chan were all fluent, effective, independent readers by the time we met them in kindergarten (Lorna told us, "I read when I was three"), and Alice, Sarita, and Saul were reading independently by March of grade 1. Najali, Zeena, and Jamal made a later start, but were reading well by the middle of grade 2. All of the good spellers continued to be excellent and avid readers, reading extensively for their own enjoyment at home as well as in school, and they ended the study able to read text well above their grade level. The three earliest readers had moved away from simple letter-sound matching spellings by the end of kindergarten; the rest had moved at the latest by February of grade 2. This rapid progress was especially surprising in the case of Najali and Zeena because their spellings had been mainly pre-sound in mid-kindergarten.

The good spellers made great use of their knowledge of sound and visual features in their spelling, but increasingly they added meaning to their spelling logic. As we saw, for example, in Chan's description of her spelling strategies in Chapter 5, there was a flexibility and a use of multiple logics evident in the reasoning of good spellers that were not apparent in the other children. As she worked on her spelling of *decision*, Najali demonstrated how the good spellers had an inquiring, exploratory, and usually persistent approach to their spellings. While spelling *decision*, she made three attempts. Each attempt resulted in the same spelling, DESICION, but she still wasn't satisfied.

NAJALI: I know there's a *d-e-s*—in the starting…[*Pause.*] Oh, no, it may be a *c*.
MARGARET: Why?
NAJALI: Because, *decide*.
MARGARET: What *about decide*?
NAJALI: It's almost a root word [*writes* DECIDION].
MARGARET: Do you have to have the *whole* root word?
NAJALI: No…[*Pause.*] I know there's an *s* in there, and I know there's a *c*, and then I know there's a *i-o-n*…And I just put them all together [*as she says this, Najali is writing* DECISION], and this looks *right*.

This kind of problem-solving was typical of the reasoning of the good spellers. All the conversations we had with these children show that they approached spelling as if there was a system to it, and as if they were able to control that system.

Unlike most of the other children, the good spellers could accurately recognize their correct and misspelled words. Like Hana in the following interview, they had an excellent ability to pinpoint problem areas in their misspellings and *spontaneously* generated viable alternatives, often generalizing across words. Unlike almost all the other children, they *wrote out* their alternative versions and compared them for correctness, taking an experimental, hypothesis-testing approach to their spelling. When Hana was trying to spell *immoveable*, she first wrote IMMO, but wasn't satisfied with it, then wrote IMO, and finally made a third, correct attempt of IMMOVEABLE.

MARGARET: Now you've just corrected *immoveable*. What was it about *immoveable* that gave you some problems?
HANA: Umm, the double *m*. I'm not sure if there is a double *m* at the beginning or not.

MARGARET: Um-hmm. So you did it *with*, and then *without*, and then you did it again at the very end. How did you decide in the end?

HANA: Just, half the way it looked, and half just because other words do that a lot. They double the *m*.

[*Later.*]

MARGARET: How did you work out there are two *r*'s in *irresponsible*?

HANA: Just the same as *immoveable*...double *r*, like, like double the consonants, when, like, you add the *e* or something.

The good spellers used these approaches in their own writing. Their self-reliance in monitoring their spellings was one of the characteristics that distinguished the good spellers from most of the other children we observed. Even when the teachers told the good spellers that they could hand in unedited rough drafts, these children were unwilling to do so. They did not want to be seen as poor spellers and felt that teachers would make judgements about them based on their drafts. They treated editing as their personal responsibility and developed effective strategies for doing it. If the good spellers were not able to fix a misspelling, they tended to look it up in the dictionary, and usually turned to teachers for help only as a last resort. Alice discussed her approaches to editing, first talking about how she monitored spelling in her journal and then sharing what she does in her story writing.

ALICE: I'll be writing it and then I'll come to a word and it doesn't look right—

MARGARET: Um-hmm...

ALICE: —so I'll think about it and I'll think about what might make it look better and then I'll put it down, and sometimes I have to work a while before I—it's right. Other times I just, I look at it and I know it, I just sort of have a feeling it's right.

MARGARET: Yeah.

ALICE: So...

MARGARET: How, when you do that [make spelling corrections] in your stories, do you erase to do that, when you're fiddling with a word, or do you have another piece of paper you do that on, or what...where do you do that? Do you put a line through it or what?

ALICE: What I usually do is—the paper goes like this, and it has sort of a line here—

MARGARET: Um-hmm...

ALICE: —and then you start writing here.

MARGARET: Yes, yes...

ALICE: And I'll go just like this—

MARGARET: Oh, in the front margin.

ALICE: —or up at the top where sometimes titles are. I'll sort of—so I can look back and I can know which ones I had trouble with and everything.

Another characteristic of good spellers that we believe is highly relevant to their spelling development is that from early in the study these children showed greater interest in the meanings and the spellings of the words used in the environment around them than was evident in the other children. The good spellers tended to recall in detail specific situations in which they had encountered and learned a word. Hana, for example, talked about how she used her experience in her parents' store to figure out how to spell *special*.

HANA: ...Because, you know, I always used to be stuck on *special* and, um, that was when I was in Milton, and I was coming here still and I was, you know, I saw it around the store a lot because, you know, "Special: 99 cents," and then I never really, never paid attention to it, but when I started to write it here [dictated spelling situations] I really started to visualize it, but then it wouldn't always work because it was too hard or whatever, but, um, then I started to, you know, when I saw the "special" signs, I would look at them and try to memorize them for when you came again.

Saul showed this same ability to pinpoint the location of a particular word he had learned. When asked how he had learned to spell *rejoice*, he told us, "Well, because at my sister's Bat Mitzvah, um, like, it's taught, it says, 'sing and rejoice,' so, and all, like, I knew how to spell the word." The good spellers noticed, and were curious about, words they heard and read, and deliberately sought out opportunities to incorporate them into their own language. This awareness of words was well illustrated as early as the beginning of grade 1 by Lorna, when she was talking about how she learned to spell.

LORNA: From watching my dad. I always watch him read, and when I hear the word, I can see the word. [*We asked what she does if her dad came to a word she didn't know.*] I'd say, like, "What does *glutton* mean?" and he'd explain it to me.

At the end of grade 3, Margaret asked Lorna how she knew the word *constantly*, which she had used in one of her stories, and Lorna remembered this incident.

LORNA: I didn't really see that in a story. I heard it. My dad was talking to a girl at his work when I was five or six, I heard him talking and he used the word *constantly* and I interrupted and asked what did it mean, and he told me and I've been using the word since.

All of the good spellers were avid readers who read for pleasure at home as well at school, so naturally their reading was a vital source of their curiosity about the meaning and spelling of words. For example, when asked how she worked out her correct spelling of *muffin* in grade 2, Zeena explained, "My sister always brings home books from the library truck for us to read at night, and then we fall back asleep, but it's called— I can't remember the name—*The Muffins*, and all those muffins are running away and everything, so that's how I memorized it."

Chan routinely "collected" words from her reading. In grade 6, among other reading she was doing, she had started *Great Expectations* and, as she explains, was finding it challenging, but followed her usual practice of listing unfamiliar words to check on later.

CHAN: I started *Great Expectations* like five months ago, but I'm still on the third chapter.
MARGARET: You're finding that hard, are you?
CHAN: Yeah.
MARGARET: Why is that?
CHAN: Well, because I guess the words are kind of old, and I was writing down all the words I didn't understand in the first chapter, which is only like two pages long, even though the words were tiny, and I had got about thirty words I didn't know.
MARGARET: And what do you do with those words? Why did you do that?
CHAN: Well, that way I can improve my vocabulary and my spelling.

While this may not have been the most effective strategy for her *reading*, it does demonstrate Chan's commitment to understanding words and their spelling. Chan and Hana, too, were somewhat unusual in that they took pleasure in the spelling of words for their own sake. Hana told us, "I just love reading and I love spelling." Chan became the grade 6 spelling champion in her school district, although she had to challenge a judge's ruling on her spelling of *hydro-electric*, producing a version of her spelling in a dictionary, to avoid being eliminated from the competition!

More typical among the good spellers was an interest in words for their use in writing. All the good spellers were active and committed writers at home and at school—in some cases, exceptionally so. At times, as in the case with Najali, their interest in writing at home only came out during our interviews.

NAJALI: I have a bunch of stories at home that I keep writing. Umm, but I never bring them to school.
MARGARET: Why?
NAJALI: Because I never have time to write them here.
MARGARET: Oh, so you write them at home, do you?
NAJALI: Oh yeah, I have hundreds of stories I have written at home.

[*Later in the interview.*]

MARGARET: So why did you start doing that [keeping a portfolio]? That's quite amazing. You're going to be a writer or something?

NAJALI: Well, actually, I don't know what I want to be when I'm older, but I really do enjoy writing.

Lorna and Alice were the most exceptional writers, but all the good spellers were engaged in their writing, showed excitement about pieces they had written at home or at school, and borrowed words from their reading. As Alice's and Hana's grade 6 writing samples indicate (see Figures 6.1 and 6.2), the good spellers used sophisticated ideas and vocabulary.

Figure 6.1 Alice, Grade 6

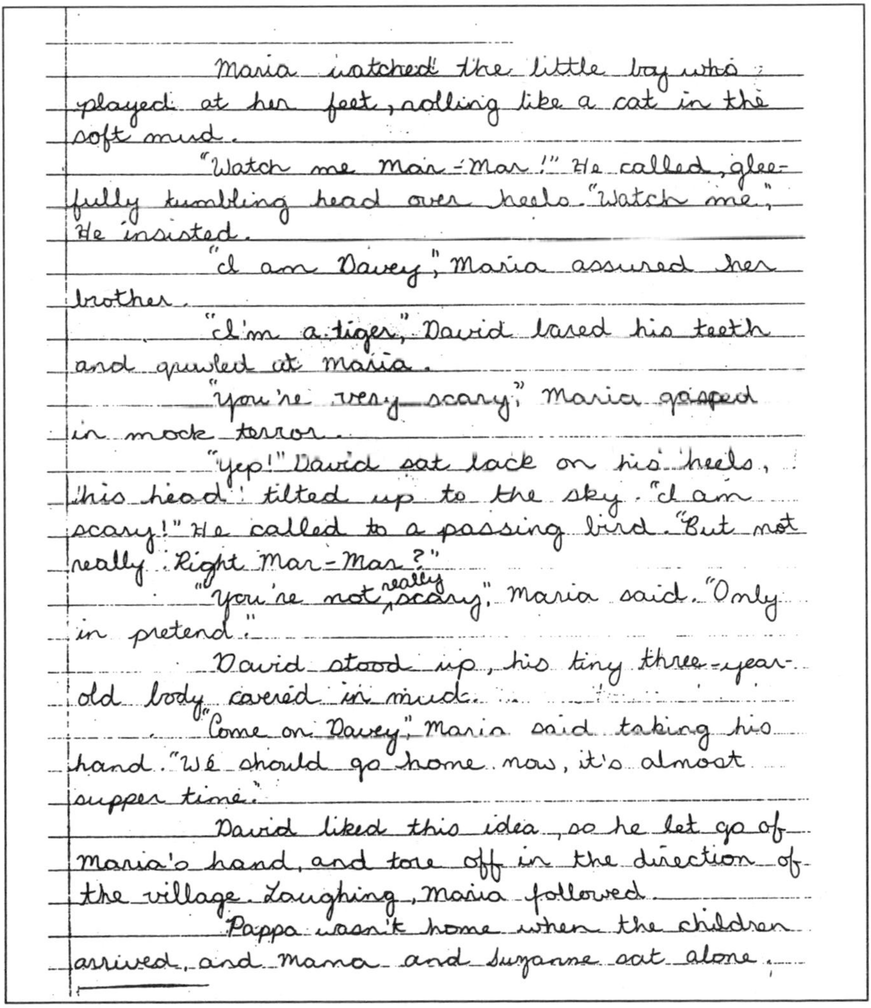
Maria watched the little boy who played at her feet, rolling like a cat in the soft mud.
"Watch me Mar-Mar!" He called, gleefully tumbling head over heels. "Watch me," He insisted.
"I am Davey," Maria assured her brother.
"I'm a tiger," David bared his teeth and growled at Maria.
"You're very scary," Maria gasped in mock terror.
"Yep!" David sat back on his heels, his head tilted up to the sky. "I am scary!" He called to a passing bird. "But not really. Right Mar-Mar?"
"You're not really scary," Maria said. "Only in pretend."
David stood up, his tiny three-year-old body covered in mud.
"Come on Davey," Maria said taking his hand. "WE should go home now, it's almost supper time."
David liked this idea, so he let go of Maria's hand, and tore off in the direction of the village. Laughing, Maria followed.
Pappa wasn't home when the children arrived, and Mama and Suzanne sat alone,

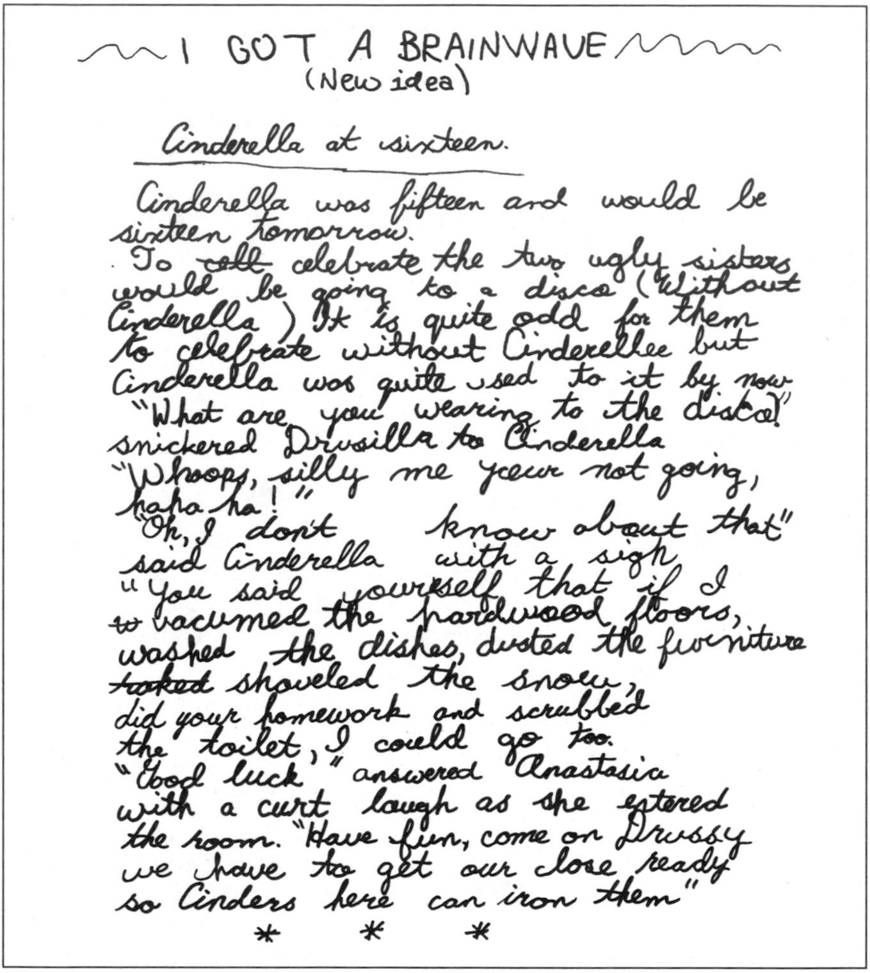

~~~I GOT A BRAINWAVE~~~
(New idea)

Cinderella at sixteen.

Cinderella was fifteen and would be sixteen tomorrow.

To celebrate the two ugly sisters would be going to a disco (Without Cinderella) It is quite odd for them to celebrate without Cinderellee but Cinderella was quite used to it by now.

"What are you wearing to the disco" snickered Drusilla to Cinderella "Whoops, silly me your not going, haha ha!"

"Oh, I don't know about that" said Cinderella with a sigh "You said yourself that if I vacumed the hardwood floors, washed the dishes, dusted the furniture shoveled the snow, did your homework and scrubbed the toilet, I could go too.

"Good luck," answered Anastasia with a curt laugh as she entered the room. "Have fun, come on Drussy we have to get our close ready so Cinders here can iron them"

*   *   *

Figure 6.2 Hana, Grade 6

It isn't surprising then, that while reading gave them (like other children we observed) the opportunities to see words in print and was the main source for their knowledge about spelling, for the good spellers, it was usually their writing that provided a place where they could try out that new language. In their writing, the good spellers drew on their reading, seeing it as a major source for generating and monitoring their spellings. Many believed that their writing helped their spelling because it provided opportunities to "practice" writing words. Zeena expressed this view, saying that writing helped her spelling because "the more you practice when you write the words down," the more you learn the words. They saw editing, more than composing and drafting, as benefitting their spelling because, as Sarita put it, "You always write, 'cause you keep writing words and words, and if you're writing rough copy and you always edit it afterwards, you can learn your words by looking in the dictionary, and check for something and know how it's spelled." Najali was especially adamant on this point, saying, "Well, there's writing my words, that wouldn't help me [spell], but by looking at it and seeing if they're right or wrong [that would help]."

All of the good spellers talked frequently about the interrelationship of reading, writing, and spelling. Sarita told us while in grade 3 that she knew a lot of spellings from her "reading and writing stories." In grade 5 Hana was explicit about this link when she talked about how she did her spelling. Like Chan, she "collected" words from her reading to use in her writing, as the following conversation describes.

HANA: Um, it depends, if, sometimes...my reading is pretty good too, and that helps me a lot.
MARGARET: How is that?
HANA: Well, I like to read a lot, and then while I'm reading, if I come to any words I usually just, if I think they're interesting, I'll keep them and then later when I'm story writing I'll use those words and also I'll have a better idea of how to spell them.

Later in the interview, we asked Hana whether she memorizes words.

HANA: ...I won't exactly memorize it, but when I come to the word I want to write and say I've seen the word before, I usually remember that I have seen the word before and I kind of try and picture the way it was spelled. And I sound it out and I'll look it up in the dictionary and if I still couldn't find it in the dictionary I would just ask adults.

Hana was very particular about the words she used in her stories, as Dennis observed while Hana was writing in grade 3. Hana stumbled over her spelling of the word *gigantic*; observing that she was erasing it, Dennis offered to give her the spelling. She took the spelling, but replaced the word with *huge*. A few minutes later, however, Dennis observed Hana going through the classroom dictionary, then returning to her desk to write the word *monstrous* a little further into the story. When Dennis teased her that she wouldn't take a word from him, but would look another word up in the dictionary, Hana replied, "Yes, but I really wanted to use *monstrous*."

The connections among reading, writing, and spelling, and especially the importance of writing to spelling, were never more evident than when we studied the development of Alice and Lorna, who, as their early stories show, from kindergarten onward, were the most enthusiastic and gifted writers in the study (see Figures 6.3 and 6.4). For Alice, the impetus to spell correctly was related to her sense of audience. For her, spelling was

Figure 6.3 Alice, Grade 1, November: *"Mom went downstairs to get paint to paint the house"*

always secondary to composing. She was writing memorable pieces (such as her story in Figure 6.3 about painting the house, which she wrote early in grade 1) before she could read independently, using mostly letter-name spellings. She moved away from simple letter-sound matching spellings only when she realized that her intended audience (an aunt to whom she had written) couldn't read everything she wrote. Both Alice and Lorna were avid readers and writers and had separate and extensive portfolios

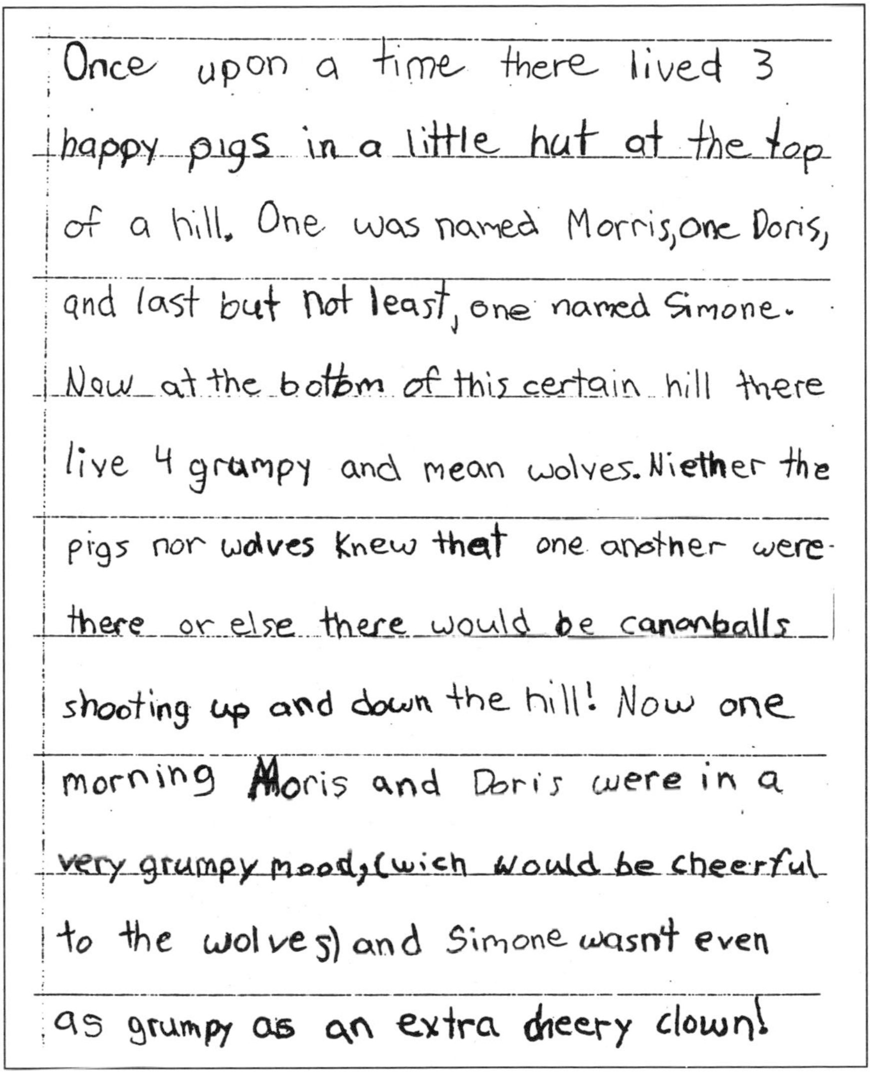

Once upon a time there lived 3
happy pigs in a little hut at the top
of a hill. One was named Morris, one Doris,
and last but not least, one named Simone.
Now at the botom of this certain hill there
live 4 grumpy and mean wolves. Niether the
pigs nor wolves knew that one another were
there or else there would be canonballs
shooting up and down the hill! Now one
morning Moris and Doris were in a
very grumpy mood, (wich would be cheerful
to the wolves) and Simone wasnt even
as grumpy as an extra cheery clown!

Figure 6.4 Lorna, Grade 2: Introduction to a four-page story, "The Three Innocent Pigs and the Four Guilty Wolves"

of their "home" writing. Alice had her own writing area at home, including a great deal of writing materials and a filing system for her pieces. She wrote poetry before starting school and was writing chapter books and plays before the end of the study. Both Alice and Lorna regularly discussed and shared their reading, their writing, and their writing ideas and drafts with their parents. Although Lorna had been reading independently since she was three, her father continued to read aloud to her at least until she left the study in grade 5.

In grade 3, Lorna talked about borrowing words from her reading for her current story. "I'm using *Irene* in a story I'm writing now, and I read that. And *furry* is the only word I used from the novel, except for obvious things." Lorna even used the books she was reading as a source for correct spellings, telling us, "Well, before I didn't know how to spell as well as I do now, I just took out the book I was reading, and I found it [the word she wanted to spell] instead of [looking for] the dictionary." It was obvious that these children lived in very literate environments, and it isn't surprising that they thought as writers. Lorna, for example, was in grade 3 when she recounted her experience writing three pieces.

MARGARET: When did you start writing stories describing what you actually did? Do you remember that?

LORNA: Well, even in grade 1, I wrote "My Newest Adventure" and I sort of got that from—I was just thinking about it and I said, "That could be turned into a story." Like, I didn't read it but I was just thinking. I was developing a story in my mind, but I didn't realize that I could put it on paper until a couple of days [later].

[*Later, she talked about a poem she had written in grade 3.*]
There's one called "The Tree of Birds." You see, every day I wake up around six, and I walk around the block, and a place in my block has this humungous pine tree with all these birds. You can't even hear yourself talking. I wrote a poem about that.

[*Later, she gave an example of how she starts to think of the situation in a story.*]
Well, one day I was almost going to write "Teresa Troll," like when she [the teacher] was reading a story to us, and it was a story about a boy who went to school, and I said, "Wait a minute! If Teresa went to school, what would happen?"

MARGARET: So when the teacher is actually reading a story, you're starting to write your own story?

LORNA: Yes.

MARGARET: Does this mean you can't actually listen to what she's saying, or what?

LORNA: Yes, I can, I can.

MARGARET: But your ideas are going on at the same time?

LORNA: Yeah, and while she was reading the story, the boy kept on getting into trouble, and I said, "Why doesn't Dorothy get in trouble and somehow lose Teresa?" like I'd lost my troll. So I combined the ideas of the book and—

MARGARET: And did you actually start to write that when it was writing time that day?

LORNA: Yes.

Clearly, Lorna viewed her world, including her reading world, with the eyes of a writer. Literacy was a vital part of Lorna and Alice's everyday lives, as it was for the other good spellers. As Alice put it in grade 6, when talking about how she became such a good speller;

ALICE: Reading—reading and writing a lot. That's what I do, like, I don't have a TV, so instead of watching a TV programme, I'll read my favourite story or whatever, and I write a lot.

Later, elaborating on how reading helped, Alice said it was because "you recognize all the words and you're seeing them a lot, so that when you're trying to write them on a piece of paper, you remember it, like, unconsciously." Explaining how writing helps, Alice said it was because "you're writing these words a lot."

Like the other good spellers, for Alice and Lorna paying attention to the meaning and spelling of words was an essential part of being an engaged reader and writer. It wasn't surprising that Alice's advice on how somebody could become a better speller was "Well, read and write—*that* just—it's doing it a lot."

Poor Spellers

The group of poor spellers, whose overall literacy development was also slow, included three children in Hampton Park (Kevin, Trevor, and Adam) and two children who started in Fulham and moved to Black Ravine School (Allan and Bryan). To these we would have added Nash, whose literacy profile, including his spelling, was very similar to the other five, but who left Hampton Park at the end of grade 4 for a special education programme in another school. The profiles of these six children are remarkably similar. They are all Caucasian boys for whom English is the language of the home, and they all entered school with a sophisticated speaking vocabulary for their age (although Adam had a speech mannerism that made it difficult to understand him at times). Their overall progress in school was very slow, and from the beginning they lagged in their literacy development compared to other children in their classrooms.

Early in grade 1 they all had a stable concept of letter, but were not able to recognize by name and sound all the letters of the alphabet, and they were not successful in concept-of-print tasks (Clay 1979), which required a rudimentary concept of word. They confused words with lines of print, were unable to point to the beginning and ending of words, and could not match words on the same page of print. In fact, it took most of these children until fall of grade 2 and the rest until the end of that grade to develop stable concepts of word and a full knowledge of the alphabet.

All of the children in this group were identified in the early grades as needing additional help, especially in reading. In spite of school policy to allow children to progress through the grades with their age peers and to accommodate special education needs within regular classrooms as much as possible, Adam and Trevor were held back an extra year, in kindergarten and grade 1 respectively, and Bryan and Allan were in sufficient difficulty to be placed in a full-time special education withdrawal programme by grade 3. In addition, throughout their elementary years this group of children was given substantial daily help from special education teachers who were assigned as additional resources within the regular classroom, and they were withdrawn daily for periods of remedial help. All but Kevin were placed in classrooms specifically designed and taught by a team that included a special education teacher in order to integrate children with special needs within a regular classroom programme. In addition, most of these children had extra tutoring at home.

Even with such additional help, this group of children in grade 4 continued to struggle with independent reading and needed considerable help with unfamiliar text. The sample reading miscue analyzes of Trevor and Kevin shown in Figure 6.5 are typical of the difficulty all of these children

Figure 6.5 Reading Miscue Analyzes. A: Kevin, Grade 4, June. B: Trevor, Grade 5, May

A

$pretting

. . . but you have to know when to stop pretending."

$pleated

"Please come down by the barn Mom," I pleaded.

Hasn't

"I'm not imagining anything. There is a bear there. Honest!"

(R) happening to wild

I walked slowly out of the house, hoping she would call

(me) back. . .

B

They have (P) (uc) familiar family

Then, half way around Otter Lake, the familiar tree

tail (P) bloated

house in the tall pine came into view. A lump bobbed up and down in

then (uc) sudden suddenly stared

Chris(s) throat when she studied the tree house she shared with her pals

every day.

had in integrating graphophonic and contextual cues as they read, and their tendency to use initial and sometimes final letters to generate words that did not make sense in the surrounding text. Their reading comprehension was usually limited to the basic details, and only Kevin reached independent reading of grade-appropriate material by the end of the study, although Adam came close.

Perhaps not surprisingly, Kevin was also the only child in the group who, although by no means a prolific reader, at some points over the course of our study referred to reading regularly beyond school requirements, and, at least once admitted to actually *liking* to read. In June of grade 4, when asked if he was a good reader, Kevin told us, "I don't know. I like reading," and at the end of grade 6, when asked what he read, he responded, "Sometimes stuff I have to read, and sometimes stuff I want to read." For most of the study Adam was at best ambivalent about reading, as the following interview with our research assistant, Fran, at the end of grade 3 illustrates.

FRAN: Do you read at home?

ADAM: Sometimes.

FRAN: How often would "sometimes" be? Twice a week? Three times a week? Less than that?

ADAM: I don't know.

FRAN: Well, try and think about it. Do you read every day?

ADAM: Maybe just a bit [*sounded doubtful*].

FRAN: Maybe—or no?

ADAM: Yeah, just a bit at school. But sometimes on Saturday and Sunday.

FRAN: Saturdays and Sundays you'll read? Or you won't? [*Adam makes a face.*] What does that mean? You don't read?

ADAM: No. [*Both laugh.*]

FRAN: What about after school and at night? Do you read then?

ADAM: No.

FRAN: All right. What types of books do you like to read when you read at school?

ADAM: Easy-to-read novels.

The other children who were poor spellers made it very clear that they neither enjoyed reading nor read much beyond school requirements. As Bryan told us, "I *hate* reading." The following conversation with Trevor at the end of grade 3 reflects the reading interests of these children.

FRAN: Do you read at home?

TREVOR: Sometimes. I'm in the middle of reading a book [a Ninja Turtle book]. I read at night sometimes.

FRAN: Every night?

TREVOR: No, sometimes. Sometimes my mom reads to me and sometimes I read to myself.

FRAN: Do you do that every night? Either you read or your mom reads to you?

TREVOR: No, not every night. Just sometimes I read. [*Asked whether he ever read magazines or comics.*] Sometimes I read comics.

FRAN: Very often?

TREVOR: No. [*Asked what he'd like to read.*] Adventure books, sort of, and funny books.

FRAN: Do you like to read?

TREVOR: Hmmm...[*seems unsure*].

Given their general slowness in developing literate behaviour, it's not surprising that these children were slow to generate readable spellings. In our dictated spelling situations, most of these children moved to fully letter-sound matching spellings around the spring of grade 2; Adam and Allan didn't produce such spellings until grade 3. In their writing at this time, most of these children wrote very little.

Adam was the exception. He was writing stories and would write industriously during daily writing time, although he rarely continued a piece beyond a single writing period, possibly because, given his limited reading skills and his incredibly messy text, he had very little idea what he had written on a previous day. Also, having caught on to the idea that letters represent sounds, Adam overpronounced each vowel sound, leading to very convoluted representations of such words as *let's* (LIEAES) and *kill* (KIAEL) in the story shown in Figure 6.6.

Although all of these children reached a point where much of their spelling contained features that could not be explained by sound alone, they reached this point very late—in most cases during the fall of grade 4. Having reached this point, however, their spellings continued to demon-

Figure 6.6 Adam, Grade 2: *"Let's kill it. I have a knife. I have a lighter. Attack. Watch out. Roar. Let's run. Back. Back."*

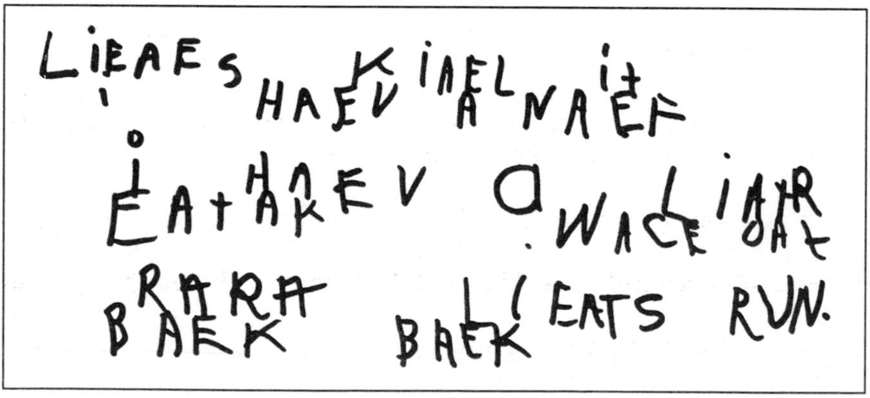

strate a great deal of uncertainty and confusion right to the end of the study. At least in their conversations with us, they never abandoned the notion that sound was the sole logic of spelling. As Trevor told us at the end of grade 6, "*Sound is the way it works.*" Even when encouraged to use the look of words to monitor their spellings, they were often unable to recognize correct or misspelled words, and they were usually very vague about where they might have seen a known word, as is evident from this conversation with Trevor.

MARGARET: How do you think you can tell when something *looks* right?
TREVOR: Like, if you've seen it before?
MARGARET: I see, and where have you seen some of these words before [e.g., TECHER, DOCTER, MAFIN]? Do you *know*?
TREVOR: Like...I don't know, I've just seen them—*places.*
MARGARET: So you don't necessarily know where you've seen them.
TREVOR: Yeah. I've just seen them.

Even when they could spot a misspelling, it was usually hard for them to pinpoint where the problem lay, let alone how to solve it. Margaret talked with Kevin about why he hadn't marked *pickle* (PIKL) as being correct.

MARGARET: Is there any particular part of *pickle?*
KEVIN: Umm...I don't know. It just doesn't seem right.
MARGARET: O.K., what about *sign* [SINE] and *signal* [SIGNL]? You didn't tick those [i.e., you didn't put a check mark to indicate you thought they were correct]?
KEVIN: They just don't look right.
MARGARET: They don't look right?
KEVIN: No.
MARGARET: O.K., what part of them doesn't look right? [*Pause.*] What about *signal*? What part of that doesn't look right?
KEVIN: I don't know [*sounds hopeless*].
MARGARET: Uh-huh?
KEVIN: It just doesn't look right.

Trevor is similarly frustrated when looking at the word *remembrance*, which he had spelled REMEMBERINS.

MARGARET: You know which part of it you're not sure about? Is there a particular part?
TREVOR: Well, *remembrance*, like I just don't know, right? So I'm not really sure.
MARGARET: Mm-hmm, what about?
TREVOR: But I don't know. It might be right.

None of these children showed any understanding that meaning related to spelling, nor did they tend to generalize from their known spellings to new words. When, in grade 6, Adam knew that his spelling of *nature* was correct, we probed to see whether he could use that knowledge to correct his spelling of *natural* (NATUL), which he recognized as being misspelled. Having painstakingly led Adam to an acknowledgement that *nature* was "sort of" related in meaning to *natural*, Margaret hit a wall.

MARGARET: "Sort of." Now, would that be a good reason for them to look like each other or not? Or has that nothing to do with it?
ADAM: No. I don't think that has anything to do with it.

Similarly, all of these children had correctly spelled *know*, but at the end of grade 6, only Bryan spelled *knowledge* correctly. Adam spelled it NOLGE, Trevor spelled it KNOLEJ, Kevin spelled it NOLEG, and Allan spelled it NOLEJE. It even took a long time for these six children to consistently use one of the most generalizable features: the *ed* past tense marker. Most only grasped it by the end of the study; at that point Trevor was still spelling *jumped* JUNPT. As can be seen from the following table, which gives examples of the words spelled correctly and incorrectly at the end of the study, these children tended to misspell common words for years.

Child	Correct	Incorrect
Kevin	LEARNED	BUZ
	PICKLE	NOLEG
	QUICK	VEW
	COMPETE	SINE
	JUMPED	GESS
Trevor	MUFFIN	TECHER
	GEESE	VUE
	DRESSING	KNOLEJ
	HAPPY	SINE
		JUNPT
Adam	YELLOW	SIGHIN
	TRAINED	NOLGE
	QUICK	BONTEN
	NATURE	PICKEL
	MUFFIN	GROSORE
Allan	DOCTOR	VUE
	KNOW	PICKUL
	EXCEPT	BEWTEY
	EXCEL	NOLEJE
		GEROSAERY

Bryan	SIGNAL	BUITY
	PROBABLY	GROSSERY
	EXCEPT	PLEACER (pleasure)
	PROBLEM	SPECHUL
		CHERPED
Nash (June, grade 4)	WIFE	GES
	CHICK	YELOW
	BUTTER	LERND
	PACK	YER
	SHOCK	KWIK

Adam didn't spell *yellow, quick,* or *muffin* correctly until the end of grade 6, and Kevin was still writing VEW, BUZ, and DOCTER at that time, despite having had these words dictated to him by us since kindergarten.

When we looked at these children as writers in the later years it was clear that they wrote the minimum required to meet teacher demands. They all told us that they did not like to write. As Trevor's book report (Figure 6.7) and Kevin's space story (Figure 6.8) from grade 6 illustrate, these children continued to write short pieces with simple vocabulary (even Adam reduced his output as he moved through the grades), and they were quite prepared to change what they had to say in order to use words they thought they knew how to spell.

It wasn't that these children lacked knowledge or imagination. From the beginning of the study Trevor's drawings were always rich with action and imagination, and as he moved through the grades his illustrations continued to be extremely creative. One of the grade 5 teachers talked about the "enormous gap between what Trevor puts down on paper and what he can say" and about the "phenomenal fund of knowledge" Adam brought to conversations on a variety of topics. Sadly, little of this is reflected in the writing of either child.

This group of children did not see themselves as having any inner resources to call upon when trying to spell a word other than "sounding out," so it isn't surprising that if their initial spelling attempts did not work out, they didn't know what to do next, other than turn to an outside resource. When he was asked in grade 6 how he corrected his spelling, Trevor's reaction was typical.

TREVOR: You can ask a teacher or a friend or something.
MARGARET: I see. Any other way that you have?
TREVOR: You could go to the dictionary.
MARGARET: And do you?
TREVOR: I've done that a couple of times.

From Trevor's tone of voice it was obvious that he really did mean a *couple* of times and that going to the dictionary was a most unusual practice

Title runAWAY Space Ship
Author Susan sAUnDers
Write a summary of the book
ther ar to Kids and
thay go to a spas senter.
     thay wanderd off.
into the spas ship
and it tok off and
thay got nokt awt
     and wen thay
wowk up thay wer
on a Aline spas ship
thay wanderd off
and fawnd a
rowm and ther was
a monster in ther

     The end
this was a pike yore
own way booke

Figure 6.7 Trevor, Grade 6

for him. By grade 6, Kevin had turned to the computer to do his writing and used its spell-checker. The others turned over responsibility for their editing mainly to their teachers or parents. When asked at the end of grade 6 how he found misspellings when he was editing, Trevor clearly showed that he abandoned responsibility.

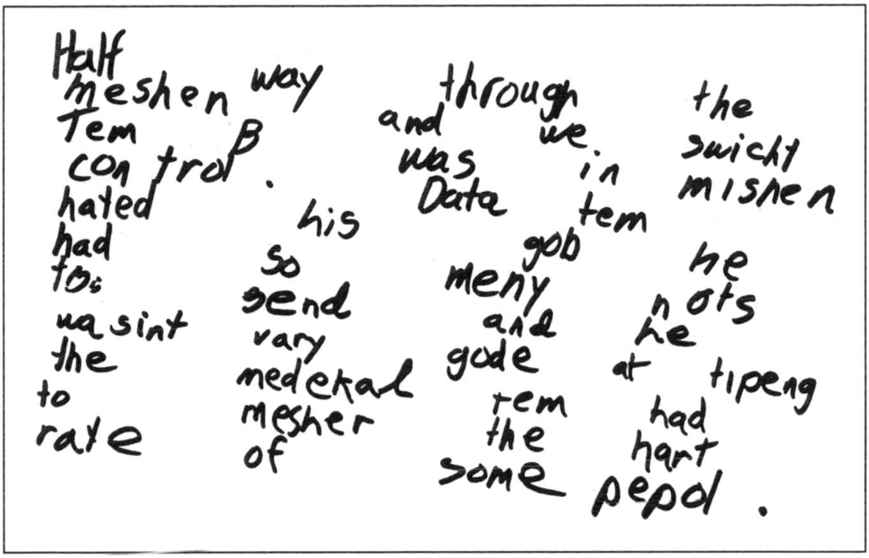

Figure 6.8 Kevin, Grade 6

TREVOR: The teacher tells you.

MARGARET: And do you find a lot yourself? Before she did?

TREVOR: Well, we're not supposed to do it ourselves—like, there's supposed to be, like, somebody, who, like—I asked a friend to, like, check the first page—that was in my rough copy, like, my rough copy was, like, a page long. And then I got the teacher to do it.

Trevor's teachers would certainly be surprised by his perception that he wasn't "supposed to" self-edit!

Even at the end of the study it was evident that these children saw the rules of spelling as strange and arbitrary. Kevin told us that spelling was "really weird—all kinds of rules and things." They were not able to make sense of it. When probed about what didn't make sense to him, Adam explained, "Well, the silent e's and all that stuff, and what to throw in and what to keep out." As Trevor put it, "English is kind of a weird language, you know!"

The contrasts between the good spellers and the poor spellers are striking. From the beginning, the good spellers behaved as though they *expected* spelling to have an underlying order, which they actively sought to understand and control. The poor spellers perceived spelling to be weird and arbitrary. While the poor spellers relied on sound as their logic for generating spellings, the good spellers were able to integrate sound, visual, and meaning knowledge as they solved spelling problems.

Literacy was a vital part of the good spellers' daily lives. They were curious about word meanings and spellings, and they adopted interesting vocabulary to use in their writing. They were avid readers who saw their reading as a major source of information about spelling. They were active, engaged writers who had messages they wanted to share, and they cared enough about their pieces to have a personal investment in editing them. What is more, they were aware of the importance of their writing for their development as spellers. In contrast, the poor spellers were at best ambivalent about reading, came to fluent reading late, and continued to read infrequently. They did not seem to see any links between their reading and their spelling; they certainly didn't appear to use them. There were no signs of the fascination with word meanings and spellings so evident among the good spellers. The poor spellers tended to write the minimum necessary to satisfy teacher expectations and took no personal responsibility for editing their writing. Even when pushed to do so, they were very poor at recognizing their correct and misspelled words or at pinpointing problems and solving them. In contrast, the good spellers were usually able to recognize their correct and misspelled words. They could pinpoint problem areas and had effective strategies for making corrections.

In the next chapter, as we describe children who were stalled at some point in their spelling development, it will become apparent that the type of behaviour and attitude that characterized good spellers and poor spellers also helped distinguish which of those "stalled" children would continue on their journey towards correct spelling and which seemed so lost that they appeared to have given up the struggle altogether.

Stalled Along the Way

At the end of the study, Sarita, a good speller, told us, "It's not like you can study spelling," and, when asked to explain that statement, went on to say, "You have to, like, have ways of learning. You can't, um, just, like, try to keep memorizing the words, like, look at the word and then try to just keep memorizing in your head, because then you're never going to know. You can't remember every single word in your head."

Sarita gave insightful advice here for the children you will now meet, many of whom believed that the route to good spelling *was* to memorize each individual word. In this chapter we look at three groups of children, all of whom appeared to stall at some point in their spelling development. The first group we refer to as late movers. These children came late to fluent reading and had early literacy profiles very similar to the poor spellers, but they began to progress steadily as spellers once they began reading fluently. The second group we call early readers–stalled spellers. These are children who were early fluent readers—earlier than some of the children who later became good spellers. In fact, they had early literacy profiles similar to the good spellers in many respects, yet they did not live up to that early promise in their spelling development. Finally, we describe the children who did not fit the early literacy profiles of any of the other groups; these children we call the in-flux group. These children were neither very late nor very early fluent readers, and at the end of the study, while some were making steady progress as spellers, a few were barely distinguishable from the poor spellers.

Late Movers

A cluster of children we found intriguing were those who, through grade 3, had beginning literacy profiles similar to the poor spellers described in the last chapter, but who took off in their spelling development after that point. This group included two boys, Joe and Thomas, in Hampton Park; a boy, Naveen, and a girl, Sangeeta, in Fulham; and a boy, Michel, and a girl, Monali, in Black Ravine. Two of these children, Sangeeta and Monali, came from homes in which English was a second language, and Naveen had additional help in English during his early school years because his articulation and phrasing were difficult for others to understand. These children did not become correct spellers by the end of the study, but they were steadily moving closer to correctness, came to have many of the characteristics of the good spellers, and did leap past many children who had had a faster beginning in literacy. As can be seen from the following table, there was a distinct difference in the quality of the spellings of the late movers by the end of the study from that of the poor spellers.

Child	Correct	Incorrect
Joe	BEAUTIFUL/LY	FETURE
	SIGNAL	COMPEAT
	CHIRPED	REJOYCE
	ATTRACTION	NATURLE
		GROSSORY
Thomas	FEATURE	GROCERISS
	PLEASE	REJUOSE
	EXCITING	MARVELLIS
	EXCEL	EXSCUES
	STAINED	SIGNLE
Naveen	STAINED	BEAUTAFULLY
	UNPLEASANT	COMPEAT
	PLEASURE	USUWAL
	KNOWLEDGEABLE	PROBABULE
	REMEMBRANCE	NATUREALLY
Sangeeta	SIGN	STANE
	COMPETITION	CHERP
	ACKNOWLEDGE	BEAUTYFUL
	FEATURING	TEARIFY
	MISCHIEVOUS	MASHINARY

Michel	FEATURING	MISCHIFF
	PROBABLY	BUSSNESS
	SEPARATE	MACANICAL
	SOLEMNITY	SOLEM
	COMBINATION	PACHENT
Monali	PLEASURE	REJOYCE
	ATTRACTION	REMEMBERINCE
	ACKNOWLEDGEMENT	MISCHEEF
	COMBINATION	IMEDIETLY
	CONDEMN	SEPRETLY

Like the poor spellers, the late movers were generally slower to develop concepts of words in print and were not generating fully letter-sound matching spellings in dictation until the spring of grade 2, nor did they produce readable text until late in that grade. Also, like the poor spellers, they struggled at first in reading and did not achieve fluent independent reading of grade-level instructional material until the end of grade 3 or, in some cases, until the fall of grade 4; but on the whole, they tended to write longer pieces with more conventional organization of text on the page than did the children who became the poorest spellers.

So what was different about these children? How did they come to progress as spellers so much better than the other late readers? One notable difference was that, once these children were over the beginning-to-read hurdle, they continued to progress steadily as readers. All were reading at least at grade level by the end of grade 6. Another difference was their attitude toward reading compared with the poor spellers. Once they became readers, they all read at home, in most cases every day, not only to satisfy school expectations, but also for their own pleasure. A typical response was Sangeeta's at the end of grade 3 when asked if she read at home, she responded, "A lot! I like reading." All these children were not only able to discuss when they read and for how long, but they could also talk about their reading preferences, often naming actual titles or novel series that they were currently reading. For these late bloomers reading became an enjoyable part of their school programme. As Joe told us at the end of grade 5, "I don't enjoy [writing] journals as much as reading [time]. I always look forward to reading."

It was remarkable how consistent these children were in their insistence that the route to good spelling was through reading. It was as if they had bought into a "learn to spell by reading" programme, believed in the programme for themselves, and were ready to spread the gospel to others. As Monali told us at the end of grade 5, reading helps spelling, "Because when you read all the words, you see them on paper. When you've seen them on the page you can remember it." Later Monali told us, "Reading and spelling are, like, together, because when you read a lot, when you read books, sometimes you catch on to the spelling...I mean, in the library there's a lot of words—there's more than a thousand words." Naveen expressed a similar understanding in grade 6, when he talked about how reading can help spelling, "because you learn more words and sometimes you might remember how to spell them." When we asked these children, "What would you tell someone who wanted to become a better speller?" Monali told us firmly, "Only two steps: studying and reading." Sangeeta suggested, "Read new books...'cause when you read, you can learn some more words from the books." Thomas told us with equal certainty, "Read!"

These children were convinced that their own progress as spellers was attributable to their reading. When asked at the end of grade 5 why his spelling had improved so much, Thomas told us, "I guess I'm reading a bit more, so I'm seeing more words and knowing a bit more." A year later, when explaining how reading had helped him, he said, "I just read a lot, I read a lot of different kinds of books, with different words, so you learn all that stuff like the *a-i*, and *ous* and *ation*, *s-h* and all that." Similarly, Monali told us, "I just got all my words from reading. I read a lot of books and for some reason they just store in my head, and then if I hear the words, I would know how to spell them." The same ideas were echoed in Michel's explanation in grade 4 of how reading was helping his spelling: "'Cause when I, um, like, see the word more often I get to know how to spell it." Naveen's account of how reading sometimes helped his writing sounds reminiscent of what we heard from the good spellers about using interesting words they had seen in their reading in their writing. He explained, "If I hear a word, how it sounds, I know what it means. And if it's a good word to use, I use it in my stories sometimes." In grade 6, Joe saw a reciprocal relationship between reading and spelling: "The spelling helped, you know, knowing the words and how to sound them out, and the reading also helped me learn new words for the spelling. You know, vice versa—each way."

We saw plenty of evidence of how these children's reading experiences had influenced specific spellings. For example, Monali, in grade 3, demonstrated the same kind of specific memory for where she had seen a spelling that we saw so often among good spellers.

MARGARET: How do you know there's a *g* in *sign* [SINGH]?
MONALI: Because, um, I'm the library monitor and when I was putting away books, one was on sign language. And I couldn't find the column [call number] because all the books were mixed up because of "reading buddies" so it took a long time, so I just remembered.

Later, when probed about how she had spelled *knowledge* [KNOWLAGE], she explained, "I'm just...when I see a word sometimes, in particularly *knowledge*, O.K.? I see—I hear—O.K., I'm reading a book about a wizard, and the wizard has a lot of knowledge, so I guess that reading books is the best way." Similarly, Michel explained how he learned about ed in grade 4: "I learned it reading books." Thomas had also explained earlier that he learned many spelling features through his reading.

Given their attention to words when they read, it should come as no surprise that around the same time or very soon after they became independent readers (the end of grade 3 or beginning of grade 4), the late movers began to show evidence of nonsound features in all of their dictated spellings and quickly moved to using the look of words in addition to sound to monitor their spellings, as Thomas explained after using visual cues to monitor his spelling of *knowledge.*

MARGARET: The look of it makes a lot of difference then?
THOMAS: Yeah.
MARGARET: What do you think is most important—the way it looks? the way it sounds? the way it means?
THOMAS: *All* of them are important.
MARGARET: Oh, are they? And how do you use them though?
THOMAS: Well, you need to be able to *see* what you're writing down—you need to be able to *tell* somehow. You can tell where the letters are. And you need to be able to sound it out or you can't spell it.

Using the look of words, they became increasingly able to pinpoint problem areas. For example, while spelling *lid* at the beginning of grade 4, Joe had initially written LIDE but then erased the *e*, explaining, "It just didn't look like it." Later in the interview, when having difficulty in spelling *once,* Joe talked about his imaging approach.

JOE: I can just remember it in my mind, but sometimes I can't make out the word. [*Pause while he tries to spell "once" again.*] I just can't see the words [letters?]. I can see all the sections of the words that I know.
MARGARET: I see.
JOE: I just, um, see it, but I can't really make it out.

Later, describing how he does his spelling, Joe elaborated.

JOE: I usually just try to spell it out—inventive spelling, trying to—try and find the letters for it, and try and spell it out. And I keep on writing down what it looks like and stuff. I try and try to remember it.
MARGARET: Well, you know, when you say you are doing inventive spelling, and you're trying to think what the letters are, how do you do that? How do you figure out what the letters are?
JOE: Well, I usually see all the letters in books and signs and stuff, so if I have a wrong word, I can tell.

In grade 6, Naveen demonstrated the importance of the look of words for his spelling when, after spelling *except* as EXCEPTE because he thought "there was a bit of sound" at the end, he decided to take the *e* off "because it didn't look right." He also knew that his spelling of *beautiful* was correct because "first of all there's usually a lot of stories about *beauty* ...and it sounds like it *looked* right."

It was evident that these children had a growing knowledge of letter-order probabilities. For example, in May of grade 5, Naveen wrote *attract* as ATRAKT, but was obviously not happy with it. When asked why, he explained, "The *k* and the *t*. Usually they're not together." With some probing, he generated a *c* to replace the *k* and said, "I think the *c*'s right." Similarly, Monali rejected *agk* in favour of *ack* in *acknowledge* because "there's rarely *agk*—it doesn't *go*. It doesn't *look* right." This is the kind of insight that makes these late movers so different from the poor spellers and more similar to the good spellers.

We also noticed that the children's knowledge of sound was becoming more sophisticated. For example, Thomas generated GEAS, GEES, and then GEESE as possible spellings for *geese* even though he was ultimately unable to recognize his correct version. Michel demonstrated a more sophisticated understanding as he explained his correct spelling of *compete*.

MICHEL: Um, "com," *c-o-m*, and then *p-e* for "pee," and then *t*, and then I added an *e* at the end.

MARGARET: Why did you add that *e* at the end? You paused a little bit before you added that *e*. What were you thinking?

MICHEL: Because this sounds like "ee," not "eh," like, so you put an *e* at the end.

MARGARET: I see, so if you *hadn't* put the *e*, how would it be pronounced?

MICHEL: Com*pet*.

The late movers often used analogy to similar sounding words to work out a spelling. When asked how he was doing his spelling at the beginning of grade 4, Joe described this approach. "Um, I usually have to just, umm, from other words I just find out what they're like. Umm, say it was *yellow*. I'll just write *yell*, and I'll find out what the other part is." Many examples of using sound analogy, like Sangeeta's generation of *stain* from thinking about *train*, were highly predictable. Others, such as Michel's reasoning when he worked on his spelling of *beautifully* in grade 5, were more surprising. Michel first wrote BEAUTIFULY, but wasn't happy with it and wrote BEAUTIFULIE, explaining,

MICHEL: Well, I know how to spell *beautiful*, so...I just put a *y*, and if it's wrong, it's probably this [*points to "ie" version*], because in a lot of words, um, like *Charlie* or something, you could put *i-e*.

MARGARET: I see. But does *i-e* look good on this one or not? Does it look right on *beautifully*?

MICHEL: Um [*looks again*], no!

Michel also used an unusual analogy when he spelled *heard* correctly.

MARGARET: So how did you figure out *heard*?
MICHEL: Well, because it *sounds* like it, like *learned*.
MARGARET: Uh-huh, like *learned*, eh?
MICHEL: Yeah. So that's how I figured it, like *heard*, h-e-a-r-d—heard.

Given their attention to the look of words and their increasing understanding of different ways to represent sound, it is understandable that the late movers, like the good spellers, all developed the practice of writing out alternative versions of a spelling to compare on the basis of look. By grade 6, Thomas gave us many illustrations of his growing ability to pinpoint a problem area in a misspelling and to generate alternatives. In this instance he is discussing his spelling of *groceries* (GROCERISS):

MARGARET: How did you know it was a *c* there?
THOMAS: It didn't look like *s* would go there, and *c* sometimes makes an *s* sound.

Later, Thomas wrote SEROUND and said that he knew that *round* was in there because of the sound and the fact that the word had something to do with *round*, but he still thought his spelling wasn't correct.

MARGARET: Now, what part of *surround* are you unhappy with?
THOMAS: The first part.
MARGARET: And do you know how to put it right? Does it start with an *s*?
THOMAS: I believe so.
MARGARET: So it's the *e* then that's troubling you?
THOMAS: It could be...I don't know. It just doesn't *look* right. [*Writes SER-ROUND.*] It's still not right.
MARGARET: No, but that double *r* is. Now, what about the *e*? What could it be?
THOMAS: *I*? [*Writes the word, changing "e" to "i," but isn't satisfied.*]
MARGARET: What else?
THOMAS: *A*. [*Writes the word again, but still isn't satisfied.*]
MARGARET: What else could it be? You've tried *e* and *i* and *a*.
THOMAS: It could be *u*.
MARGARET: Try that and see.
THOMAS: [*Rewrites with "u."*] I think that one's it. [*Points to SURROUND.*]

At first, we believe, the children's writing alternatives was prompted by encouragement in our interviews, but the approach soon became spontaneous, not only during interviews but also when writing. Sangeeta told us that one thing she did when writing was "write the word over, and if—then I write one more word, rewrite more words underneath it, and I'll check which one is right." At the end of grade 6, Thomas described a similar practice. When asked if he ever tried alternative spellings, he responded enthusiastically "Yeah. Sometimes I, like, look at words and compare them, and lots of times I write all the different versions on the side of the paper or whatever, so that I can see, and I look down and check out the ones that *look* right, and I take the other ones out, and I write that one down [in his text]." When asked what he might tell people to help them to get better at spelling, Thomas said, "Compare with other words—write it a few times down, and then limit it, you know, write it down and keep making assessments and stuff." Again, this approach of writing and comparing alternative versions was one used by every good speller.

These late movers also often referred to the concept of root word (although they didn't usually use that term) as they described their approach to spelling (as Thomas did when he was working on *surround*), and we wondered whether they were in fact using meaning to help them spell. Usually we found that their reasoning had more to do with sound, as the following conversation with Michel in May of grade 5 illustrates.

MARGARET: Why do you think that *especially* [ESPECIALY] looks so much like *special* [SPECIAL]?

MICHEL: Because [*pause*] you know there's an *ee* on the end, because... and then you could *hear* the word *special in* it, and then you just add the *y*.

MARGARET: Do you think there's any reason *why* the word *special* [is] in there?

MICHEL: I don't know why it's in there, but it sounds like it's in there.

Later Michel conceded that meaning could be connected with spelling, "in *some* words—and this could be *one*: *excel* and *excellent*...but only a few, I think." In November of grade 6, Michel was still talking about roots in terms of sound, when he used his spelling of EXCELL to get to EXCELLENT because "it sounds the exact same, then I just put *ent*." Asked whether the fact that they looked so much alike had anything to do with their similar meaning, Michel dismissed the suggestion, saying, "No, I wouldn't think it has anything to do with meaning." Even when he recognized *except* as the root of *exception*, he still reasoned, "I guess it's just the way it sounds." However, in February of grade 6, discussing why his spelling EXPLAIN was so similar to his EXPLAINATION, he said it was because "it's a root word," and by the end of grade 6 he was allowing that he *sometimes* used root words. "Not very often, but sometimes."

Like Michel, by the end of grade 6 all the other late movers came to recognize root words when asked, and at least occasionally considered using them to generate their spellings. For example, in the fall of grade 6, after spelling *compete* correctly, Thomas changed the *a* to *e* in his spelling of COMPATITION to spell it correctly, because "that's *compete*, and *compete*'s more or less in *competition*." Similarly, he pointed out that "*Natural* is *nature* and then *this* part," pointing to the *al*. Margaret then asked whether words that have similar meanings, like these, would be spelled similarly, and Thomas answered immediately and firmly "yes," and went on to point out his spellings of *grocery* and *groceries* as an example. Nevertheless, he didn't initially use his correct spellings of *know* and *knowledge* to spell ACNOLAGE. Questioned about the similarity of meaning, Thomas tried the *w* and then immediately said, "Maybe there's a *k* in there as well," tried it (ACKNOWLEG) and decided there was. Monali wrote *lawyer* correctly in one of her grade 6 stories and when asked how she remembered there was a *w* replied, "Like, lawyers usually have something to do with the law, so I just remembered, like, *lawyer*."

Still, like even the good spellers, the late movers were ambivalent about meaning-spelling links, often seeing meaning in terms of synonyms. Around the beginning of grade 6, we heard an example of this ambivalence when Michel talked about why KNOW and KNOLAGE didn't have to be spelled more similarly because of meaning.

MICHEL: I don't think they should be spelled the same because things can mean the same, but they don't have to be spelled the same.
MARGARET: For example? Give me an example of that.
MICHEL: Um [*pause*] *run* and *jogging*.
MARGARET: I see. They sound very different though?
MICHEL: Yeah.

It's clear from comments like these that the concept of meaning, particularly as it relates to spelling, is complicated and caused much confusion and contradictory thinking as the children tried to use meaning as an approach to spelling. Such great potential for misunderstanding needs to be taken into account when educators design instruction on the role of meaning in spelling.

As the conversations with the late movers illustrate, a key difference between them and the other late readers who became poor spellers was that the late movers had a confidence that spelling was something they could achieve. They were able to develop a set of approaches to help them solve the problems that everyday spelling posed, without making them dependent on others to produce correct spellings. As early as the end of grade 3, when Joe was struggling in trying to sound out words, he had confidence that he could do it. He told us that he usually knew the "last or the first" letter, and when asked how he worked out the rest he said, "It takes me a while, but I can do it." Monali displayed this same confidence when, at the end of the study, she described how she did her spelling. "Sounding out, and then looking at it and then I—if it's—I look at a different word, a word similar to the spelling if it doesn't look right, and then I'll use it. And if it *still* doesn't look right, I'll ask the teacher." Clearly, unlike the poor spellers, asking the teacher was a last resort for Monali.

Another important way in which the late movers differed from the poor spellers was in their greater sense that there was a system in spelling, although they were certainly ambivalent about the existence and nature of such a system. Thomas's response, at the end of grade 6, to the question "Does spelling make sense?" demonstrates this ambivalence.

THOMAS: No!

MARGARET: Why not?

THOMAS: Because there are *so* many different things. *This* rule is *sometimes*, but not *all* the time. And then, like, you can never put these two letters beside each other, and then there are *exceptions*.

MARGARET: Is there *any* kind of system in it at *all*, do you think?

THOMAS: *Yeah.* I think there *is.*

MARGARET: What is the system then, do you think?

THOMAS: The way you do letters, and the way you can put them together. But I think there are a lot of, sort of, *dumb* rules, and so many exceptions, and everything—you can do *this*, but you can't do it when… [*voice trails off*].

MARGARET: So you think those rules are dumb. Do you think they might have a reason behind them?

THOMAS: They might have a reason, but I just don't know them.

Although at the end of grade 6 some of the children, especially Sangeeta and Naveen, still tended to talk about spelling more as a matter of learning individual words, even they had a sense of rules that enabled them to generalize about spelling. For example, when Sangeeta correctly spelled *featuring*, she explained, "I didn't write it with the *e*, I take the *e* and put the *i-n-g* on it." We observed many such instances of generalizations across words, which reflected at least an implicit sense of system. When spelling *jumped* correctly, Joe said firmly, "I just know it has *e-d*." When asked how he knew, explained, "'Cause it's, like, a way of ending the word *jumped*." Even when challenged that the ending sounds like a *t*, he replied, "Yeah, but it's only—it has to be an *e-d*."

In some instances, the children were more explicit about the underlying sense in spelling. When we asked Joe at the beginning of grade 6 whether spelling made sense to him, he said that it did; when asked to elaborate, he talked about using words he knew to figure out unfamiliar spellings. Joe told us, "Um, just getting more of the facts of how there can, some—if you can't get one word right, think if there's any others that might be the same about it." Monali, speculating on an explanation for silent letters, summed up the sense that there is a system, but that she hadn't grasped it, saying, "There should be a *reason*."

The profiles of the late movers as writers were also interesting. Although by no means bringing the passion to their writing that we saw in most of the good spellers, it was evident that in most cases, the late movers worked diligently in their writing. In fact, "conscientious" was a common word used by their grade 6 teachers when describing their progress and attitude as writers. This conscientiousness is evident in the samples of work from the children characterized as late movers shown in Figures 7.1 through 7.4.

Unlike the poor spellers, the late movers tended to take more personal responsibility for at least an initial check for misspellings in their writing, usually checking in the dictionary. There were differences among the children in their attitude to correct spelling in their drafts. Naveen acknowledged that correct spelling was a concern for him even in "the

Figure 7.1 Naveen, Grade 6: *"Then something jumped on me"*

then something jumped on me! el scremed "Ahhhh !!" the thing coverdd my mouth. it had a knife. it was going to push it in my stonic then el wokeup. el looked at Jbray's bed. he wokeup to he said "el had a horrable dream". they talked when they were getting dressed they both had the same dream. when they went into the kichen they told their mother they didn't wont to go to camq their mother said ok.

The End

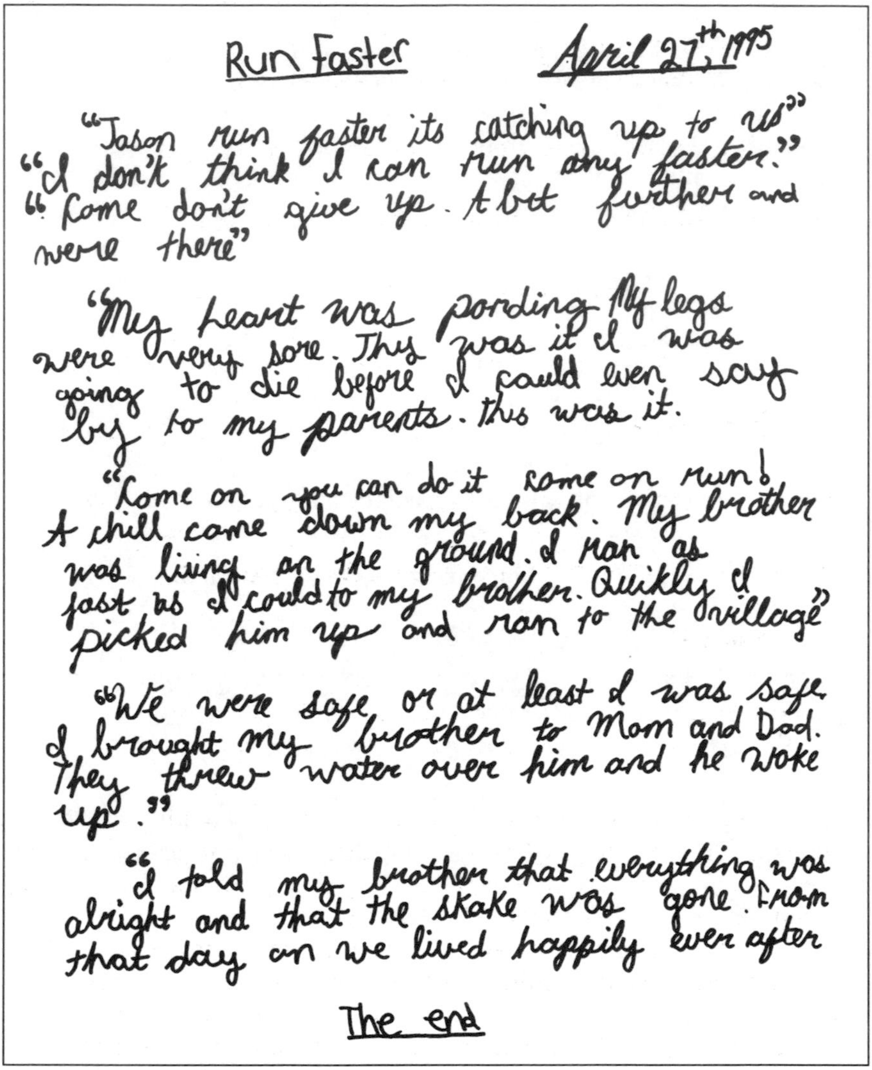

Run Faster April 27th, 1995

"Jason run faster its catching up to us"
"I don't think I can run any faster."
"Come don't give up. A bit further and
were there"

"My heart was pording My legs
were very sore. Thy was it I was
going to die before I could even say
by to my parents. this was it.

"Come on you can do it come on run!
A chill came down my back. My brother
was living on the ground. I ran as
fast as I could to my brother. Quikly I
picked him up and ran to the village"

"We were safe or at least I was safe
I brought my brother to Mom and Dad.
They threw water over him and he woke
up."

"I told my brother that everything was
alright and that the skake was gone. From
that day on we lived happily ever after

The end

Figure 7.2 Michel, Grade 6: *"Run Faster"*

rough copy a little bit, and the good copy, *yes*!" Joe told us that, until grade 5, not being able to spell well got in the way of his writing "because, you know, if you don't know how to spell a word, you don't want to bother asking people," so he would write less and said he would "replace the word with a simpler word." He thought that good spelling would matter. "If I was really proud of a story it would. If I didn't really feel proud of the story [for] me, I don't think it would." The rest of the children tended not to be concerned about spelling in their rough drafts. As Monali put it, "To

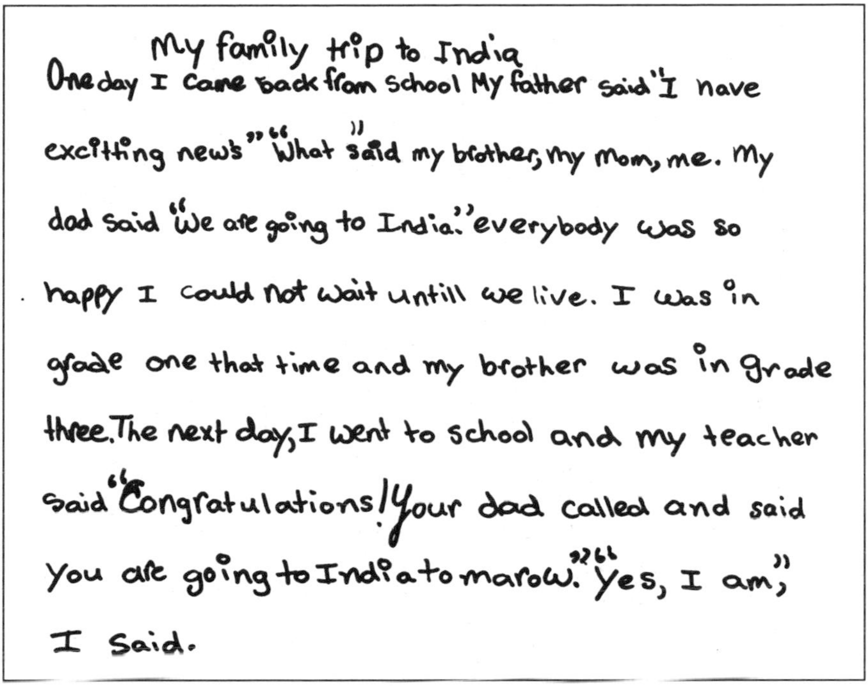

My family trip to India
One day I came back from school My father said "I have
excitting news" "What said my brother, my mom, me. My
dad said "We are going to India." everybody was so
happy I could not wait untill we live. I was in
grade one that time and my brother was in grade
three. The next day, I went to school and my teacher
said "Congratulations! Your dad called and said
you are going to India tomarow." "Yes, I am,"
I said.

Figure 7.3 Sangeeta, Grade 6: *"My Family Trip to India"*

me, spelling doesn't really matter. It's just when I'm writing to get the thought down." Similarly, Thomas definitely did not like correcting spelling as he wrote, "I don't care, I just keep going. You look for spelling and you get really bored and you lose interest."

It was clear that all the late movers preferred reading to writing. Monali was most explicit about the preference, explaining, "because, like, when you're writing you have to think about everything. Everything has to make sense right? But when you're reading, you don't have to think about all that stuff, like, 'Why doesn't this make sense?' You know, professionals and stuff won't make that mistake." Thomas and Joe were ambivalent about rewriting final drafts. Thomas enjoyed researching new topics but found it "boring" when it came to writing down what he'd learned, and said, "I don't like, uh, writing and rewriting. I just do the first draft and then that's it!" Joe also pointed out that the best part of writing is "the reading up and writing down, not the rewriting!" But he continued, "Well, no one I know really likes writing up a second copy over again, but—the good copy—but, you know, it's part of the project, so I made myself enjoy it." Such conversations suggested to us that these children were beginning to show a willingness to become invested in their writing.

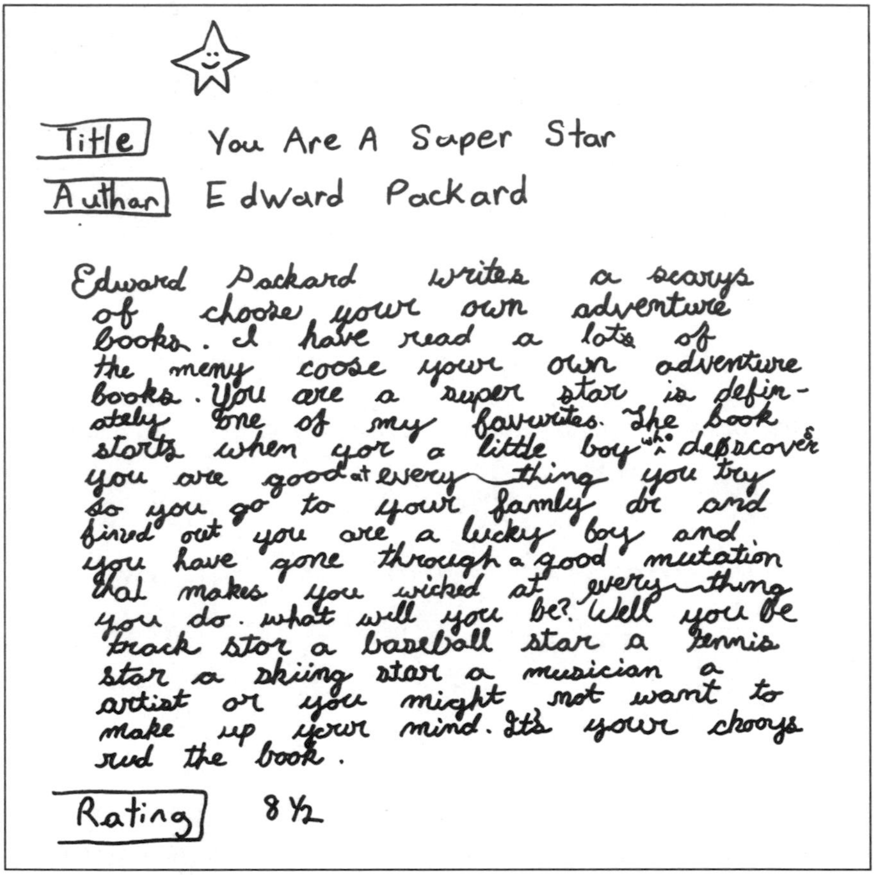

☆

Title You Are A Super Star

Author Edward Packard

Edward Packard writes a scarys of choose your own adventure books. I have read a lots of the meny coose your own adventure books. You are a super star is definately one of my favurites. The book starts when yor a little boy who desscover you are good at every thing you try so you go to your famly dr and finrd out you are a lucky boy and you have gone through a good mutation that makes you wicked at every thing you do. what will you be? Well you be track stor a baseball star a tennis star a skiing star a musician a artist or you might not want to make up your mind. Its your chooys rud the book.

Rating 8 ½

Figure 7.4 Thomas, Grade 6: Book Report

Unlike the poor spellers, by the end of grade 6, many of the late movers saw writing, and not just reading, as helpful to their spelling. Sangeeta saw writing as beneficial because, she said, it provided opportunities to "practice" spelling. As she told us in grade 5, writing helped her spelling, "because if you write lots of words and you get it wrong and you check it again and it's right, then you get practice by correcting it." When, at the end of grade 6, Margaret asked Sangeeta, "Well, looking back over the years, what have you done in school that's helped you become a better speller?" Sangeeta replied, "I write books. I write lots of stories." Again, there was a focus on words in her explanation of how writing helped: "Because it's, um, you're, like, writing words and you don't know how to spell them; you try; and if it's right, you know how to spell that word then." Naveen had a similar response in grade 4 when asked if writing helped spelling. "Yeah," he said, "because writing makes you a better writer, and then you'll learn more words. And if you keep on repeating the word out in your story, you'll learn it." At the end of the study he told us, "Pretend you're writing and you get one wrong, then the next time you use it in another story, you might get it right this time because you did it already, and you know how to spell it right." By the end of grade 6, Michel saw a clear link between writing and learning to spell. As he expressed it, "The more you write, you'll know more stuff [about spelling]." When asked what he'd tell somebody who wanted to become a better speller, Michel said, "I would, um, tell them to, um, do, like, *spelling* things, like a short story." In this, and in many other attitudes and behaviours that distinguished them from the poor spellers, these late movers grew more and more to resemble the good spellers.

Early Readers–Stalled Spellers

Whereas the good spellers, as a group, showed us a way to attain success in spelling, we were fascinated, though somewhat troubled, by a group of children whose early literacy profiles looked very similar to those of the good spellers, but who did not become correct spellers by the end of the study. This group included four girls, Toshi, Catrina, Yoko, and Elly, and three boys, Julian, Braden, and Paul, in Hampton Park; and one girl, Dhara, in Fulham. For all of the children but Dhara, whose home language was Hindi, English was the language of the home. During the last three years of the study, three of the girls in Hampton Park were selected for a weekly half-day withdrawal programme for children who were gifted. It should be said, though, that despite the fact that they did not make it into our category of good spellers as defined by our study, Catrina was seen by her teachers as a "very good" speller, and Elly, Julian, and Dhara were seen as "above average" on the basis of their performances in class spelling tests and their spelling in edited writing. Certainly, these were diligent children who could learn words for tests and who had learned to use various resources (including parents and computers) to produce edited, final copy. By the end of this section, you will be able to judge whether what we demonstrate about their ability to generate and monitor spellings, plus their understanding about how spelling works, justifies our description of these children as stalled.

To begin, the following are some of the words that these children spelled correctly and incorrectly at the end of grade 6. On the one hand, these children certainly had a respectable set of sophisticated words that they knew how to spell. On the other hand, almost all of the incorrect words below they thought were spelled correctly!

Child	Correct	Incorrect
Toshi	APPEARANCE PLEASANT	REJOYCE RESPONSABLE ACTKNOWLEDGE MISTIUFUSS EXHEL
Catrina	FEATURING PLEASURE ESPECIALLY RESPONSIBILITY	ACKNOWLEGE SIGNIFICENT MISCHEF EXCELL SUROUND
Yoko	LEARNED STAINED	REJOYCE ATTRAKTION PLEASER SIGNLE KNOLGE
Elly	DEFINITION PLEASURE BEAUTIFUL SURROUND FEATURING	IRESPONSOBLE UNHAPPIELY ACTRACT BUTTEN KNOLAGE
Julian	SIGNIFICANT ESPECIALLY BEAUTIFULLY CONFIDENTIAL GROCERIES	APPEARENCE EXELENT REJOYCE CHERPED MISCHEVE
Braden	FEATURING NATURAL NATURE	MARVALES PLESHER NOLAGE BUATIFULL ATRACTSION
Paul	APPEARANCE ATTRACTION UNPLEASANT RESPONSIBILITY SPECIAL	DEFFINITION MISTIUFUS CHURPED GROCREYS KNOLAGE
Dhara	REJOICE ESPECIALLY ATTRACTION NARRATIVE EXPLANATION	KNOWLAG MISCHEIF BUSSNISE CONSONCE SOLOME

The children in this group were early readers, all able to read independently by the end of grade 1 or, in many cases, much earlier. Braden and Toshi, for example, were solid readers of grade-appropriate text by November of grade 1, and Julian and Elly were reading in kindergarten. In fact, Elly was reading very sophisticated text when we first met her, although at times, when reading some of the very advanced texts she chose to share with us, she appeared to be "word-calling," perhaps trying to impress us rather than attending to meaning. Some independent pleasure reading was built into their daily classroom schedule, and all the children continued to enjoy reading at home, although (except for Elly) without the obvious passion we saw among the good spellers. Also, as the children moved up to grade 6 we noticed that, for many, reading at home was increasingly done only to fulfill school expectations or was losing out to other activities in their busy lives. When asked whether he read much at home, for example, Julian told us, "I try to, but I don't really get much done." Toshi echoed this low priority for reading, saying, when asked if she read every day, "Whenever I can fit it in." Still, regardless of their day-to-day involvement as readers, many were described as "very good" or "excellent" readers by their teachers, and all were reading at, or above, grade level at the end of the study.

With the exception of Braden, who held onto letter-sound matching spellings until the beginning of grade 3, this group, like the children who became good spellers, had moved beyond letter-sound matching spellings by spring of grade 2. In fact, through grade 3, most of these children appeared to be developing similarly to the good spellers. For instance, as with the good spellers, there was a marked increase in the number of their correct spellings and, as their reading helped them realize that some of their spellings were not correct, we heard frequent references to spellings not "looking" right. Also like the good spellers, they developed (albeit in some cases less rapidly) more sophisticated ways to represent sound in their spellings, including the use of analogy to the sounds of other words they were coming to know from their reading. Looking back at our summary observations from that time, we see that we predicted a rapid move in these children's spelling development. It was a move that never came.

In grade 4, it became apparent that there were distinct differences between the understanding and approaches of these about-to-be-stalled early readers and those of the children who later became good spellers. With the wisdom of hindsight, we can see that the signs of some of these differences had been in place earlier. As we described in Chapter 4, once children learn to read, they have available to them a large and vital source of information about spelling that has the potential to inform their understanding of the sound, visual, and meaning logics that underpin English spelling. There appeared to be qualitative differences in what these stalled spellers learned about spelling from their reading compared to the good spellers. As we saw earlier, the good spellers seemed to be fascinated by

words, often remembering in detail where they had seen or heard an interesting word, and they noted spelling features, perhaps because they deliberately sought ways to use such words in their own writing. The early
readers–stalled spellers, in contrast, did not appear to display this kind of
interest in either the meanings or the internal features of words. Perhaps
when they read they focussed only on the meaning of the text as a whole.
Such a focus on meaning is desirable for efficient reading, but it would
seem that this group of early readers, unlike their good spelling peers, did
not also read with an eye to their needs as writers and spellers. They certainly demonstrated poor visual memory for words they'd read, especially compared with the good spellers. A clue about this came from a conversation with Julian in the spring of grade 3, when Margaret asked him
whether he thought that knowing a spelling had something to do with his
reading.

MARGARET: And if you know it, *how* do you know it? Where does that
    come from?
JULIAN: I just learned it.
MARGARET: Do you think it has anything to do with your reading? Do you
    think?
JULIAN: I don't know.
MARGARET: Do you still read a lot?
JULIAN: Yes, but if I read, if it was a word that I come to that I didn't know,
    say like *bravely* or *excellent* [words that had just been dictated to him]
    and I didn't know that was the right—something like a couple of let-
    ters, and I didn't know what it *said*, and then I wouldn't know how to
    spell it, so I couldn't learn it from the book. I would have to ask some-
    body what it said, and then I'd know that and then I'd learn it off by
    heart.
MARGARET: Oh, I see. Are there words that you can read in a book—for
    example, *excellent*—words that you know that you've read, but you
    just can't exactly remember?
JULIAN: Yeah.
MARGARET: For example, you haven't ticked *special* [SPESHELL]. Now,
    have you read *special* in a book anywhere?
JULIAN: Yes, I have, but I can't remember how to spell it.
MARGARET: What about *button* [BUTEN]? Is that a word you think you've
    seen?
JULIAN: Yeah.
MARGARET: What about *eagle* [EGGLL]?
JULIAN: Yeah.
MARGARET: So there are a few words that you've seen. So how do you
    think that works then? There are words that you can read in a book
    and understand, but you can't spell?
JULIAN: Well, 'cause I *zip* through that page usually.

MARGARET: Oh, so you read it but you're not sure how to spell it when you've finished?

JULIAN: Yes, because I usually read books really *fast*.

MARGARET: Oh, do you?

JULIAN: And I'd remember what would happen in the story, but I wouldn't remember all that. Like, if an eagle flew overhead [in a story], I wouldn't remember that until, like, if somebody was sharing something, they wouldn't tell, "Meanwhile, an eagle flew overhead," and then I'll forget about that part if I was sharing.

MARGARET: I see, but you'd have read it and seen it, but you wouldn't necessarily remember it?

JULIAN: Yeah.

MARGARET: You mean, you wouldn't remember it happening or you wouldn't remember how to spell it?

JULIAN: I wouldn't remember how it happened—I wouldn't even remember it.

MARGARET: Oh, I see. That's how it happens, is it?

JULIAN: Yes, if you read it over again, you'd see it and remember it, usually.

MARGARET: I see.

Clearly, Julian is at best ambivalent about the relationship between his reading and his spelling knowledge. Similarly, even though Catrina claimed that reading helped her spelling she was equally vague about how that relationship worked. Margaret asked Catrina how reading helps people become good spellers and she replied, "I read a lot and then the words *automatically* go into my head." She betrayed her lack of confidence in this approach, however, adding, "But I don't really think about them." After listening to these children, it seems to us that the process by which reading helps spelling may be far from automatic.

Lack of attention to the internal features of words might also explain some other behaviour that characterized these spellers. For instance, they were very poor at judging which of their spellings were correct. At the end of grade 3, when we asked the children to identify the words in the dictated list they thought were correct, all but Julian identified more than twice as many words correct than were actually correct. In Braden's case, of twenty-nine words he identified as correct, only ten actually were. Even at the end of grade 6, we noticed a serious overestimation of correct spellings (see Table 7.1)

In addition, most of these children, as can be seen from Table 7.1, rejected spellings that were correct. Dhara and Julian, who were most likely to identify errors, were also most likely to identify correct spellings as incorrect, demonstrating, perhaps, an overall lack of confidence in their spelling. Yoko did not tend to overestimate her correct spellings, but this was probably because she didn't take the risk of making *any* decisions

Table 7.1 Estimations of Correct Spellings by Early Readers–Stalled Spellers at the End of Grade 6

Name	Identified as Correct	Identified and Were Correct	Correct but Not So Identified
Toshi	16	3	PLEASANT
Catrina	22	8	0
Yoko	7	1	0
Elly	19	7	BEAUTIFULLY (preferred BEAUTIFULY)
Julian	21	12	ESPECIALLY COMPETITION GROCERIES ATTRACT
Braden	19	6	NATURAL
Paul	29	14	ATTRACTIVELY
Dhara	34	19	ATTRACTIVE BUSY BUSINESS

about her spellings. This lack of confidence may also explain why we noticed that, in contrast to the good spellers, these stalled spellers held onto misspellings over long periods and frequently lost spellings they previously had correct. For example, Catrina had SHOCK in the middle of grade 2, had lost it in favour of SHOK by the end of that grade, and then held onto SHOK well into grade 4, even though she had other *ck*-ending words correct long before that.

The following conversation with Paul illustrates the difficulty these children had in monitoring for correctness. Paul had written PACK, TAC, and QUICK, and Margaret probed about the *ck* he had not generalized.

MARGARET: How is it that *tack* only has a *c* and *pack* has a *c-k*? How come?
PAUL: Well, I'm not sure.
MARGARET: How would you work that out then?
PAUL: I don't know.

MARGARET: If you're not sure, why did you put a *k* on, then? 'Cause you've got a *k* on *quick* and you've got a—

PAUL: Well, I know how to spell it [*tack*], but I don't know *how* I know how to spell it.

MARGARET: Oh, so you know how to spell *tack*, do you? And you know how to spell *pack*, do you, and *quick*?

PAUL: I don't know, I guess.

MARGARET: Which one did you think you knew how to spell of the three?

PAUL: *Tack*.

MARGARET: *Tack*. You think you knew how to spell it, but you don't know *how* though. You've never seen it anywhere?

PAUL: No.

MARGARET: But you know it's different from *pack* and *quick*, do you?

PAUL: Yeah, I just know how to spell it, but I don't know *how* I know to spell it.

Like Paul, the other children in this group were inflexible in their approach to the misspellings they believed were correct. We very frequently heard "I just know it" as justification for a particular spelling, whether correct or incorrect, as we did from Elly, who, in spite of realizing that *know* is in *acknowledge*, insisted that she didn't need the *w* in her ACTKNOLAGE because "I just know how to spell it." Another common response was that they "knew" a spelling was right because they'd seen it. For example, Catrina was adamant that her spelling EXELL was correct "because I've *seen excel!*" Such rigidity and certainty was in marked contrast to the more flexible and tentative reasoning of the good spellers as they worked on their spellings. We were perplexed by this group's rigid confidence in misspellings and wondered how such intelligent and diligent students, well advanced in their reading ability, could be so sure of so many incorrect spellings. How could they *not* be troubled by some of their spellings? We suspect that the operating principle the children used to identify problems was the notion of "ease of production." If, during the dictation, the children seemed to stumble or ponder over a spelling, they were more likely to say they were uncertain of a spelling attempt than if they had produced the word with relative ease. What they appeared to monitor primarily was not, in effect, the spelling produced, but *the act of production itself*. We also believe that when children such as Elly and Catrina referred to words "looking" right, they really meant that they could *read* the spelling—if they could read it, it should be right. We observed a similar inflexibility in these children's approach to the misspellings they *did* recognize. For instance, even when they had begun to use "look" to monitor their spellings, they were less able to move beyond a global "It just doesn't look right" to pinpointing problem areas in a misspelling. In the middle of grade 4, when Braden was asked which of his spellings he wasn't sure about, he indicated VYOU, SHUV, and BUTAFAL.

MARGARET: Well, with *view*, is there a *part* of it that you're not sure about, or what?

BRADEN: No, just the look of it.

Even when Margaret tried to probe about whether the beginning or the end of *view* didn't look right, Braden wasn't able to pinpoint the problem and decided that both the beginning and the end were correct! Similarly, when probed about *shove* and *beautiful*, it was "just the look of it" that made Braden think they were wrong.

There were also numerous times when these children were able to recognize that a word was misspelled, but selected a part as problematic that was, in fact, correct. This was the case in the following conversation with Paul in December of grade 6.

MARGARET: You didn't mark *natural* right [NATCHURAL]. Is there a *part* of that that's bothering you?

PAUL: Umm, the ending.

MARGARET: What? The *a-l*?

PAUL: *U-r.*

MARGARET: *U-r-a-l?*

PAUL: Uh-huh.

MARGARET: That's actually right—the *u-r-a-l* is right.

PAUL: Oh.

Given their difficulty in pinpointing problem areas in their misspellings, it wasn't surprising that most of these children were loathe to generate alternative spellings. Of this group, only Julian, Elly, and Dhara made the kind of multi-attempts at their misspellings that was so typical of the good spellers. Even so, Elly made it clear that she didn't use multi-attempts in her writing, preferring just to "picture" the word in her mind, "because I don't like writing very much." It was remarkable how tidy and unaltered the spelling sheets of the other children in this group were. From the beginning of her move away from letter-sound matching spellings, Toshi had to be encouraged to generate even *one* alternative version, and never did it spontaneously. The following conversation, during which Margaret pushed Toshi to try an alternative, may explain why Toshi didn't use this technique.

MARGARET: Tell me if there are any words there that you are not sure about.

TOSHI: *Sailor* [SALER].

MARGARET: What is it about *sailor* that you're not sure of?

TOSHI: The *a*.

MARGARET: So what could it be? [*Toshi begins to write an alternative version:* SYLE.] A *y*? Does that look right?

Perhaps because such early attempts sometimes took her even further from the correct spelling, Toshi became increasingly resistant to generating alternatives. Even when our probing pushed them to consider, and even in some instances to verbally generate, an alternative, these children tended to actively resist *writing* an alternative. This meant that they did not visually compare alternatives in the way that the good spellers did so spontaneously and effectively. For example, at the end of grade 5, Braden had correctly spelled NATURAL, then spelled NATCHER, and immediately used a caret to insert *ch* into *natural* to match his spelling of *nature*, which led to the following conversation.

MARGARET: Well, if they're spelled similarly—you just told me that, and I'm telling you there isn't a *c-h* in *natural*—you were right the first time you spelled it, what would that tell you? Try to figure out how to spell *nature* then.

BRADEN: *N-a-t-u-r* then.

MARGARET: *N-a-t-u-r*? Is that the end of it?

BRADEN: Yeah. Er, *nature*?

MARGARET: Yes. *N-a-t-u-r*?

BRADEN: No. *N*...

MARGARET: Try it down here. [*Braden did not rewrite it.*]

BRADEN: Yes, that's what it would be [NATUR would be correct].

Similarly, Catrina, at the end of grade 6, inserted an *a* correctly into her initial spelling APPERENCE after some discussion with Margaret, but still wasn't sure if it was correct. Margaret asked her if she thought it would be better to write the whole word so that she could compare the two versions. Catrina explained, "I usually put things above," because if she rewrote, "then I'd have to erase the whole rest of the word." Nevertheless, Catrina still couldn't decide whether or not the *a* was correct. "I don't really know, like they look mostly the same to me, if I had it there or not. 'Cause, like, if I just went and looked at the word, I'd just know it was *appearance* even if it has an *a* or without an *a*."

Elly and Julian were unusual in this group because they seemed more able to pinpoint problem areas when they first moved away from using simple letter-sound matching than they were later. As mentioned earlier, they were also among the few in this group who frequently and spontaneously tried multi-attempts at their spellings. Margaret had the following conversation with Elly at the beginning of grade 4 about her spelling process, and it sounds very like that of the good spellers.

MARGARET: So, how do you do your spellings now? How do you actually set about doing it when I asked you? For example, with *chick* you wrote it twice [CHICK, *then* CHIK, *then crossed out the incorrect version*]. And with *peck* you wrote it three times before you were satisfied

[PEK, PEEK, PECK]. What were you thinking when you got to *chick*, for example. You first of all wrote it with *c-k*, and then you wrote it with a *k* just without the *c*. Now, what was going on there?

ELLY: Well, umm, I read lots of books and sometimes I just have to put the word down twice and see what one's right. Like, umm, sometimes I look at a word once, umm, like just quickly write it down, then look at it quickly, and I, umm, don't actually see if it's right or wrong, and then I write it down a second time, the second time looks wrong, and then I go back to where it was right.

At the end of grade 4, Elly was still able to pinpoint the problem, in, for example, NATCHURE and NATCHUARULE. She gave this analysis of her attempt.

ELLY: Well, when you get to *n-a-t*, it's all right, but when you get to *c-h-u-r-e*, it doesn't look right.

MARGARET: Is it all of the *c-h-u-r-e* or just part of it?

ELLY: The *c-h*—in both *nature* and *natural*. In *natural*, it's *arul*.

In spite of this, Elly did not rewrite *nature* and only changed *natural* to NATCHURUL. In fact, at this point, she uncharacteristically was rewriting very few of her spellings.

During the latter half of grade 4, Elly's spelling development showed signs of stalling. She had developed sophisticated ways of representing sounds, though perhaps she relied too much on whole word analogy, but she tended to use the information in a piecemeal fashion, segmenting by sound (usually into syllables) and representing each sound segment with a combination of letters (in the case of a syllable, often a like-sounding whole word), but without seeming to pay sufficient attention to the look of the resulting spelling. We also think she monitored for correctness by checking whether each sound segment was represented in her spelling— that is, whether she could read it. At this critical time, when in order to move forward she needed to *integrate* sound logic with visual logic, Elly appeared to be clinging to sound as her dominant logic. Although she seemed to use her visual memory to generate sophisticated representations of sounds, she continued to monitor words by checking their sound or their readability. As a result, the sense of the look of words she derived from her reading was overridden by her concern to represent each sound discretely. Needless to say, this approach produced misspellings such as EXSIGHTING and BUTY which surprised us, coming as they did from a child who had been reading such words since kindergarten! Thus, by the beginning of grade 5, Elly's ability to pinpoint problem areas and to generate sensible alternatives seemed to be declining rather than growing. We see this in her discussion of her spelling BUTY.

MARGARET: You didn't seem totally happy with *beauty*. Are you happy with it?

ELLY: No.

MARGARET: Why? What's wrong with it?

ELLY: Well, where I put the *y*, I don't know if there should be something between the *t* and the *y*.

MARGARET: But you think it's *b-u-t*—that part's all right, is it?

ELLY: Uh, um, yes. That part's fine, but I know there's supposed to be something in between.

At this point Elly lost confidence in her ability to spell and showed a growing tendency to turn to outside resources, as the following conversation demonstrates.

MARGARET: How do you do your spelling now?

ELLY: Not very well [*giggles*].

MARGARET: When you don't know how to spell a word, how do you figure it out?

ELLY: I just think about it.

MARGARET: Yes, but what do you think when you're thinking?

ELLY: About where I've seen the word before.

MARGARET: Can you most of the time think where you've seen the word before?

ELLY: Usually, not always.

MARGARET: And if you can't think where you've seen it before, then what do you do?

ELLY: Try and sound it out.

MARGARET: And does that usually work?

ELLY: Sometimes it does, sometimes it doesn't.

MARGARET: And then what would you do, if it doesn't seem to be working?

ELLY: I usually get the word wrong.

MARGARET: You get the word wrong then, do you?

ELLY: Yeah, because there's not many ways—sometimes if you go back again and think again, and again, but in our spelling tests [in class], we usually don't have much time to do that.

MARGARET: No, but what about when you're writing though?

ELLY: I ask someone, or I look it up in the dictionary.

Whereas good spellers quickly learned to integrate sound and visual logic, it was characteristic of the stalled spellers that, like Elly, they tended to generate their spellings in sound bits without seeming to notice how the bits fitted together in the look of the whole word. This produced some strange results, such as Braden's ECSQUES and ATRACKSHON.

These stalled spellers had even more difficulty integrating meaning features into their spelling. For example, we observed a great deal of confusion in the children's understanding of the past-tense *ed* marker. Not until the middle of grade 5 was the past-tense marker a stable feature for Toshi. At the beginning of grade 3, she used *t*, *et*, *d*, and *ad*; when asked how she decided which to use, she said, "I never know." Later, when asked why she had used *ed* for some words and *d* for others, her response was "I don't know, I just put it." When probed, she gave an explanation based on sound, but told us that "mostly you can have both *ed* and *d*." By the beginning of grade 4 Toshi wrote TRAIN'D but couldn't explain why: "I don't know, I just put it in." At that time we also saw Julian using apostrophe *d* to mark all past tenses. We also noticed that many of the children used *ed* correctly when the past-tense marker sounded like a *t* (as in *chirped*) *before* they used it correctly for past-tense verbs that ended with a *d* sound, such as *learned*, which they spelled with a *d* alone. Braden's explanation was typical: "If it sounds like a *t*, try *ed*." This reflects a logic based on sound, rather than an understanding that past-tense markers, no matter how they sound, mark a change in meaning. The stalled spellers were also poor at generalizing spelling features from one word to another. Paul's grade 4 spellings ATTRACT, ATTRATCHON, and COMPITION are typical, showing a lack of generalizing both semantic and syntactic features. Margaret asked Toshi, who had produced the spellings ATTRACKSON and DEFINISHION, about how she had ended *attraction*.

MARGARET: Do you know any other way to end words that end in *shun*, by the way? Are there any other words that you know that end with that kind of sound and are spelled differently from that? [*Pause.*] See, I noticed with *attraction* you've only got an *o-n* there, and you have an *i-o-n* here [*in definition*]. Is it usually *i-o-n* or is it usually *o-n*?
TOSHI: *I-o-n.*
MARGARET: So it could be *attraction* with an *i-o-n* as well, could it?
TOSHI: Yeah [*but Toshi doesn't try the "i-o-n"*].
MARGARET: Does that look right—*attraction*?
TOSHI [*after a pause*]: Yeah.

These children had even greater trouble integrating the logic of derivational meaning. Once again, as the following conversation with Catrina at the end of grade 6 indicates, sound took precedence, even though initially she talked about the "look" of the word. Catrina had written RESPONSIBILITY, but then IRRISPONSIBILITY, and when asked about the inconsistency explained:

CATRINA: I think spelling, like, it has to look right too. Like, I just can't, like, if I had *irresponsibility*, if there was an *e* in there it wouldn't look right to me. [*When asked what "irresponsibility" meant, she continued:*] It means that you're not really responsible, and that you don't get on with what you have to do.

MARGARET: That's right. So it means the opposite of *responsible*. So why would the *responsible* part of it change? It's like saying "not responsible."
CATRINA: Er, it's more of a sound of an *i* than an *e*, I guess, like—I think the *i* has the "ih" to it more than the *e* does.

Even though Catrina had other relevant information to bring to bear in making this spelling decision (she understood the meaning connection between the words), it was overridden by a spelling logic based on sound. This was typical of many conversations we had with the stalled early readers. These conversations indicated their reluctance to modify their understanding of sound to accommodate their knowledge of visual and meaning features in words. As a result, they were bound to be frustrated as they increasingly encountered words that could not be successfully generated only by sounding out.

Their problems really went back to the point at which they were moving beyond simple letter-sound matching in their spellings. Although they were including features that could not be explained solely by sound, they remained confused about how other logics could be used to generate and monitor spellings, particularly about how to integrate these logics when they might come into conflict. Because of this confusion, and because they could really control only one part of the spelling system, they quickly reached a dead-end and could not generate alternatives.

We noticed that these children had more difficulty than we anticipated in defining words. Again, this may be a reflection of their general lack of interest in words per se. Such difficulty hampered their ability to recognize and use root words in spelling, as we saw, for example, when Dhara was attempting to spell *prosperity* at the end of grade 5.

MARGARET: I want you to spell *prosperity*. What are you going to do? How are you going to tackle that? That's a big word, *prosperity*. What will help?
DHARA: I think, uh, root word.
MARGARET: What is the root word of *prosperity*?
DHARA: The meaning is, uh, [*pause*]. The meaning of *prosperity* is, uh...
MARGARET: What if you had lots of wealth? You're quite *prosperous*. So *prosperity*. [*Pause.*] Try it and see. [*Pause.*] So, how are you going to do it?
DHARA: Pros-pare-a-tee. First I'm going to try anything. [*Writes* PROSPARATY.]
MARGARET: O.K., now, so what do you think the root word of that is? Now, you have a go at it. Can you think of a word that has something to do with, you know, gaining wealth? [*Pause, then Dhara says something quietly.*] Yeah, what was that word you just said?
DHARA: *Spare*?
MARGARET: No, I thought you said something else. Is there a word that looks like something familiar?

DHARA: I don't know. [*Pause.*] *Pare?*

When asked how a person learns to spell, this group of children was most apt to see the solution as learning every word (not surprising, given their apparent inability to generalize successfully across words) and clearly believed that spelling was more arbitrary than systematic. We heard as many responses of "I just guessed it" and "I was just taking a wild guess" from these children as we did from the poor spellers. It isn't surprising, then, that all of these children turned to outside resources to monitor their spelling in their writing. Elly told us in grade 6, "If I don't know how to spell a word in my story, I just write it and wait for somebody to correct it." Toshi said that asking a parent at home or her teacher at school was her best way to get a spelling right. Asked for an alternative strategy, she mentioned looking up the word in a dictionary, but admitted that she didn't do that very much. Julian had virtually given up on trying to understand spelling and did all his work at home, using, as he told us, his computer and his parents for help.

JULIAN: And then when I'm done, I go back to the beginning and then check it all again.
MARGARET: But you don't do too much checking with your eyes. It's more the computer does it.
JULIAN: Well, I do sometimes, like when I take it out, my parents either highlight things or look for things that they can highlight.

By the end of the study, we could not even get a sample of his unedited copy. Julian, like many of these children, knew that correct spelling was important in school, but had abandoned hope of being able to spell correctly himself, and so had developed effective strategies for meeting the requirements of the school. Braden even found a proofreader at school!

MARGARET: Do you change words a lot in your stories? [*Braden indicates no.*] So you just put them down and then what?
BRADEN: I just start going onto the next sentence or whatever.
MARGARET: When you've finished what happens?
BRADEN: Well, I get Miss S. [his teacher] to check it and make sure the spelling's right.
MARGARET: And then? Does she tell you what the right spelling is?
BRADEN: Then, if it's wrong, she corrects it, and then I do it in good copy.

Like the poor spellers in the study, all these children (except for Dhara) saw editing as somebody else's role, usually their parents or teachers.

Writing was not a favourite activity for any of these children. Elly and Catrina enjoyed their writing but would rather read or do other activities

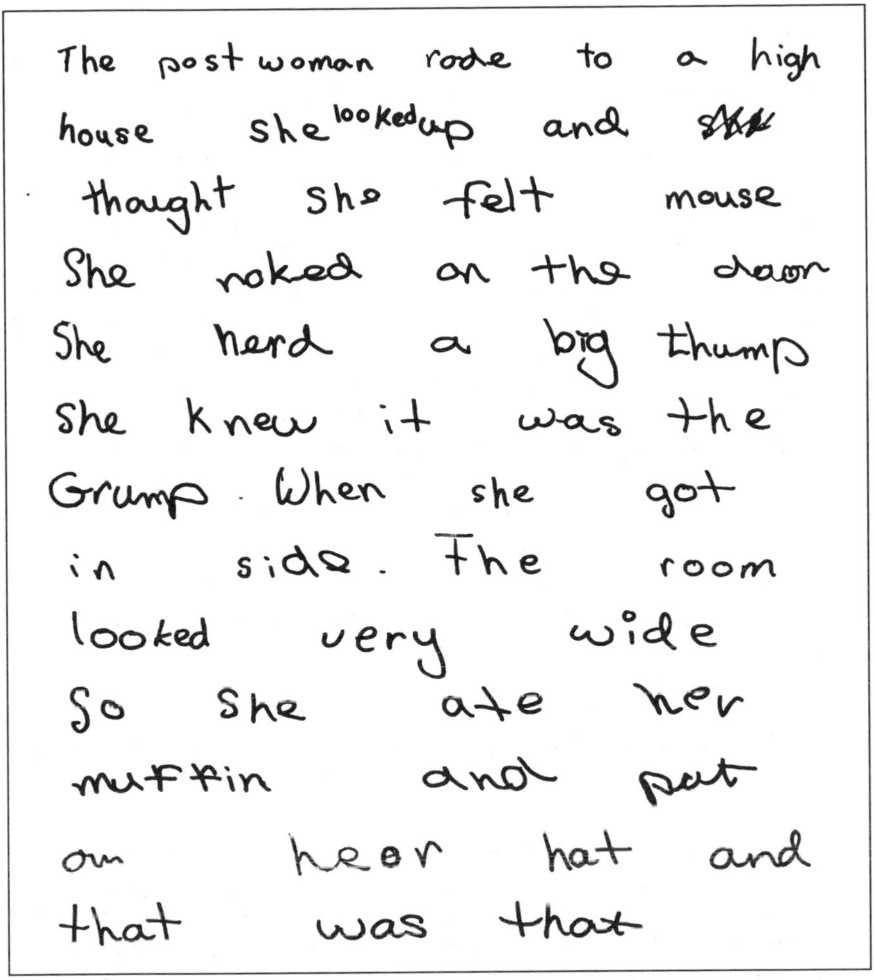

The post woman rode to a high
house she looked up and still
thought she felt mouse
She roked on the door
She herd a big thump
she knew it was the
Grump. When she got
in side. the room
looked very wide
So She ate her
muffin and put
on heor hat and
that was that

Figure 7.5 Braden, Grade 6: *"The Postwoman"*

than write. The writing samples of this group demonstrated their commitment to meeting the requirements of their teachers (although in some cases, such as Braden and Paul, just barely), but without the sense of engagement we saw in the writing of the good spellers (see Figures 7.5 through 7.8). Their teachers saw their work as acceptable, but noted that it often lacked evidence of the risk-taking in plot and vocabulary they might have expected from such good readers. At the end of the study, although these children still had a lot of confusion about spelling, we saw signs that Catrina, and perhaps Elly, were beginning to progress again. Interestingly, these signs of progress coincided with greater engagement in some pieces they were writing at the time.

Snow White and the swin Dwarfs

DEAR SEWIN DWARFS, HERE IS THE POSHION
YOU ORDERD TO REVIVE YOUR OAN MRS WHITE

TWO BAT WINGS ONE WOGELE
TAIL, ONE DRAGON'S TOUNGE, ONE HAND FULL
ACITIC / ACED → OF GIANT HAIR, ONE TABLESPOON OF
PTERODACTYL DROPINGS, AND A LEPRICON'S
TOE INTO A COLDRIN PRE HEAT TO 108060°
FOR 8 HOURS STIR WHEN READY AND
GIVE TO MRS WHITE PLEASE SEND $1,000,000000
TO 153 OFF THE WALL AVE P.O. BOX 12345
SEND $99.99 SHIPING & HANDELING

Figure 7.6 Paul, Grade 6: *"Snow White and the Seven Dwarfs"*

Figure 7.7 Catrina, Grade 6: *"Chapter 1"*

Chapter 1

"Mom, I'm home! And I have great news!"
I ran to her and knocked a glass of
leamonade out of her hand, the glass
shattered on the floor.
"Oh, Samantha Jane Newton! Look at the
mess you made!" She buried her face in
her hands.
"But mom, I have great news," I whined.
"Oh all right tell me your great news," she
sighed.
"Okay. Today Mrs. Grately, our drama teacher
announced that a new student would be
attending our class. She auditioned late, but
got in. Guess who this person is!!" I didn't
even give her time to guess, "Katie Parsons!!"
Maybe this is a good time to tell you who I
am. My name is Samantha Jane Newton.
Prefferably known as Sammy or bam.

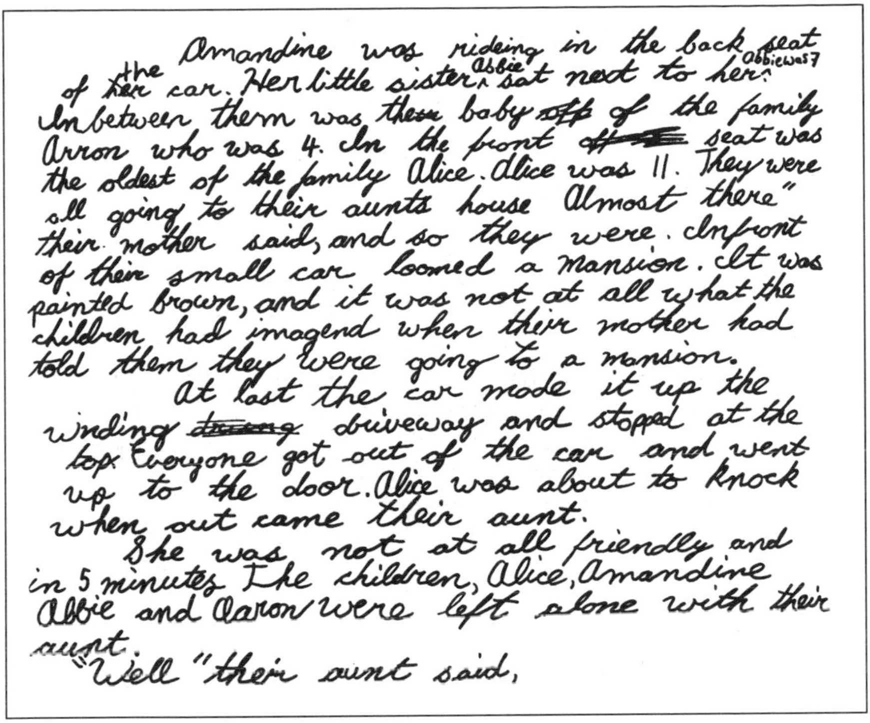
Amandine was rideing in the back seat of ~~her~~ the car. Her little sister Abbie sat next to her. Abbie was 7
In between them was the baby ~~off~~ of the family Arron who was 4. In the front ~~of the~~ seat was the oldest of the family Alice. Alice was 11. They were all going to their aunts house Almost there" their mother said, and so they were. Infront of their small car loomed a mansion. It was painted brown, and it was not at all what the children had imagend when their mother had told them they were going to a mansion.
At last the car made it up the winding ~~driveing~~ driveway and stopped at the top. Everyone got out of the car and went up to the door. Alice was about to knock when out came their aunt.
She was not at all friendly and in 5 minutes The children, Alice, Amandine Abbie and Aaron were left alone with their aunt.
"Well" their aunt said,

Figure 7.8 Elly, Grade 6: *"Amandine"*

Children in Flux

None of the children we will now describe fits neatly into the groupings we have already looked at, but we believe you would recognize them in your own classrooms. They include, for example, Vang, who was not speaking English when we met him in kindergarten and required ESL help throughout the study, but was bright, highly motivated, and a successful learner on all fronts in grades 1 and 2. His progress then came to an abrupt stop when behavioural difficulties, probably related to the turmoil in his life history, affected all his learning. By the end of the study, spelling was the least of Vang's problems. There was also Louisa, who from the beginning wouldn't take risks and was very dependent in all areas of the curriculum on her "best friend." Louisa gave more of her attention when writing to trying to produce beautifully handwritten and illustrated pieces than to what she wanted to express. Then there was Vikram, who, like Vang, learned English in school and received ESL help until the end of grade 3, and who hid a bright mind behind a rather secretive manner and, in his early writing, beneath a sea of letter reversals. In all, this "group" included a boy, Donny, and a girl, Starr, from Hampton Park; three boys, Vang, Kareem, Vikram, and two girls, Shauna and Louisa, from Fulham; and a boy, Parviz, from Black Ravine. They were neither early readers nor very late readers. Except for Donny, who needed some assistance into grade 3, they all became independent readers of grade-appropriate material during grade 2 (around the same time as Najali, Zeena, and Jamal, three of the children who became good spellers by the end of the study). They were also using letter-sound matching spellings by the end of grade 1, and, except for Donny, had begun to include nonsound features in their dictated spellings by the end of grade 2.

These children did not cohere as a group and, in many cases, had more in common with some of the other groups than with each other. While none of them were correct spellers by the end of the study, a few, most notably Kareem, Parviz, and Vikram, had at least some of the characteristics of the good spellers. (Interestingly, the homes of all three spoke English as a second language.) Some of the others, such as Donny, Starr, and Vang, were difficult to distinguish in many respects from the poor spellers, although, as can be seen from the following table, their spellings were of marginally better quality.

Child	Correct	Incorrect
Donny	BEAUTY	GROSERIE
	DEFINITION	MARVELISE
	EAGLE	STAYNED
	PLEASE	SPEACIL
	GEESE	APERRANCE
Starr	BEAUTY	KNOLAGE
	LEARNED	GROCERIS
	EIGHTY	APER
	DEFINE	DEFANITION
	BRAVELY	COMPITIITSHTION
Vang	BEAUTIFUL	NOLEDGE
	PROBABLE	CHARPT
	TERRIFIED	MACHANICAL
	MISCHIEF	MISCHEVOUS
	SEPARATE	SEPERATLY
Kareem	CONSCIENTIOUS	SIGHN
	MECHANICAL	SPEICAL
	DECISION	NARREUTER
	PATIENT	EXPLAINATION
	CONDEMNATION	CONDEM

Vikram	ATTRACTION	EXCELINT
	ACKNOWLEDGE	KNOWLIDGE
	EXPLANATION	SEPPERRATE
	TERRIFY	MISCHEFUSS
	PATIENT	EMIDIETLY
Shauna	GROCERIES	CONSCIENCEOUS
	NATURALLY	UNPLEASENT
	MACHINE	
	PROBLEMATIC	
	FEATURE	
Louisa	FEATURE	VEAU
	GROCERIES	DEFFIGN
	HAPPILY	TERRIFIE
	TERRIFIED	MACHANICLE
	DECISION	ATRICTIVE
Parviz	SOLEMN	ERESOPONCEBILE
	MISCHIEVOUS	SOLEMNETY
	NARRATOR	CONSIONS
	ACKNOWLEDGEMENT	PACHONT
	APPEARANCE	PROSPARITY

Many of these children had attitudes and approaches to reading, writing, and spelling that we observed also among the early readers–stalled spellers. For example, most of these children read more at school than at home. Silent reading was built into their classroom programmes and, in some classrooms, was required as homework as well, so the children in this group continued to read (at the end of the study all but Vang and Donny were reading at grade level), but their reading tended to be more to meet teachers' and parents' expectations than for their own love of it. As Parviz put it in grade 6, "I'm not *crazy* about it." He added, "I'm not exactly a reading person like *other* people. I read *sometimes*, like maybe I read [at home] five minutes or ten minutes." As they moved up the grades, reading at home tended to lose out to other interests and homework. Even Kareem responded "No way!" at the end of fifth grade when asked if he read in his spare time, although, as you will see, his attitudes were undergoing a major overhaul at the time. Even though Kareem, Louisa, and Shauna appeared to enjoy their writing times, they saw writing as a school expectation and not as an activity they would choose to engage in for their own enjoyment at home. Parviz and the poorest spellers in this group, Donny, Starr, and Vang, wrote the minimum they could get away with, even in school. These varying degrees of commitment to composing and spelling can be seen in the grade 6 writing of Donny, Shauna, and Kareem (Figures 7.9, 7.10, and 7.11).

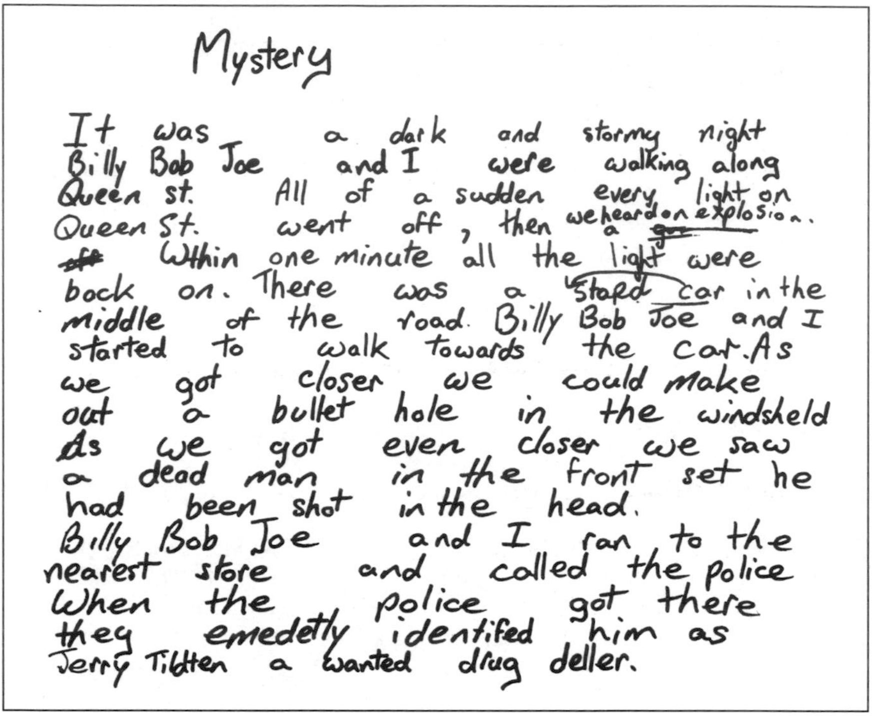

Mystery

It was a dark and stormy night Billy Bob Joe and I were walking along Queen st. All of a sudden every light on Queen St. went off, then we heard an explosion. Within one minute all the light were back on. There was a stoled car in the middle of the road. Billy Bob Joe and I started to walk towards the car. As we got closer we could make out a bullet hole in the windsheld As we got even closer we saw a dead man in the front set he had been shot in the head. Billy Bob Joe and I ran to the nearest store and called the police When the police got there they emedetly identifed him as Jerry Tibtten a wanted drug deller.

Figure 7.9 Donny, Grade 6: *"Mystery"*

Donny had attitudes and approaches similar to the group of poor spellers, although he was more advanced in concept-of-print tasks, used letter-sound matching, and moved beyond sound-only features earlier than they did. Donny required assistance in reading through much of grade 3 and looked from that perspective very like the slow developers. It was, however, difficult to tell whether Donny's achievement truly reflected his ability, because his reading performance seemed to be influenced by his resistance to being successful lest that would lead to demands to read more challenging text! By a combination of charm and a show of helplessness, he managed to get his peers to help him to complete a lot of his classroom work, and he took a similar "I can't do this" approach to the reading and writing tasks we gave him. Donny avoided engagement in reading and writing throughout the study. He continued to read at school because it was required but, by grade 3, told us that he *"never"* read at home "because I usually go out to play with my friends." He did the minimum amount of writing and restricted what he wrote to words he thought he knew how to spell, "'cause it's easier and faster." At the end of the study, when asked how he worked out words when writing, he told us, "Usually I know most of the words already. I do that purposefully. I don't use words I don't know how to spell." He went on, "If I do need to use a miss. Swamp would give 12 deten tions a day, never give treats, always yell, and ~~was always the had~~ and never smiled.

One morning miss. swamp didn't come to school, everyone was wondering were she was ~~Miss Rose~~ mr. ABITER the princeapble phoned miss.swamp. "RING RING" went the phone finaly miss swamp piked up the phone "Hi" she said "Hello miss swamp why aren't you at school today?" "I'm vary ill, I must stay in bed" "Fine but your class is going to be in miss. Roses class Well your gone!"

Figure 7.10 Shauna, Grade 6: *"One morning"*

word that I don't know how to spell, I just sound it out and, if it's wrong, the teacher will correct it." Clearly, Donny took no responsibility for editing his writing; in fact, he behaved as if the very suggestion that he should was a strange one. When Margaret asked if he ever looked over his work, Donny interrupted her and declared emphatically, "No! Mr. C. [his teacher] does that!" He explained later how the editing process worked, telling us, "My teacher edits it. I print it out [on the computer] and he writes on the paper and everything. And I just go back on the computer and correct the mistakes." He acknowledged that even if he did read it through himself,

Sindy whispered "where do you live anyway?" Johny asked. "On the street," she replied as tears ran down her cheeks. "Why didn't you tell me?" Johny quiried. I was embarrossed and thought you wouldn't be my friend, she answered softly. Their

(18)

conversation was interrupted by the teacher. "Would you like to share your comment?" No it's alright," Sindy blurted out. "Okay class we are going to start a unit on the supernatural and we'll start on a project. Partner up." Mrs. Rogers announced. Johny and

(19)

Figure 7.11 Kareem, Grade 6: *"Sindy whispered"*

he really didn't find much to correct, while his teacher did. Although Donny was perhaps the most explicit about where he thought the responsibility for editing lay, we noticed that most of the children in this group saw editing as something their teachers did, more than their own responsibility, even though self-editing and peer editing were teacher expectations in all the classrooms.

In contrast, Kareem was reading independently by midway through grade 2 and moved beyond letter-sound matching spellings by the end of that grade. But at that point his spelling development slowed as his commitment to schoolwork in general declined. As he candidly described it later:

KAREEM: I was sort of on my slant downward on my education. I thought education was garbage, you know. So I was, "O.K., fine, yeah, forget it, forget it." I never—so I never did my homework. I never did my spelling. And then my journal—so, like, to keep the teacher [thinking] that I had it done, I would always lie. And that's how I got myself in deep trouble. That was my worst year in school [grade 4]. And then, in grade 5, I realized I can't keep this on. I got in trouble for all that, and I didn't think it was worth it. Because I thought, "O.K., yeah, *sure*, I can do this now, but then what about in grade 6, when every single day, every homework you get, the teacher has to check it. Then, I'm really in trouble." So I just stopped from then. And my dad gave me real lessons, like gave me, like a few, um, a few hours of stuff. And then, after that, I got caught up with my work.

Indeed, Kareem did take charge of his learning. By grade 6, he began to move ahead in all areas, including spelling, and deservedly won the school prize for the child who made the most progress during grade 6. At that time, Kareem developed many of the behaviours we observed among the good spellers. For example, he became a very engaged and enthusiastic writer, so eager to talk about his stories that it was difficult during our interviews to keep the focus on spelling. Kareem constantly shifted the conversation back to an animated description of the plot and characters of his current story. He clearly saw himself as a writer talking with another writer.

MARGARET: I'd like to talk with you again about your writing.
KAREEM: Yes, and you'd like a copy of my story too.
MARGARET: Yes.
KAREEM: So, how's your book coming along?

In addition, Kareem showed the same interest in the meanings and spellings of words that we observed in the good spellers. In the following conversation he remembered learning words from his spelling list by looking them up in the dictionary.

MARGARET: And *especially* [spelled correctly] was one of those words?
KAREEM: Not in our list, but in, er, in some cases, when I would find a word, wonderful words—*nonpareil*—some words in French—something like—Can I write it for you?
MARGARET: Yes. [*Kareem writes* NONPARIEL, *then changes the "ie" to "ei."*]
KAREEM: E-i, I'm not sure, something in French—*nonpareil*.
MARGARET: So, when you looked it up, you saw the word *especially* in the definition, did you?
KAREEM: Yes, it said, "something, something, something *especially* unique."

Kareem made many references to how reading was a source of his writing vocabulary and his spellings, which suggested that, like the good spellers, he read with an eye to his needs as a writer. For example, in February of grade 6, Margaret asked how he knew the correct spelling of *different*.

KAREEM: I just *knew* it.
MARGARET: From reading, or from writing?
KAREEM: From reading mostly, 'cause that's where I get *most* of my words. When I read a book the same word keeps popping up, maybe ten or twenty times, you know, it probably soaks into my mind.

And later:

MARGARET: What about your writing? Do you think *that* helps [your spelling]?

KAREEM: When I read?

MARGARET: Well, I was thinking writing—when you write stories like this one, for example.

KAREEM: Right, when I read it helps my writing, 'cause that will give me a bit of the ways they use the words—like *frantically* [used in his story], the ways they use some of these words.

Like some of the good spellers, Kareem saw writing as a place to use the new words he had read; he perceived that the benefits for his spelling came from editing his writing. At the end of grade 5, he mentioned these ideas:

MARGARET: Now, how do you do your spelling, Kareem?

KAREEM: Well, right now, most of the time, what I do is, when I'm reading a book—mostly novels, like, the words are in there...

MARGARET: Uh-huh.

KAREEM: Mostly, especially if some words, like, describe the character, they keep on going, like, in the book, several times.

MARGARET: Yes...

KAREEM: So, by the time, when I'm trying to read that word—which doesn't take me that long, I sort of look at the letters—I sort of memorize it that fast, and then, when I'm writing a story, then, the first time, if I get it wrong, then I go back to my teacher and get it checked, and I'll look it over again, and I'll see what my mistakes were, and I'll sort of memorize what I got wrong.

Perhaps not surprisingly, given this emphasis on the look of words at this time, Kareem, like the good spellers, generated new spellings by writing down and comparing alternatives.

In grade 4 Kareem was adamant that meaning had nothing to do with spelling, but by the end of grade 5 he began to think about meaning when he was working on a new spelling. For instance, when he was explaining why *know* was in his spellings KNOWLEDGE and ACKNOWEDGE, he talked in terms of the possibility of meaning similarities influencing spelling.

KAREEM: Yeah, because in *knowledge* and *know* [they] are practically almost the same I'm not sure if it's probably, or mostly, 60 percent of a chance of its always working out.

MARGARET: I see, you mean that it will be like it—

KAREEM: If they almost mean the same, they'll be alike.

MARGARET: Yeah.

KAREEM: I'm just taking a pretty wild guess—I mean, a 60 percent chance.

MARGARET: Oh, I see. So you do use that, do you?

KAREEM: Yeah.

Later, in grade 6, Kareem showed us how he integrated sound, visual, and meaning logics to generate his correct spelling of *beautiful*.

MARGARET: With *beautifully* [spelled correctly], how did you know that there were two *l*'s in the *fully* part?

KAREEM: Um, well, I remember, like, a few, like, in my story writing, in my chapter book, I remembered about *fully*, like, "Cindy might not be *fully* recovered," and all that, so that's how.

MARGARET: I see. So, how did you do *beautifully*?

KAREEM: Well, I wrote *beauty*—*b-e-a-u-t-i*—not actually *beauty* with the *b-e-a-u-t-y*, because that would make *beauty*. But in *beautifully*, instead of putting the *y*, I put in the *i* and added *fully*.

With these kinds of understandings, Kareem was on the verge of joining the good spellers. Unfortunately, this was by no means typical of the reasoning of the children in this group, many of whom more closely resembled the early readers–stalled spellers (or as we have shown, even in a few cases, the poor spellers) in the ways they approached spelling. For example, they tended not to see any system in spelling, rather perceiving it as a matter of memorizing individual words. Louisa, for instance, in grade 4, knew that *sign* (SIGHN) and *signal* (SIGNEL) were related in meaning, but did not think that they should be spelled more similarly "'cause they're said differently, and they're different words." She held onto this view, as the following conversation in grade 5 illustrates.

MARGARET: Do you think spelling makes a lot of sense then?

LOUISA: No [*nervous laugh*]—not really.

MARGARET: Why not?

LOUISA: Well, 'cause every single word is different. Like they have silent letters, and...[*voice trails off*].

MARGARET: So, how do you think that someone learns to spell then?

LOUISA: You just have to memorize spellings.

Similarly, Vikram was telling us at the end of grade 5 that to learn to spell, "You just learn different words." When probed about whether becoming a good speller was therefore a matter of luck or whether there were things you could do to become a good speller, he said, "There are things you can do. You can take all the words you don't know how to spell and write them down, and ask someone to check it, and you can memorize them." Belief in the randomness of spelling was also expressed by

Parviz as late as grade 6 in the following conversation, as Margaret was trying to probe his spelling of *pleasant* (PLEASANT):

MARGARET: Are there any reasons why words are spelled a particular way, and not another way?

PARVIZ: Well, not really. Like, mostly people make words, right? So, they just thought, like, somebody first made up the alphabet, and then someone made up some funny words, and said, "This is the meaning of them."

MARGARET: So it's pretty much just a matter of chance, then, is it? [*Laughs.*]

PARVIZ: Yeah, if this was the first year that the earth was made, we could probably make up some funny words too, like *agarum* and we'd say the meaning and stuff.

MARGARET: But you don't think that there's a real reason why the *e* and the *a*—*please*—is in *pleasant*, then? There's no real reason for it to be there?

PARVIZ: No, I don't think so.

Even later, when Parviz was able to recognize the roots of words, he rejected the idea that they would help him to generate words.

MARGARET: And where do root words come in for you?

PARVIZ: Not at all.

MARGARET: Not at all—why not?

PARVIZ: Because I just don't use them.

MARGARET: Why don't you? You don't find them useful?

PARVIZ: No, not personally.

MARGARET: Why is it not useful?

PARVIZ: Well, because it could lead you off the wrong track...

MARGARET: So, what does *not* lead you astray then? What's the most reliable thing to use, then, for you? I mean, what do you find the most reliable thing to use?

PARVIZ: Sounding out.

Given such perceptions, it isn't surprising that neither Vikram nor Parviz became correct spellers by the end of the study, in spite of the fact that they had earlier both demonstrated a good visual memory for words and continued to add to their knowledge of how sound can be represented in English spelling. Neither child successfully integrated meaning aspects of spelling into their understandings. In fact, except for Kareem, the rest of the children in this group shared these beliefs in the arbitrariness of spelling and did not tend to generalize across words. Also, as can be seen from Table 7.2, like the early readers–stalled spellers, they frequently overestimated the spellings they thought were correct and had

Table 7.2 Estimations of Correct Spellings by "In Flux" Children at the End of Grade 6

Name	Identified as Correct	Identified and Were Correct	Correct but Not So Identified
Donny	19	9	COMPETE SIGNIFICANT
Starr	21	6	SAILOR HAPPILY STAINED EIGHTY LEARNED
Vang	52	18	HAPPILY
Kareem	32	16	MISCHIEF CONSCIOUS
Vikram	52	33	
Shauna	36 *(with help)*	29	MISCHIEF
Louisa	48	23	USUAL USUALLY
Parvis	39	28	PROBLEMATIC ABUNDANCE

varying success in pinpointing and solving problems, often rejecting the correct spelling alternatives they had generated. For example, at the beginning of grade 5, Starr thought that her spellings STEND, BOUTEN, and NATHIRE were correct and, even in the middle of grade 6, she firmly rejected her correct spelling of *stained* in favour of STAIND.

The following conversation with Shauna demonstrates the kind of confusion that results from treating spelling as arbitrary.

MARGARET: How come *beauty* you spelled b-u-t-t-y, and *beautiful* you spelled with the *e-a-u* [BEAUTFUL]. Why are they different?
SHAUNA: Oh, I just think so.
MARGARET: Why would that be?
SHAUNA: Because, they sort of—they might, they, they mean sort of the same, but they're also just like, like *sign* and *signal*—they're different words.

MARGARET: Oh. And if they're two different words, even if they mean similar, or even in this case, they sound quite similar—*beauty* and *beautiful*—they can still be spelled totally differently, can they?

SHAUNA: Yeah.

MARGARET: So how do you decide then?

SHAUNA: Well, this one [BUTTY] I just sounded out, and this one [BEAUT-FUL] I sort of think I knew.

MARGARET: Oh, so *beautiful* you knew, but *beauty* you sounded out?

SHAUNA: Yeah.

MARGARET: Now, why wouldn't it help you? So if you knew how to spell *beautiful*, that doesn't help you to spell *beauty* then?

SHAUNA: No.

MARGARET: Why is that?

SHAUNA: Umm, I'm not sure. I'm just going to try something out. [*Writes* BEAUTTY.] No, I think it's—umm…

MARGARET: You're pretty sure it's *b-u-t-t-y* even now you've tried it?

SHAUNA: Yeah, 'cause this doesn't even look right.

MARGARET: Oh, doesn't it? O.K.

Shauna had lots of the basic knowledge about these words to work towards a more correct spelling, but was unable to use that knowledge in an effective manner, and in fact was confused about how her knowledge would fit together.

As we look back at the various groups of spellers we have described over these last two chapters, so much seems to depend on how they approach their own reading and writing and use their literacy to help them as spellers. The good spellers were all among the best readers in the study and derived both sense and pleasure from their reading. But it's obvious that while reading was a necessary condition for good spelling, it was certainly not sufficient. The early readers–stalled spellers illustrate that being a reader—even a very good reader like Elly or Catrina or Julian—is not enough in itself to guarantee good spelling.

So what is it that the good spellers brought to their spelling that most of the other children did not? As we have seen, an important difference is that the good spellers were committed writers, and as such they approached their reading, as they did their general environment, with the mind-set of *writers*. As they told us, they paid attention not only to the meaning of what they read, but also to how authors expressed their meaning; they looked for interesting words and phrases to use in their own writing.

The good spellers did not slow down to read in a word-by-word fashion. They read efficiently as well as effectively. Nevertheless, they did notice unusual or interesting words and surprising spelling features. They were able to recall and reconstruct words they had seen in their reading or elsewhere much more accurately than did the other good readers. Also, even if they hadn't seen before a word they were spelling, they made better hypotheses about how it *could* be spelled than the other children were able to do. It seemed that they brought to bear in their spelling a high level of knowledge of print—Frank Smith's (1978) "nonvisual information"— that enabled them also to read so well. The other good readers in the study possessed that knowledge, but did not appear to use it to the same extent in their spelling. It seemed that the commitment of good spellers to use print as writers gave them a greater investment in attending to the conventions of print, including spelling.

We believe that a major reason for this difference is that the good spellers approached spelling with the assumption that there was a system to it, an orderliness about the ways words are spelled that they could make sense of. Their reading provided prime opportunities to hypothesize about, and make sense of, that system. In contrast, many of the other children saw spelling as arbitrary; they didn't believe that there was any system to spelling, so why *would* they try to make sense of it while reading or in any other way, for that matter? While all the good readers constructed meaning as they read, it seems that, for the good spellers, making meaning included making sense of spelling.

When it came to writing, early readers–stalled spellers like Catrina and Elly tended to recognize problems in their spellings only when they had trouble generating them or when they generated spellings that they could not reread. Even when they did recognize misspellings, they weren't good at correcting them. Their method of approaching spelling seemed to be "If I can write it easily and read it easily, it's probably right, and if it isn't, someone else will correct it." In contrast, when good spellers were faced with generating spellings, they used their knowledge and their sense of system to make reasonable choices and select increasingly correct renditions of words.

A *Context for* Instruction

MARGARET: *How do you get to be such a good speller?*
CHAN: *I guess from reading so much.*
MARGARET: *It wasn't, you know, from the lessons the teachers do, then?*
CHAN: *Well, those are sort of like side dishes, side orders.*

To this point, we have described the children's spelling behaviour and understanding within the context of their reading and writing development, but with little reference to instructional context. We have done this because the focus of our study was not the teachers and what they were teaching, but the children and what they appeared to be learning—the understanding they were demonstrating through their spellings, their spelling behaviour, and their conversations about spelling. Of course, the children were always spelling in their classroom and their home environments. Inevitably they would share their perceptions of the influences of both home and school as they talked about how they had learned to spell and about the sources of their knowledge about spelling. We also learned about both environments when parents talked with us about their children and when teachers each year told us about their programmes and about the children's progress as they worked within those programmes.

So what did we find out about the instructional context for the children in our study? As we said in Chapter 2, as a group the children learned within many classrooms over the years, and any generalized description would fail to capture the natural diversity among the teachers and their programmes. Nevertheless, there were some patterns in the instructional environment, many of which we mentioned in Chapter 2 and that bear repeating here.

Teaching Spelling and the Context of Literacy

Spelling was directly taught in all the classrooms we observed; these teachers cared about spelling. As Catrina told us in grade 3, "We have spelling and we usually have spelling tests, and I get a lot of it because Mrs. H. is teaching us a lot about it." As we noted in Chapter 2, very few of the teachers used an actual spelling text (a "speller") as the basis of their programmes, but most of the programmes included the kinds of weekly word lists and speller-like word study activities that we believe are typical of spelling programmes in many classrooms. A key difference from the practice of using a speller was that the words studied were usually drawn from the classroom reading and writing programmes. At least by grade 4, and in most classrooms by grade 3, the children had words to learn in preparation for weekly spelling tests. These words were usually taken from commonly misspelled words in the children's writing, published lists of most frequently used words, and words connected to current classroom thematic units. In some classrooms the children were allowed to choose the words to be learned, and some teachers gave activities related to the test words to be completed by the children between the time of the pre-test (usually on Mondays) and the test (usually on Fridays). With the exception of a few teachers of the earlier grades who integrated spelling instruction entirely within their writing process programmes, all of the teachers had regularly scheduled times each week when they gave direct spelling lessons, usually with follow-up activities. In the earlier grades, when the children were learning to read, these lessons were often linked to reading as much as to spelling needs, and focussed on sound patterns in words (for example, lessons on segmentation, phonics, and rhyming).

From around grade 3 onward, although there continued to be lessons on sound patterns, instruction also included lessons on syntactic features, such as prefixes and suffixes, and on the grammatical functions of words. Vocabulary study included meaning features such as homonyms, synonyms, and antonyms, although our conversations with the children suggested they often saw these as sound—rather then meaning—features. In at least some classrooms, there were lessons on word families and roots, although the latter term was not necessarily used. It was clear from what the children said that teachers provided spelling rules and mnemonics as part of their instruction.

Through all the grades, in response to the needs they observed in the children's writing, teachers regularly linked spelling directly to the classroom writing programmes through lessons on such topics as vocabulary building and editing. From grade 3 onward, teachers expected the children to edit their own writing for misspellings. When pieces were being completed for "publication," this self-editing was followed in most classrooms by peer editing, before the writing was handed to a teacher for response.

During the years when the children in the study were moving through grades kindergarten to 3 in Fulham and Black Ravine, teaching writing, using process approaches based on the work of Donald Graves and his associates, was a school district initiative. This involved a great deal of joint teacher planning, consultative support, and teacher development on the writing process and designing writing programmes in these schools during the early grades. This may explain the remarkable spurt of catching up we observed at that time in the Fulham–Black Ravine group, who on the whole began in kindergarten behind the Hampton Park group, but who reached at least comparable levels of development by the end of grade 2. The teachers at Hampton Park were also offered professional development on teaching writing during the years when the children were moving through their early grades. It is not surprising, then, that all the children were offered substantial opportunities to write during their early years in school. In grades 1 to 3, a regular daily writing time of from 40 to 60 minutes was usually scheduled, with considerable choice of topic and form given to the children. The children's writing tended to be mainly personal narrative, story, or poetry. Although in most of the Fulham–Black Ravine classrooms this kind of regular writing time continued through grade 6, albeit sometimes for shorter periods, we noticed a decrease in regular writing time in some of the Hampton Park classrooms. In grades 4 through 6 across all three schools, we noticed a marked increase in writing in nonnarrative forms, such as research reports on a topic linked to social studies and responses to reading. In some classrooms (again, more commonly in Hampton Park) the nonnarrative writing tended to replace rather than be added to narrative writing; this resulted in relatively less writing being produced overall than in earlier grades.

More of the good spellers, and even the late movers, were in Fulham or Black Ravine; most of the early readers–stalled spellers were in Hampton Park. We wonder whether the reduction we observed in writing time during the upper grades may have adversely affected the spelling development of some of the children, coming as it did when they had moved to using features in addition to sound and were at a key stage in trying to understand the complexity of English spelling. Any decrease in opportunities to write decreases opportunities to engage in spelling in the context of writing—something we observed to be vital to the development of the good spellers. The good spellers were not only highly committed to making the most of any opportunity they did have to write in school, but were also writing at home, and so would not be as greatly affected by a reduction of school writing time as would the children who only wrote at school.

When we reviewed the writing samples collected in grades 4 to 6 at Hampton Park during that time, we found that many were produced as part of a class unit and were often in nonnarrative forms, such as research projects often completed over several weeks and brought to published form after a final editing by the teacher. (In fact, the higher the grade, the more difficult it was for us to obtain first-draft writing.) While producing writing for publication obviously offers many desirable experiences to a writer, it can lead to less writing, in terms of generating new text and more copying of already written text to produce "good copy." Also, as we have seen, although the good spellers, and others who were progressing steadily in spelling, took personal responsibility for careful editing before handing their writing to a teacher, the poor spellers (including many early readers–stalled spellers) were inclined to abdicate responsibility for editing to their teachers. The process of producing more polished pieces may therefore have inadvertently resulted in these children's actually having *less* concern about spelling!

Reading was consistently given much attention in the classroom programmes as the children moved up the grades. They had daily opportunities for pleasure reading of their own choosing, as well as a variety of teacher-guided reading. This attention to reading seems to have paid off in the children's spelling development. As we pointed out earlier, all of the children moved beyond simple letter-sound matching in their spellings, in most cases in a timely fashion; and the children demonstrated all kinds of understanding about spelling gained from their reading. In fact, as pointed out in Chapters 6 and 7, when we asked the children how they had learned to spell, they overwhelmingly attributed their progress to their reading. But when we asked them about the helpfulness of what they had learned from their teachers, they all interpreted those questions as referring to either their learning of lists of words in the classroom programme, or to particular rules or lessons their teachers had taught—that is, they didn't think of spelling instruction in terms of their reading programme. This suggests to us that the links the teachers made between reading and spelling may have been more implicit than explicit.

The Children's Perceptions of Instruction

We doubt that the direct spelling lessons the children received were a potent factor in the development of the good spellers. Certainly they did not attribute their development to such instruction. They were adamant that they were good spellers as a result of their reading and writing a lot; they rarely mentioned classroom spelling lessons. Even when asked explicitly whether classroom lessons had helped, they, like Chan in the quote at the beginning of this chapter, saw them at best as "side dishes." When we pressed Alice at the end of the study on whether she had been taught helpful things about spelling at school, she laughed and said, "Not really. I just spelled." When we looked back at what she had said earlier about instruction, we found that in grade 2 she had valued the help her teacher had given in correcting some "important" misspellings while responding to her writing. But she made it clear in grade 3 that, while she found it easy to learn the list words for the weekly test, she did not find the words especially useful.

ALICE: Yes [I do learn to spell in class], but I find the spelling in class really easy. We're doing words like *plain, hello*—like that.
MARGARET: In a speller?
ALICE: Yeah, I'm doing grade 4 spelling, but it's still very easy.
MARGARET: Are the words ones you'd want to use in your writing?
ALICE: No.

In grade 6, however, Najali saw some value in her word lists. "Well," she said, "spelling just gives me new words. When I study them for a test, um, the way I study them sometimes helps me." We noted Najali's use of "just" and the fact that it wasn't so much the words to be learned in themselves that sometimes helped but "the way" she studied them.

Still, some of the children, especially early readers–stalled spellers such as Catrina and Elly, set great store by the word learning and direct spelling instruction their teachers provided. When asked how she knew about *ed* in fall of grade 3, Catrina replied, "My teacher told us about it—well, at the beginning of the year, she said, 'This is…some people put *e-d* in their books and some people *don't*; they put *t* at the end instead: because it *sounds* like a *t*, but it's really an *e-d.*' So she goes *e-d* on the chalkboard, like *this* [*demonstrates*] and she writes it, then she puts a *t* on the chalkboard and she underlines it." In fact, at the end of the study when she was talking about what had helped her become a speller, "Paying attention to the teacher" was the first thing Catrina mentioned. And indeed she did pay attention: she could recall in detail specific spelling lessons, and she frequently referred to them as the source of her knowledge about spelling.

Unfortunately, many of the children tried to apply misunderstood or half-remembered spelling "rules" they had been told about, which only created confusion and added to their sense of spelling as arbitrary. For example, Kareem and Julian had trouble applying the "*i* before *e*" rule. Kareem was attempting to spell *special* and wrote SPECIEL. He explained, "I'm not sure if it's *e-i* or *i-e*. Sometimes you have a saying of, um, 'I before *e* only after *c*, but then sometimes I find words like that and that *confuses* me sometimes." In grade 5, Julian was so confused that he tried to apply the rule to his spellings of *compete* and *competition*, which he had spelled correctly but wasn't sure about. He recalled, "Because, well, the—*usually*, unless there's a *c* before the—um, before the *i*—Wait! It's usually before *e* unless there's a *c*—unless there's a *c* before it...*I* before *e* except after *c*." Clearly, misunderstandings can result when children are given rules they learn by rote!

Even when they correctly remembered the rule, the children often had trouble generalizing it. Elly, for instance, correctly spelled *featuring* and when asked how she knew about dropping the *e* explained, "In one of our spelling books it gives you hints with your words and that's one of them: when you add *i-n-g*, you drop the *e*." But when asked if that was always the case, she replied, "I don't think *always*. I think that with *coming* you *don't*. It's, um, I forget the golden rule there is for them...There's supposed to be a golden rule thing but I forget it." Given such confusion about relatively simple generalizations, it isn't surprising that so many of the children were lost when it came to the complexities of derivational relationships.

Another factor that figured in the children's reflections on their learning was their experiences at home. When the good spellers talked about what helped them learn to spell, they referred as much, in some cases more, to help given at home as at school. Even for many of the children who had not become correct spellers by the end of the study, the most memorable parts of their learning to spell were experiences they had at home. The nature of the help varied. Sometimes parents gave very traditional assistance, such as setting out word lists to study, but especially for the good spellers the help was linked to reading or writing. Typical was the description by Jamal: "I just, well, my mom used to sit down with me when I was small, same with my baby sister, and she, we just went through books, and reading."

Thinking About Change in Teaching Spelling

In general, the instructional context of the classrooms in our study was one in which, on the one hand, the children wanted to learn to spell and tried to use the instruction the teachers provided for them and, on the other, the teachers cared about the children's spelling and tried to teach them how to spell correctly using the kinds of instructional approaches that we believe are typical in many classrooms across North America. But, as we have shown, in spite of all those good intentions, most of the children were not spelling correctly by the end of grade 6 (of 37 children, only 9 were included in our group of good spellers) and, more troubling, too many appeared to be stalled in confusion. Clearly, we educators must change our thinking on how to teach spelling.

Our work with the children has convinced us that spelling can be, and needs to be, taught; but the focus of instruction needs to change in order to take into account the sense-making nature of spelling. The idea of the systematic nature of spelling needs to be emphasized in instruction, so that children will learn the tools that enable them to solve the problems they will encounter in spelling throughout their lives. Children need to be involved as informants about their own processes and understandings and must be encouraged to develop a sense of control over the decisions they make about spelling. This view of instruction calls for the teacher to be proactive in encouraging children to think about spelling as systematic, leading them to develop insights into how spelling works, and helping them to monitor their own processes and spellings.

We aren't alone in calling for instructional change. The thrust of recent work on spelling in books, journals, and conferences has been to encourage a rethinking of spelling instruction. Clearly, instruction has not yet changed to match new knowledge about what spelling is and how it is learned. Like us when we began our study, many teachers refer to spelling as one of the "mechanics" of print, distinguishing it from the meaning-making processes of composing and comprehending text. Such a view has too often led to learning to spell being treated as a primarily rote-learning process, and to spelling instruction being given in isolation from reading and writing. Educators still make the mistake of having children focus on learning a list of specific words rather than on learning how spelling works *across* words. One change in instruction has been to draw the words to be learned from the children's own writing or from classroom themes instead of from lists supplied by the creators of spelling texts. This may make the words being learned more immediately usable and might individualize the process; but learning specific words does nothing to cause children to think about the systems that produce the spellings of those words, or to use their knowledge of the words to generate and monitor other spellings.

Sometimes (and we've certainly done this) teachers use their knowledge of systems and of conventional spelling to give a child clues to solving a problem—for example, by encouraging a child to listen to the sounds in a phonetically consistent word or by asking a child to recall a rule that, although highly imperfect, applies in the particular situation. While on the surface this would appear to be offering a higher level of help, it hides the reality that, in order to become effective spellers, the children themselves need to go through the process of using what they know about print to generate and test various possibilities as they make spelling decisions. Teachers can Socratically lead children to spell a word correctly, but the children must learn the process suggested in the teachers' questions in order to become good spellers. A focus on learning individual words is risky because it may give children the message that spelling is a random, word-by-word activity. As we have shown in earlier chapters, many of the children we worked with believed this to be so.

We suspect that many teachers themselves see spelling as more arbitrary than systematic; at least, they give that impression to their students. Even when that is not the case, it is likely that their own knowledge of the spelling system is largely implicit or relatively poorly understood. For example, they may teach spelling as a solely sound-based system long after that is useful.

The changes in instructional approach that we suggest require a radical shift in teachers' own notions and beliefs about spelling. If we teachers do not believe that spelling has logical, negotiable patterns, how can we hope to help children develop that insight? We are not advocating that teachers go through an intense course on English spelling as a prerequisite for changing their approach to instruction. A more productive route—certainly one that we found rewarding—is for teachers to join as co-investigators with their students in a search for system in spelling, or for teachers to withhold their expertise and let the children develop insights into language. This approach allows teachers to share their own decision-making process in spelling—weighing options, trying alternative versions, and so on. Also, when teachers model an exploratory, inquiring attitude towards spelling, they are more likely to inspire similar interests and attitudes in their students. We noticed in our conversations with the children that when we took this kind of stance towards a spelling problem, they, too, tended to become engaged with the problem, often seeming to forget that we might have some expertise on the subject. We are convinced from our own experiences that this shift in approach will encourage greater interest in spelling as a system on the part of both teachers and children, and will lead many teachers to seek out resources to expand their knowledge.

The goal should be to encourage all students to approach the demands of spelling with the behaviours and attitudes of the good spellers. As we explained earlier, the children who succeeded as spellers had a very stable and common profile directly linked to their success. Their behaviour was that of good *learners*; like learning to talk, or to read, or to do mathematics, they approached learning to spell as a sense-making activity. They viewed spelling as a problem to be solved, one that they could solve, and they used what they already knew about print to find solutions to the challenges they faced as they spelled. This basic orientation was demonstrated early on, and was marked by their tendency to explore possibilities and to generalize across words. They developed the ability to take into account multiple logics and were especially adept at using the look of words to make decisions about spelling. All the good spellers were readers and writers. Not only did they know how to read and write, they *did* it. They read and wrote beyond school requirements, for personal purposes. These children took ownership of their spelling. Correct spelling was important to them because they valued their own writing and wanted to see it responded to favourably, but they were not usually inhibited by issues of spelling when they composed their pieces. These children were also supported at home. Each child who became a good speller had direct support from someone who built on their interest in words or in writing or reading, and who helped to provide insights into spelling that the children could use to understand the system. Parental support alone isn't enough; there were many children who did not become successful spellers, but whose parents cared about their success and offered similar kinds of support to that enjoyed by the good spellers. Nevertheless, home experiences can play a major role in contributing to children's growth as spellers.

We are confident that the skills and attitudes demonstrated by successful spellers can be taught to more children. To do this, however, requires a reconception of what spelling instruction should look like. From the start, instruction should approach spelling as problem-solving, emphasize a search for its underlying system, and lead children to look to their own expanding resources to find the means to solve spelling problems.

A key element in improving how spelling is taught is to ensure that spelling be well embedded in literacy. It isn't a coincidence that the good spellers were prolific readers and writers; nor is it surprising that progress in spelling requires engagement in written language. After all, reading is a vital source of information about spelling, and writing provides both opportunity and need to put those understandings into use. Teachers may need to be more intrusive in developing children's awareness of how their own reading and writing can provide them with insights about spelling. While the good spellers seem to have reached this understanding on their own, most children need help if they are to become effective problem solvers. We also wonder whether teachers have sufficiently capitalized on the reciprocal nature of the various facets of literacy. For example, working with letter-sound relationships as children construct their early sound-based spellings can enhance their understanding of graphophonemic cues as they learn to read. The same reciprocal benefits would apply to letter order probabilities and visual features of word structure and to the meaning aspects of spelling. For example, the generalization that words that are spelled similarly often have a similar core of meaning can modify and extend children's understanding of word meanings and of connections among words, which would enrich their reading and writing. This potential benefit occurred to us when we saw how many children rejected the idea of a meaning connection between *nature* and *natural* even when they had spelled the two words similarly because they had definitions of each that did not overlap. Helping children see that similarity in spelling suggests a possible link in meaning can lead them to a greater understanding of specific words, which in turn can benefit their reading and writing.

Another key ingredient in instruction is to keep teaching informed by what the children are actually doing and thinking as they spell. Growth in spelling lies not just in a larger number of correctly spelled words, but in a deeper understanding that spelling is systematic. In fact, as demonstrated earlier, not all growth is signalled immediately by an increase in correct spellings. This means that teachers need to be aware of how spelling develops, so that they can identify both growth and arrested development in their students. Intervention will only be useful if it fits into the child's own emerging understanding.

One kind of intervention we found useful was to ask questions that encouraged the children to think about how they made spelling decisions and that, when appropriate, created dissonance. We tried to make our questions open-ended: "How did you know that?" "Why do you think it works that way?" and so on. We capitalized on any opportunity to nudge children's thinking, especially when we saw signs of movement through a new feature that might signal that new information was coming into play in the child's spelling. For example, when a visual feature appeared where previously only sound was represented, we typically pointed out the new feature and asked why it was there. Through questioning, we also drew the children's attention to any features in their spellings that were in conflict with the explanations they were giving of their decision-making process. Often the children were surprised by such questions, probably because they were unaware that they were making use of a new feature in their spelling. Our intention was to help them become more aware of the feature and to consider its implications for their other spellings. At the same time, such questions provided the children with words and concepts they could themselves use when thinking and talking about their spelling process.

Asking questions is especially useful when children show signs of moving away from purely sound representations, but it doesn't hurt to start asking questions as soon as they begin learning how to read. Just don't be surprised if your questions meet with stony silence for a while! We found that until the children began to make some sense of print as they learned to read there *was* no dissonance for them with different logics for spelling, and we would expect them to tell us (as they did) that they "sounded out" their spellings. An analogous experience was one Dennis had when he was watching a magician with his three-year-old son, Toni. Dennis asked Toni if he knew how the magician had done an especially challenging trick, and was surprised when Toni responded that he did. When Dennis asked how it was done, Toni explained, "It's magic!" There was no dissonance for Toni.

What we found to be important was to keep asking questions even when the children didn't have answers, because what often happened was that our questions eventually led the children to think about some aspects of spelling and moved them toward new understandings. We saw many demonstrations of the benefits of this kind of internalizing of questions. As Hana told us when explaining how she came to use meaning much more in her spelling: "Well, it just sort of happened, but also when you keep asking me these questions, it sort of makes me think of it *more*." While we were able to ask questions in a one-to-one context, there is no reason why this sort of enquiry cannot be explored in small groups or even whole class situations. An important prerequisite for this approach is a genuine curiosity about what children are thinking and doing. It is also helpful if questions are informed by an understanding of how spelling develops; but teachers can increase their own understanding of spelling development, as we did, by observing and listening to the children.

The need to embed instruction in children's emerging understandings may cause panic in the heart of every dedicated teacher. Every class is filled with children who have different understandings and are clearly at different points in their development, not only in spelling but in every other aspect of cognitive and social development. Fortunately, as we have shown, there is an overall pattern to children's development that can guide the focus for instruction. At times teachers will want to address specific understandings with individual children or with small groups of children. But a focus on spelling as a system and an emphasis on problem-solving allow for activities that can involve the whole class. Children will bring their own level of understanding to the class's spelling problem, and some children will consolidate their understanding while others will be led to new insights.

In short, whatever the grouping, instruction will be more successful when it is embedded in an overall programme that encourages children to think about how spelling works, and that helps children develop a sense of ownership over spelling and a language with which to talk about spelling and its problems. This kind of teaching can be extremely rewarding; and it encourages the development of critical problem-solving, which should be at the heart of all education.

Instruction

MARGARET: *When you're doing spelling, there is some sort of system to it, then? It isn't nonsensical?*
CATRINA: *No, like it—like it—I mean if, if you tried to analyze spelling— I've never done that before—but, like, if I tried to do that, it wouldn't really make sense, like, you'd just throw a whole bunch of letters on the page...*

Unless you've just opened the book at this chapter, it should not be a surprise that we begin our discussion of spelling instruction by considering the classroom first as a centre of literacy development. Our study has shown us how deeply rooted spelling development is in the development of the children as readers and writers. Children learn about spelling through their encounters with print, and they get to try that knowledge out as they write. If children do not have a strong literacy programme, including extensive opportunities to read and write in a variety of forms and for a variety of purposes, including their own pleasure, they do not have an effective spelling programme.

Having said that, we must add that our observations over the eight years of the study convinced us that while such a reading and writing programme is essential, it is not enough to enable most children to attain a level of understanding and performance that we would describe as correct spelling. As we have pointed out, of the 37 children we were able to work with, only 9 could be considered good spellers at the end of our study; and while some others show the promise of continuing to develop steadily, too many appear to be seriously stalled in their development. Consequently, we believe that most children need teachers who are proactive in building on the experiences a good literacy programme provides, in order for children to understand the systematic nature of English spelling and to see themselves as effective problem solvers in their attempts to produce well-spelled text. To help children make these links, teachers must provide activities that will help children focus explicitly on aspects of spelling and will help them construct a workable understanding of the interrelated logics of spelling. Some of these activities should be directly linked to the reading and writing experiences of children; others might initially stand apart from actual reading and writing, but should still be embedded in an exploration of language. Ongoing reading and writing are essential because it is through reading and writing that children can integrate their knowledge about language.

The starting point for any effective spelling instruction is finding out where the children are in their spelling development—so that is where we begin.

Finding Out What Children Already Know

When we began our study, we assumed that the main source of information about the children's spelling behaviour and knowledge would be the result of analyzes of their correct and misspelled words in their daily writing, in much the same way that miscue analysis provides a window to their reading process (Goodman 1973). These analyzes did provide essential information about what spelling knowledge the children were actually using as they composed and edited their written pieces. But you will doubtless have noticed that many of the insights we have shared in these pages came not from analyzes of word lists, but from conversations we had with the children about spelling as they wrote the words we dictated to them three times each year.

The list of words we dictated grew over time and was designed to include spelling features that we expected would give us insight into the growing understanding the children were developing—for example, how they came to include certain spelling features and logics in their repertoire. Usually, as each child learned a correct spelling, we removed that word from the list for that child and added others that had similar spelling features or new features we wanted the children to work with. In a sense, as mentioned earlier, the process is like miscue analysis in that we had to keep the level of difficulty high enough to force the children to misspell, because we believed that misspellings would give us better insight into the logics the children were using as they generated their spellings. In the end, our dictated lists, compiled over the years for the children in our study, provided a rich source of information about each child.

We recorded each child's spelling on a large chart, which gave us a concrete, visual record of the child's development over the years. When we shared these records with the children, their parents, and their teachers in the study or in workshops, they could quickly see how the children grew as spellers. The teachers wished they had this kind of information available to them in their classroom. Well, they can! We think that developmental records like this should be included in children's portfolios or ongoing records and move with them from grade to grade. Such a record is useful not only to teachers planning instruction, but also to children, who can get a sense of their own growth, and to parents, who can see how their children are learning.

Why a List?

A reasonable question, and one we asked ourselves, is why dictate a list of words to monitor spelling growth when the children are producing spellings in their writing every day? After all, the most authentic testing ground for spelling knowledge is in the context of composing text. Given our own preferences for contextualizing learning and assessment, we at first had some discomfort with the notion of presenting lists of words outside the context of authentic writing situations. Over time, however, we came to appreciate that *both* sources of information are important if one wants to get a fuller picture of what children know and that if we wanted to push to the outer limits of the children's understanding, a carefully constructed set of words has distinct advantages.

For example, we quickly saw that, especially in their early years, the vocabulary most children used in their writing, even over several weeks, did not represent the range of spelling features we could include in a constructed list. Also, when writing, some children tended to use a small set of "known" or copied words repeatedly, which made the majority of their spellings correct. We also noticed that, at least until the later grades, certainly well beyond the time when they were spelling by simple letter-sound matching, the children did not display in their writing the knowledge we saw reflected in the dictated spellings. For example, when we were seeing many nonsound features in the children's dictated spellings, we still saw only letter-sound matching in their writing. This lag is understandable given the competing demands of composing and spelling, especially when children are at an early point in their learning in both processes.

Another advantage of the lists over compositions was that we were "on the spot" to observe the children as they generated the dictated words, and could talk with them about what they were doing and why they were doing it. This was especially important when the children were broadening their understanding. In contrast, it was always a matter of luck whether we were present when comparable things were happening as the children were composing. We often found ourselves asking questions about process after the fact, or possibly being obtrusive when the children were trying to compose. These after-writing questions were more useful towards the latter half of our study, when we were reviewing the children's writing portfolios with them. They were less productive in the early years, when the children had trouble reading what they had written, let alone remembering how they had done it. Of course, classroom teachers would have more daily opportunities to "catch the moment" during children's writing times, but with the demands of working with many children in the classroom, they too would probably find dictated words useful.

On balance, then, we came to see tremendous value in monitoring the children's spelling behaviour, knowledge, and attitudes while they were responding to the dictated words.

Where Did the List Come From?

We didn't go about reinventing the wheel. Our starting point was a list of words developed by Mary Ellen Giaccobbe (personal correspondence). We included ten of her list words in our first dictated activity and followed with ten more. Later we added words from the Gillet and Temple feature list (1986), and words suggested by Henderson and Templeton (1986) and Henderson (1990). Along the way we added words that we felt would give us more information on particular features or logics and words such as *rejoice*, which we had noticed from children's writing would suggest particular insights into spelling.

The list must be seen as organic and should include some awareness of local vocabulary, accents, and usage. For example, Giaccobbe's original list included the word *zero*. In the United States, this word invites children to use the letter-name "zee" in generating their spelling. We were working in Canada, however, where the name of the letter *z* is "zed," so we replaced *zero* with *hero*, which slightly suggested letter-name, but also called on children to use word analogy, with both *he* and, in time, *hear*.

It was never our intention to have children be bombarded with all the words on our list. We began asking children to spell just ten words for us. A few of the children in kindergarten could not do this, and we accommodated them. By the end of the study, we were asking children to attempt between twenty-five and thirty words in one sitting. We dropped words when we felt children had reached the stage at which they could spell a word independently. In retrospect, we may occasionally have been too eager to drop words: we wish we had better information on some children's ability to retain correct spellings. Classroom teachers, who see their students daily, would have a better sense of when a spelling has been achieved.

In general, you'll probably need to use between ten and twenty words in order to see some pattern, with the higher number more useful in the upper elementary grades. Your best guide in selecting the initial words from our list would be what you notice your students are doing in the context of their writing. Take a look at a recent piece of writing (in the case of younger children, a few pieces) and see what logic they seem to be using in their spelling and what features already appear to be in their repertoire. We hope that Chapters 3, 4, and 5, on patterns in spelling development, will help you to do this. Remember, often the children's misspellings give you more information about their knowledge than their correct spellings.

Perhaps it would be helpful if we showed you some of the kinds of thinking we went through when we analyzed children's spelling. Like us, you have probably seen spellings just like the ones below. These we gathered from different children over the years of the study; they are typical spellings of the words *game*, *yellow*, *view*, *chirped*, and *sign*. As you look at each spelling, you might, as we did, consider what knowledge about print the children would have to have in order to come up with such a spelling.

YLO	YALO	YELLO	YELLOE
RYSTY	GM	GAM	GAEM
U	VU	VYOU	VIEW
CRPT	HRPT	CHERPD	CHURPED
SIN	SINE	SINGE	SIGHN

As you can see from this set of spellings, some of the approaches are easy to discern. Some of the spellings, like Michel's RYSTY, his early spelling of *game*, show that the children knew that words are spelled with strings of letters; they used whatever letters they knew at the time to produce the words. Spellings such as U, GM, and VU suggest that the children were making connections between letter names and the sound of the words. All of the children at some point used their knowledge of letter names to spell; GAM, YLO, VU, SIN, and CRPT (or HRPT—you can hear the "ch" in the letter name "aitch") were common results. The addition of *e*'s, even when overgeneralized, as for example in SINE, YELLOE, and SINGE, suggest a growing awareness of the role of *e* in modifying vowel sounds, and a move away from a sound-only logic. Such spellings as GAEM and VIEW signal a growing awareness of the significance of the way words look. Many children borrowed known words to help them spell unknown ones; this resulted in such spellings as VYOU and SIGHN.

Having done some of this preliminary thinking about your students' approaches to spelling, you might select words from the feature list that would give you an opportunity to confirm (or modify) your preliminary thinking about the children's spelling logic and to introduce some new spelling features to see how the children work with them.

Given the competing demands on your time, you may be wondering if you could dictate a single list of words to the whole class at once. The difficulty we see in doing that is that the further the children move up the grades, the greater the range you will find in their spelling development (as in all other areas of learning) and therefore the greater would be the challenge to construct a single list of words that would provide you with the information you need for all your students. In addition, we found that some children moved through our lists quickly, easily incorporating new features, while others would hold onto a misspelling for years. A compromise might be to dictate a set of words to small, homogeneous groups of spellers. You might use such occasions to have conversations with the group around the logics they are using. We would urge you, though, to try to find time—even if it's just twice over the school year—to sit down with individual children for conversations about spelling in the context of even a few carefully selected, individualized dictated spellings. This would allow you to observe the children's spelling in process, and to listen to what they tell you about their thinking. You have seen in this book what wonderful informants children can be. It would be a pity not to capitalize on such a valuable source of information.

Why Use a Developmental Feature List in a Classroom Programme?

The goal of using a developmental feature list of spelling words like the one on the next page is to learn about your students' current understanding of spelling so as to provide a basis for instruction. It is not to have the children learn the words on the list. Inevitably, from time to time, some words on the list will be included in whatever spelling instruction occurs in a classroom. In fact, sometimes teachers in our study included some of these words in the lists they gave the children to learn for weekly spelling tests. When that happened, the children were not always able to spell the word correctly for us afterwards, although they were often convinced that they had spelled it correctly because they had it "right on the test." It seemed that for most children only when they included the particular features of a given list word in their other spellings would they reliably incorporate the features, even in the word they had "learned."

Take a few minutes now to read through the words on the list. The words are placed in the order we generally used them in our study. We began in kindergarten with the first ten words in the first column and added the second group of ten words in grade 1 as the children became able to cope with longer dictations. As children correctly spelled these twenty words, we added words with new features, maintaining a list of about twenty to twenty-five words for each child. We dictated words three times each year; this may be a useful pattern for you, too.

Having read this far, you'll have a lot of insight into the kind of information we were able to collect from how the children in our study spelled

A Developmental Feature List for Monitoring Children's Understanding

rag	shed	beautiful
six	puppy	beautifully
game	puppies	special
nice	geese	featuring
yellow	year	probable
kiss	exciting	improbable
hill	excuse	probably
muffin	know	invite
back	knife	invitation
hero	eagle	exception
camp	teacher	attract
doctor	feature	attractive
drive	brave	attraction
yell	bravely	grocery
pickle	sign	groceries
quick	signal	terror
late	please	terrify
once	pleasant	terrified
butter	pleasure	acknowledge
batter	knowledge	usual
wife	city	usually
shock	cities	connect
stained	compete	connection
trained	competition	responsible
chirped	nerve	irresponsible
jumped	nervous	irresponsibility
learned	rejoice	condemn
chick	beauty	condemnation

these words. The beginning words draw on letter-name and sounding-out approaches. It's also important to include a few two-syllable words for young children, to see how the children might balance sound across a word; also, include a few words like *yellow* and *kiss*, which children are apt to recall from their environment. At this early stage, particularly when the children generate unusual spellings, it's a good idea to ask the children to pronounce the words they are writing. Naveen, for example, wrote LIND for the word *lid*. When we asked him to say the word he had just written, he pronounced it with an "n" sound. Early on, we started looking for sophisticated representations of sound, particularly the silent *e* and "ck," "sh," and "ch" usages. We also begin to look for letter doubling. These told us that the children were beginning to use knowledge gained from reading, either to make more sophisticated letter-sound patterns or to include features that cannot be accounted for by sound.

As the children's understanding grows, expand the list to include syntactic features, such as past tense endings, plurals, adverbial endings, and prefixes and suffixes. We wanted to see how consistently the children would apply these features. In other words, would the children see that syntax is itself a part of the logic of meaning, that it works regardless of the sound of the word? We were also interested in how children would blend words. Would they show an awareness of the integrity of the root word and, at the same time, be willing to modify their spelling when pronunciation comes into play? For example, do children keep the *e* when adding *ly* to *brave*, but drop it when they add *ly* to *probable*? Finally, our list also includes words that share common meanings and common spelling features, but not necessarily similar pronunciation.

A key insight you can gain from working with the list is the extent to which children use knowledge from one word when trying to figure out another word. In the early set of words, for example, there are several words that include the *ck* combination. If a child correctly uses the *ck* in *back*, you should see if *pickle*, *quick*, and *shock* also are spelled with *ck*. If these words are spelled with a *k* only, you might ask the child to spell *back* again and see whether this triggers a change in any of the spellings. If not, you may want to ask the child about the different spellings. This questioning strategy can also be used later, if children ignore meaning and revert to using sound alone to spell new words—for example, spelling *know* correctly but then spelling *knowledge* as NOLAG.

Another useful strategy is to ask children who are at the upper end of sound-based approaches to spelling which words they are sure are spelled correctly or incorrectly. This kind of question is not useful earlier, because at that point spellers are not working towards conventionality. It becomes important later because good spellers have a much greater awareness of their own knowledge than do poor spellers. This strategy also reinforces what we constantly told children during our conversations about the dictated words: that these words are hard and that we were amazed that they spelled so many of them correctly. The children should know that you are simply trying to find words they can't spell, as opposed to words they spelled "wrong." This takes the pressure off, as does asking the children themselves to identify misspelled words.

Working with lists of words with developmental features will help you identify the kinds of instruction best suited to particular children. In the rest of this chapter, we present various instructional approaches linked to information about the children gained from using the words on our list. The goal is to embed instruction in the children's own development.

Working with Children as They Read and Write

Our study demonstrated a clear link between what children do as they read and write and how they develop as spellers, and much successful instruction can capitalize on this link. There are four different starting points: getting children started as readers and writers; helping children read like writers and spellers; working on writing and proofreading; and using a known-word list.

Getting Children Started as Readers and Writers

Because early spelling development is directly related to children's becoming literate, the most important instruction for spelling growth is instruction that helps children learn to read and that gives them opportunities and reasons to begin expressing themselves in print. In this sense, all activities that introduce children to the pleasures of books and provide insight into how print works on the page are, indirectly, spelling activities. In short, our first focus should be on getting children started on the road to literacy.

As teachers, you know that regularly reading to young children is an essential starting point for literacy development. The greatest value of this, of course, is that it introduces children to the wonderful world of books, so you don't want to destroy this pleasure while trying to use literature to teach about text. At the same time, the value of making text *accessible* to children as they are read to is clear. Many children, like Lorna, trace their first understandings about literacy to following along with their parents as they were read to. It is difficult in a classroom to replicate the kind of intimacy Lorna and other children enjoy as they sit close to their parents and listen to stories, but teachers have found creative ways to share books that make the text highly visible to the class during the reading. Using Big Books, chart paper, or an overhead projector can allow teachers or children to point to the text as it is being read aloud. Such early experiences with print provide children with information from which they build their concepts of letters and words. These fundamental concepts of print (Clay 1979) are the building blocks to future growth.

When you read aloud to children they need to see that print carries the meaning—that the words you are saying are there on the page. The goal is to help the children grow in their understanding of how these marks on the page (letters, words, punctuation) work. If children are to be able to talk about letters and words, and if they are expected to read and write, they have to know what letters and words look like on the page and how they match what is being read aloud. In other words, teachers need to help children establish a concept of letter and a concept of word in print.

Teachers of young children have more ways to help children to build these concepts than we could ever think of, but here are some activities that could be considered.

◆ Children can do *letter hunts*, looking first, perhaps, for a letter from their own name, or for the "letter of the day," or, eventually, the common letter in an alliterative string. The teacher would have the children see the letter and hear the repeated sound, thus moving them towards an understanding of the relationship of letter and sound.

◆ Children can "read along" in predictable pattern books, perhaps with the teacher or the child pointing to the text as it is read.

◆ Children can listen for beginning sounds in words, and then can listen and look for other words that have that sound. Alert children will realize that sometimes the same sound comes in words that start with different letters (*cat, kitten*), or that all words starting with the same letter may not start with the same sound (*toss, throw*). This is not an idea that needs to be driven home, although teachers can draw attention to it. The main goal here is to help children form an awareness of a relationship between sounds and letters.

At the same time that children are beginning to understand text from a reader's perspective, they can begin to explore how written words work from the perspective of a writer, by actually generating text. One of the things we have learned is that one does not have to wait until children have learned to read, and have been taught to write all the letters and spell core vocabulary, before expecting them to write. In fact, for some children like Alice, writing is the way to literacy. We cannot list all the ideas that have been generated over the past years on how teachers can invite children into engaging with writing, or how to support them, but we do want to celebrate those efforts and point out that they have a direct impact on children's learning to spell. Remember, too, that spelling instruction is intended to support writing, not that the primary purpose of writing instruction is to support learning to spell!

At the beginning teachers need to provide whatever support is necessary to get the children started, but they need to do this in ways that leave as much responsibility in the hands of the children as possible. We have shown how difficult it was for the least literate children in our study first to hear and identify a sound, then to link it to a letter, and then to remember how that letter was formed. These children were more than willing to let their teachers, peers, volunteers, or anybody else take over the whole process for them. Teachers have to maintain the right balance in giving children support but keeping them involved. Here are a few ideas to consider when trying to keep that balance.

◆ Children who are unsure about the look of specific letters need to have the letters of the alphabet as readily available to them as possible. On their own desk is preferable to having them only on wall displays because, as all teachers know, much can be lost (including time!) on trips across the classroom to look up a letter. Besides, the more accessible the information is, the more likely it will be used.

◆ Most children respond well to being encouraged to "just write it out the way you think it goes" to get their messages on paper. (This is what is usually called "invented spelling.") But some children, for a variety of reasons, resist writing independently. Providing a scribe for them may help as a temporary measure, but this merely postpones the day they will need to risk writing for themselves. To encourage independence it sometimes helps to let these children know that they will be given help spelling one or two words of their own choice once they have made a genuine effort to try to write on their own.

◆ If children do need the help of a scribe to get started, it is important to keep the children as actively involved as possible in understanding the process by having them connect what is being copied with their own knowledge of print. They might be asked to identify the letters being written. They might also be asked what sound in the word a particular letter connects to.

◆ When children are just beginning to write, the focus need not be on having letters perfectly formed. In fact, almost all the children in our study, and some who became the very best writers and spellers, reversed letters. Some used capital letters for lowercase letters (like e) whose directionality they were unsure of, even after they had moved to a general use of lowercase forms.

◆ Children may need help segmenting words and representing sounds. Our weaker students had difficulty "holding onto" a complete word as they segmented it. They would get lost in the word. When we or a classroom teacher or aide were able to keep the focus on the word by repeating what the children had completed and encouraging them then to repeat the word and attend to the next sound they were saying, the children were able to segment the word more effectively.

◆ In the beginning stages, we see nothing wrong in encouraging children to "sound it out," although it should be remembered that children's ability to progress later in spelling will depend on their ability to disregard this advice! It might be better to invite children to say how they might figure out how to represent a word. Children are likely to say, "I'll sound it out," to which the teacher can reply, "Go ahead and try that." In this way, teachers can get diagnostic information about how children approach spelling without signalling what may be a partially useful approach as the definitive way to do it.

We know that we are repeating here many approaches that may be well known to teachers who work with young children, and we don't wish to recreate texts on teaching reading and writing. Our point is that these kinds of activities are valuable for helping children to learn about *spelling*. We think it is important that teachers who, as we mentioned early on, are likely to be besieged by concerns about spelling development understand the relationship between early literacy development and spelling development and make the link clear for concerned parents or administrators.

Helping Children Read Like Writers and Spellers

We noticed a basic difference between children who progressed as spellers and those who didn't in the way they approached text. The stalled spellers, many of whom were enthusiastic and effective readers, tended to read for the message alone and paid less attention to how the message was constructed. The good spellers also paid attention to the content of the text, and were no less efficient as readers, but, in addition, they paid attention to the *form* of the text. They noticed words and also how authors constructed their meaning. Frank Smith (1982) calls this "reading like a writer." Teachers therefore need to create activities and ways of reacting to text that will help children read as writers—and as spellers.

Early spelling development depends on children's becoming independent readers. Children need to become aware of the stability of print. They need to be able to find words repeated at different points in the text. They need to expand their understanding of letter-sound relationships, and they need to explore how written words work from the perspective of a writer. Here are a few possibilities for working with early readers.

◆ Children can be asked to say some of the words they have already read, then to isolate the sounds (segment into phonemes) and point out where the word says each sound. Children should be looking at the beginning, middle, and end of words.

◆ Children's rhymes provide lots of opportunities to look for words that have the same sound at the end, and children can find these words and see how the words make that rhyming sound.

An early focus on sound is probably appropriate for most children. Certainly in our study the vast majority of the children began their awareness of spelling by thinking about the logic of sound. Still, there will always be children like Joe, for whom sound was not a very useful tool. What he needed was lots of experience with simple, repetitive, but meaningful, text in order to develop a bank of known words. Joe progressed when he read, and reread, a small set of simple stories until he had a core of known words. This core was extremely useful, as it gave him resources to use in his writing and a body of words the teacher could use to help him explore how words work, and to help him develop at least a rudimentary sense of the logic of sound, which is part of the overall picture.

Even though most children in a classroom will probably be focussing on sound, at the same time they will be developing a set of words that they are familiar with from their environment and experience.

We saw evidence of children's becoming effective readers in their spelling. Increasingly, we saw features like the silent *e* or consonant doubling that could not be explained by sound alone. Teachers can make links between the words children use in their writing and their reading, asking children where they've seen the words they are using. As well as encouraging children to continue reading and to seek out their interests through books, teachers need to help them to read like writers and to think about what the author is doing that they like. If they look for them, they will see ideas or words they could use in their writing. Reading moves children as spellers from being content to represent sounds in their own way to trying to approximate conventional spellings. Rereading favourite passages gives children opportunities to focus more on the "look" of text and how authors construct meaning, because they are freed from the focus on content when they reread.

As children begin to enjoy the pleasures of independent reading, teachers can use the reading experiences to help children develop greater awareness of, and interest in, the ways words are used to express meaning. As we saw among the good spellers, curiosity about word meanings can lead to awareness and interest in spelling.

Children can be encouraged to collect words from their reading and possibly look up the etymology of some of them. We are not suggesting they keep long lists, but rather lists that contain a few words the children have noticed—words they are curious about or are perhaps interested in using in their own writing. Such lists can have particular focusses, depending on the kind of reading and writing a child is engaged in. For example, a child who reads stories from a different historical period might collect especially interesting terms that are not used much today. Or a child whose stories are filled with characters can begin to collect words from novels that describe characters in interesting ways. By the end of elementary school, children are often reading in very specialized areas. They might be encouraged to collect the specialized vocabulary they encounter. Such a list may be especially useful because it is apt to reflect the child's interest or may provide an opportunity for the teacher to demonstrate meaning links between words. An interest in space, for example, may lead a child to record words like *supersonic* and *extraterrestrial*, which give the teacher a chance to explore the meaning logic in words.

The important thing is that the lists be manageable and relevant so the children become engaged with a few personally chosen words that they may want to use in their writing.

Reading, then, can provide important clues about how spelling works. In the beginning, for most children the instructional focus is on how print works, and its relation to sound. Increasingly, teachers need to lead children to consider how words look and what they mean, and how authors use words to inform and delight. By reading like writers and spellers, children can use their reading more effectively to help build a picture of how words work. They develop this picture through their writing.

Writing and Proofreading

In our study, there appeared to be a close relationship between children's engagement in writing in a variety of modes for a variety of purposes, and their learning about spelling. One of the features of language arts instruction over the last fifteen years has been the reintroduction of regular writing into daily classroom activity. As we have said before, writing requires children to use their knowledge to generate spellings. In the beginning, then, spelling instruction needs to focus on encouraging children to compose and share their writing—to get started as writers. Nevertheless, teachers can ask questions that will help children think about the spellings of the words they are writing.

◆ Such questions as "Where is that 'nn' sound that we hear?" or "I see a g in the word [night], but I don't hear one. How do you know it's there?" help children start to think about the look and sounds of words.

◆ When the children say that a word doesn't "look right," it is helpful to encourage them to try to pinpoint the problem area by asking such questions as, "Where doesn't it look right?" or "Does it look right at the beginning [or middle or end]?"

◆ Drawing attention to the length of words can be useful. For example, ask, "Is this word too long [or too short]?" or "Where could a letter be taken out [or included]?" Questions like these provide clues for children about how they might work with the look of words in their spelling.

◆ Questions such as "Can you think of other words that look like this?" and "Where do you remember seeing this word before?" encourage children to think back to their visual bank of words from their reading and their environment as they spell. You recall that the good spellers were able to generalize across words and often referred very specifically to where they had seen a word before. It may be useful to encourage children to make these kinds of connections.

The intent of these questions is to embed them in the children's minds, so that they might ask themselves such questions as they try to generate spellings. Such questions also reinforce the notion of system in spelling—that there are reasonable expectations of how words might be spelled.

Children often ask teachers to give them a spelling. When they ask us for spelling, we are usually supportive—that is, we provide the spelling, *but only after the child makes an attempt.* Again, the idea is to encourage independence on the part of the child, but it also allows the teacher to see how the child goes about spelling, and it also provides a chance for the teacher and the child to compare the correct spelling with the attempted version.

If the word is one the child will use regularly, it may be a good idea to have the child use the teacher's version to *learn* the word. If so, at some point the teacher should check to make sure that the child's version is correct, lest the child take away an error that he or she believes is correct "because the teacher told me."

Should a child become overdependent on a teacher or a peer for spellings, or become too concerned with correct spelling, a request for a spelling can be answered, "I think this is one you should try to figure out on your own."

Eventually, without dropping the focus on composing and sharing writing, it is important to get children involved in proofreading and correcting their public copy. At the earliest writing stages, conventional spelling is not the goal and should therefore not be an issue. When children "go public," however, teachers must exercise their responsibility to protect their young writers and ensure that their writing conforms to the particular expectations of the audience. Sometimes teachers can meet with parents and be successful in adjusting parents' expectations, so that they can appreciate their children's early attempts at representation. At the same time, teachers need to introduce children to the process involved in bringing written pieces to completion, and children can develop a sense of pride in carefully produced work. Teachers cannot be expected to proofread and copy every piece of writing that they or the children would like to publish. In some situations, parent volunteers or "buddies" from older grades can help out. Often, however, children will be expected to copy out their own final, corrected text. Children also may have their own reasons to recopy corrected text for particular pieces or particular audiences and should be encouraged to do so, as this also helps them understand the writer-reader relationship. While there is value in "going public" with a piece of writing, we don't believe that this value is directly related to the act of recopying, because copying corrected material does not seem to help children become aware of either their errors or their correct spellings.

Once children move beyond simple letter-sound matching, teachers are placed in a real dilemma over proofreading. At this point, children are aware of the mismatch between their spellings and conventional spellings, and conventionality becomes a reasonable expectation for the writer and an instructional goal for the teacher. We noticed from our study that successful spellers are characterized by their understanding that proofreading is their responsibility, whereas poorer spellers tend to pass that responsibility off to peers, teachers, or parents. We also know that learning to proofread effectively is a challenging and long-term process. A child's early attempts will be far from adequate, and if that opens the writer up to criticism, it may inhibit his or her developing confidence and sense of voice. How then to introduce a concern for proofreading while still protecting the writer?

It is important to understand what is meant by proofreading and how it fits into the writing process. Writers first focus on composing or drafting text. Then, if the piece is to have any further life (not all pieces will) it usually requires rereading and revising—making decisions to add, take out, or alter content, working on elements of style and structure that will make the piece more effective. Finally, prior to a piece's going public, writers proofread, checking that the spelling is accurate, that punctuation is conventional, and that the piece will not be poorly received on the basis of how it is presented. "Going public" with a piece of writing they care about usually helps children understand the value of carefully prepared, accurate work. Alice, you recall, was awakened to her responsibility to work toward conventional spelling when her mother told her that although her aunt enjoyed receiving her writing, she had real trouble understanding it.

Of course, no writing process is ever so neatly divided into stages. Writers proofread as they compose, and sometimes revise when they proofread. Nevertheless, having understood that writers approach text differently at different times, we have to help children see that they have to read differently when they proofread than they do when they compose. Stalled spellers tended to be troubled by spellings only when they were having trouble generating them, and were more apt to interpret a word as "not looking right" when they had difficulty reading it. When they proofread, they still tended to read for meaning, not paying attention to the appearance of words. It is this attention to appearance that teachers have to foster. The first step is to begin speaking of proofreading as a writer's responsibility and providing clear expectations about what that means in practice.

A reasonable expectation is to give children a high responsibility (that is, to expect total accuracy) for correcting a limited number of words. The known-word list (which we discuss in detail in the next section) and lists of common words can form the basis of early expectations for correctness. A teacher, when reviewing a proofread passage and seeing many words from those lists still uncorrected, should indicate only that the passage contains incorrect words that the student should have caught and leave the student with the problem. If the work has been proofread but only a few words have been missed, the teacher might help the child by indicating in what paragraph or line the errors remain.

At the same time, students should be expected to identify problematic words or areas in words beyond the known-word list, so that the teacher, aide, parent, or peers can work with them to correct the text. Initially, children might only be expected to identify words they think are incorrect.

Soon, however, teachers can expect children not only to identify words, but also to identify where the spelling problem is within the words. The next step is to have children suggest plausible alternatives.

We strongly advocate that children *write* their alternative versions as they attempt to correct a misspelling. They can then be encouraged to make visual comparisons of their alternatives and select the one that looks the best. All the good spellers in our study used this strategy, yet it was shunned by the poor spellers and many of the other children. While the good spellers spontaneously generated two, or even three, possible alternatives and compared them before selecting the one they would use, other spellers told us they made comparisons in their heads, or were apt to either make the change internally in a word or cross out or erase one version before generating another. In any event, they rarely had a basis for comparing spellings. When we encouraged them to produce separate spellings for comparisons during the interviews, those who had been reluctant to use this strategy found that they usually could make better choices when they had written alternatives.

Children still need help and protection as they attempt new and difficult spellings and formats, but teachers and peer editors should *support* the children, not take responsibility from them.

Finally, over time, children need help to develop their ability to proofread effectively. As we have said, reading as a proofreader requires one to pay attention to the look of words and to try to ignore the overall meaning of the text. Various approaches are possible and children should be encouraged to experiment until they find the one that works best for them.

◆ A ruler can be used to reveal the text word by word, which will make it difficult for children to "chunk" words into meaning units.

◆ Writers can read from the bottom up, or in reverse order on the line.

At times, children misspell words in text that they actually know, or that the teacher suspects they know, how to spell correctly, and they miss those words when proofreading.

◆ To bring the writer's attention to such words, a teacher can make a list of such errors and use them as a spelling dictation. Our experience would suggest that the child will actually spell many of the words correctly from dictation and can then use the correct versions in proofreading the original writing. One of the effects of this exercise will be to demonstrate to children that they are not using all that they know about spelling when they are writing and proofreading their pieces.

◆ Children who approach spelling unsystematically often spell the same word differently throughout a text. Again, a peer or teacher can identify this behaviour and ask the children how they can decide which of the versions is correct.

Such activities continue to emphasize the look of words. Children should also develop other aids to personal proofreading.

◆ Children can keep in their writing folder a proofreading guide to their most common errors and, when proofreading, should include a specific look for idiosyncratic problems.

◆ A child who regularly confuses *there*, *their*, and *they're*, for example, can develop a personal way of knowing what word to use when, and should be encouraged when proofreading to stop at every such word to check and make sure that the correct word is used.

◆ Children can be encouraged to think of patterns, word types, or common homophones that give them problems, and to include a separate check for those patterns and problems as they proofread.

◆ Children can also be encouraged to make use of textbooks and dictionaries to confirm or check on specialized or unusual vocabulary.

◆ Children should also be thinking about where they have seen a word or used it before, as a way of efficiently checking for correctness.

Using a Known-Word List

From the earliest grades, all children have words they know how to spell. We believe this important knowledge is not taken advantage of as much as it could be in spelling programmes. If children developed a list of the words they know how to spell, this growing list could serve three very important purposes. First, it would demonstrate to children their growing understanding of spelling. Children need to have their growth demonstrated to them in order to help them retain what they know, but also to build up their confidence as spellers. Second, the list would serve as a basis for continued learning. Through the study of known words children can explore how words work and learn to generalize their knowledge to new situations. There are advantages to working with known words. The list would contain much of the children's up-to-the-moment implicit knowledge about spelling, and word study based on emerging correct spellings can better move from the known to the unknown. For example, children might have recently added the word *jumped* to their list of known words, but give no evidence in other spellings that they have understood or generalized the *ed* feature. Instruction can capitalize on this one word to help these children understand and generalize this feature across words. Further, because the words are known, children can consider questions about why a word is spelled a particular way without worrying whether the word is correct. A third use of the known-word list is its role in proofreading, as mentioned in the previous section.

There are various ways to develop such a list. In the early grades the words might come from children's own environment and their writing. The known words may include a few words that have special importance to children, such as their own names and words whose sound suggests their spelling, such as *mom* and *no*, several of the small connecting words, such as *a*, *the*, and *and*, and some basic pronouns, such as *I*, *she*, and *he*. Very quickly it will become impossible to include all known words on a list, so some decisions about what to include will have to be made. We suggest that the words be those that are regularly used, words that have been problems in the past, and words that reflect control of new features or logic in a child's spelling.

Lists of known words can be kept with children's writing, part of a portfolio or other ongoing record that moves from class to class each year. If the list grows at the rate of 100 to 150 words a year in the later grades, by the end of elementary school, the list might include 500 to 1,000 words. While this historical list would provide useful information, teachers may wish to develop a more manageable subset of recent words. The important thing is not the number of words being added to the list at any time, but the inclusion of words that will be regularly *used* by the children in their writing and learning about spelling.

As we talked with the children in our study, we found that the poor spellers greatly overestimated the number of words they felt they "just knew." We also realized that such a response to the question "How did you know how to spell this word?" reduces the possibilities for teaching. For this reason, we feel that the children's list of known words should be closely monitored. A word must be spelled correctly over a period of time in order to make the list. Children may nominate words, but should demonstrate their knowledge before it can be added. Teachers may also wish to nominate words for the list. For example, they could identify common words or common errors and have children learn to spell the words they use often but do not spell correctly.

Children need to learn a basic approach to learning words. For some a useful approach is the following: look at the word—especially for tricky or unusual parts; say the word aloud, attending to parts that don't sound the way you expect; cover the word; try to see the word in your mind; write the word; check the word. If the word is incorrect, repeat the process concentrating on the specific part or parts that were not correct. Children can be encouraged to apply this approach—or another that is effective for them—to learning selected words that teachers feel would help them as writers. Should children continue to have trouble with a word or, as sometimes happened in our experience, abandon a correct spelling, that word should be relearned or dropped from the list.

In the earliest grades children might be expanding their list at the rate of two or three words a week, but by grade 6 children could be adding five or more words a week. Clearly, teachers cannot be the sole monitors of this list, nor should they be. Here are some possible strategies that would make monitoring more manageable:

◆ During certain writing times for young children, teachers can ask the children to leave their word list out with the new entries clearly visible, so that teachers can check these words as they circulate around the room.

◆ There can be periodic sharings of new known words, in which children display their words on cards or on overhead transparencies. This has the advantage of requiring children to rewrite the word.

◆ At regular intervals, perhaps monthly, children can give a list of their additions to a peer partner. Peers can confirm the spellings, and then each partner can test the other for accuracy.

◆ The known-word list can become a focus of a short conversation as part of regular writing conferences.

◆ Children can ask their parents to test them on a set of their known words.

All these activities support the idea of ongoing monitoring, an important part of using known-word lists and working with children's writing.

Work with the known-word list can begin very early. As mentioned earlier, the first word young children are likely to know is their name. Teachers thus automatically have at their disposal a list of words familiar to everyone in the class, each of which can probably be written and read by at least one person in the class. Furthermore, most teachers of young children have name tags of their pupils; the following activities could make use of that resource:

◆ The children could find their own names from the set of name tags.

◆ Children whose name starts with a particular letter could stand up and show their name tag so that the class can confirm the letter. Teachers might ask, "Do you see the *R* at the beginning of *Ravinder*?" and ask if there is anyone else not standing whose name begins with *R*. Children can then do the same activity with last letters, or with any letter.

◆ The children could group names by common initial letters.

◆ Similar activities to the ones above can be used with a focus on the names' beginning sounds instead of the initial letters.

◆ The children's attention can be drawn to names like *Catrina* and *Kareem*, where different letters make the same sound, or *Glenna* and *George*, in which the same letter makes different sounds. We believe that teachers should simply point out such facts and move on. The idea is to sow the seeds of the children's own analysis, not to drill the class in letter knowledge.

◆ Focus can then move to sounds in different parts of the name. For example, teachers might ask, "Whose name has the sound 'mmm' in it?" The class can then listen for the sound and try to find where the name has that sound.

◆ Attention can be directed to the look of names. Children can be asked to think about whose name would have lots of letters in it and whose would have only a few, or what names would have the same number of letters in them. Then they could check the lists, find the names, and count the letters.

As the known-word list begins to grow, children can be encouraged to use this knowledge to generate new, correct spellings. Teachers may ask children, for example, "If you know how to spell *cat*, what else can you spell?" Most children will probably adopt a rhyming strategy, but others may change letters at the end of the word. Either approach is fine. If children do use rhymes they might be probed to see whether they can also change end sounds; but the emphasis here is not so much on teaching new strategies as on leading children to use their current strategies to generate new words.

In this case, and in many others related to analysis of how words work, *the questions become the curriculum!* Teachers needn't be alarmed or rush to get an answer. If they get no response to the query "What would this word be if it started with an *r*?" teachers can leave the problem with the children by saying, "I'll leave you to think about that." The aim is to get children thinking about the possibilities, and to invite them to take a problem-solving stance.

Generalizing can be encouraged by having children group words on their list. For example:

◆ As previously suggested, early grouping can be done around issues of sound—for example, grouping words that start the same or that have the same sound in them.

◆ Teachers can ask children to account for all the sounds in particular known words, asking, "Can you show me where the 'nn' sound is?" or reversing the question, asking them to account for letters that don't appear to be sounded?: "How do you know that that letter [e.g., the silent *k* in *knife*] is there?"

◆ Children can be asked to look at words on their list to see whether sounds are always made the same way. When they see that they are not, they can identify different ways to make a sound, and perhaps group words that use a particular pattern.

Even when children are beginning to include spelling features that cannot be explained by sound alone, it is likely that they will still be trying to explain their spellings according to sound. This kind of work makes them aware of the complexity of sound and the need for other considerations in their spelling. The advantage of teaching this awareness through the known-word list is that the list will demonstrate to children that they are already acting on these complex concepts and that, even though they are complex, these concepts reflect a system that is quite within their capacity to understand.

As children start to show more conventional elements in their spelling, the known-word list can become the basis for their move into proofreading, and their generalizing can focus more on elements beyond simple letter-sound correspondences. Here are some relevant classroom activities:

◆ The children should be encouraged to become responsible for checking their work to be sure no word from their known list is spelled incorrectly.

◆ All spellers have a relatively small list of personal problem words or patterns. Children should be aware of what these problems are and should be encouraged to develop their own ways of solving them. Teachers cannot give individual children the specific mnemonic that will help; these must be generated by the individual child if they are to be meaningful. The question to ask is, "How are you going to remember how to spell this?"

◆ To encourage children to think about words and reflect on their learning, they can be asked, "Where did you learn that word?" or "Where specifically have you seen it?"

◆ Word building and generalizing from the known-word list can help children explore analogies using different letter patterns (for example, *ight*, *ough*, *exc*) or rules (*ed* or different plural forms).

◆ Children can start to group words according to meaning families (for example, *here*, *where*, *there*, *beauty*, *beautiful*, *beautifully*).

As teachers encourage children to explore word building, it is important to ensure that the children pay attention not only to what is added to words, but also to how the addition changes the word. *Beautifully*, for example, doesn't change *beautiful*, but *beautiful* does change *beauty*.

Word building from the known-word list can emphasize the various logics used to generate correct spellings. Increasingly children should seek meaning connections between words and should take words from the list and build related words. As they do this, they should be made aware that these additions are units of meaning, so attention to how the meaning changes is as important as how the spelling changes.

As the children encounter the challenge of adding suffixes and prefixes (for example, how to add *ly* to words ending in *e*, like *brave* and *probable*, or what to do when the prefix ends in the same letter as the first letter in the word the prefix is being added to, as in *irresponsible* and *immoveable*), they need to consider the patterns in these blendings and also make visual comparisons. Increasingly they should verbalize their thinking.

Creating Dissonance

One technique we found very useful was a technique we call *creating dissonance*. Children's spellings, as we have said, contain a lot of implicit knowledge. As teachers, we don't always know what knowledge children are actually using, or what aspect of a spelling they are explicitly aware of. We also found that children tend to cling to rationalizations that fly in the face of their own practice. Creating dissonance is a way to encourage children to challenge their own assumptions. The following excerpts from a discussion with Kareem demonstrate how dissonance works to make children aware of their own understanding and to help them develop a more refined sense of how words work. The discussion took place when Kareem was in grade 6. It involved his correct spellings of *pleasure* and *narrative*. The discussion actually moves through two levels of dissonance, as, Kareem first turns to sound to justify his use of *ea* in his correct spelling of *pleasure*.

MARGARET: Do you know why there would be an *a* in there? Because it sounds like it should be *ples.* Why is it *e-a-s*?

KAREEM: Umm...To give it, like, you know, to make it a long vowel, like "plee."

MARGARET: Why would you need a long vowel?

KAREEM: Well, you wouldn't need a long vowel. It's probably to make the *e* have the proper sound. Instead, 'cause the *a* would make a—the *e* and *a* together would make a different sound than just the *e* itself.

MARGARET: Yeah. What kind of sound would it make?

KAREEM: Eh, "pleh-zure" [*extending the vowel sound*]. The "eh-eh"—it would make it a bit longer...

MARGARET: Looking at *pleasure*, is there a word that you know, maybe in—the whole word may not be there, but there's a word that means something like *pleasure*, it has a meaning connection to *pleasure*.

KAREEM: Yeah, well, not...

MARGARET: What?

KAREEM: I got *leisure* instead.

MARGARET: Ah, I see.

KAREEM: Yeah, you take off the *p* and you've got *leisure*.

MARGARET: Yes, I see. Anything else in there that you can see?

KAREEM: Yeah, *sure*. *Sure* is in there.

MARGARET: Yes, but *sure* doesn't really have much to do with the meaning of *pleasure*, does it?

KAREEM: No, it doesn't.

MARGARET: Is there any other word in there that has something to do with *pleasure*?

KAREEM: Um, yeah, *ease*! Like, *pleasure—ease*. Maybe when I'm having a pleasurable time, I might be at ease—instead of, like, stress.

MARGARET: Yes, but what about *please*? If *ease* is in there, *please* is, but *please* isn't all in there.

Later, the discussion resumes in the context of another word:

MARGARET: So what is the root word of that [*narrative*]?

KAREEM: *Narrate*. Yes, with one *e*—one letter could be missing sometimes. Ah, *pleasure*—even though one letter's missing, that could mean that maybe *please* could also be part of *pleasure*, then, could be the root word.

In the end, Kareem realized that his own work contradicted his personal "rule" that the root word must be kept whole in any derivative and, at least for the moment, he abandoned his mistaken rule. When discussing *pleasure*, Margaret's purpose was not to resolve the dissonance, but to leave the problem with Kareem. In this case, the problem resurfaced quickly, in the word *narrative*. At that point, Kareem was able to make the connection to *pleasure*.

As children move to incorporate different logics, dissonance becomes a useful tool not only to help children generalize from what they know, but also to help them explore the reasoning behind spellings. The following activities can be helpful:

◆ Teachers can point to a place where letter doubling has occurred (*butter*, for example), and then to an instance where it hasn't (*hoping*) and challenge the child to explain how he or she knew to do it one place and not another.

◆ Teachers can use known words to compare with misspellings where a pattern used in a known word hasn't been used and ask a child why the pattern would hold in one instance but not in another—for example, a double *t* in the correctly spelled *butter*, but not in the child's spelling of *batter* (BATER). This can lead teachers to ask "How do you know it's right?" and perhaps get a more complete response than "I just knew."

Investigating the Logics of Spelling

The work we have proposed in relation to reading, writing, and the use of the known-word list embeds spelling in the regular, ongoing activity of children within their reading and writing programmes. At the same time we recognize that the teacher can play a role in helping children deepen their understanding of how words work through involving children in activities that systematically investigate the logics of spelling and ultimately how these logics relate to each other. The kinds of activities we propose here are intended to awaken an interest in words and encourage children to think about how spellings come to be. Although some children will learn specific words from these activities, that is not their overriding purpose. We believe that most of the learning will come as the children apply the knowledge they work with in their own writing. The activities we describe here are not some new spelling panacea: teachers will be familiar to some degree with most of them.

We try to show how these activities can best be presented to help children actively problem-solve about spelling, and try to demonstrate that the activities themselves need to have a purpose consistent with the concepts about how words work, which leads to good spelling. Almost any activity can be adapted to involve some purposeful problem-solving. Word searches, for example, don't involve a lot of deep thought, and, despite their seeming emphasis on the look of the word, are not useful for reinforcing this concept, because their purpose is to hide and distort the look of words (representing the letters in reverse order, for example). But the activity can have some value if the emphasis is put on letter patterns, if children are encouraged to look for common letter patterns to see whether a word is hidden. In other words, teachers have to develop a critical attitude toward spelling activities and adapt them for specific purposes.

One activity we have real problems with, because it seems to reinforce the notion that spelling is random and lacks meaning, is searching for "little words in big words." Some of the discussions we had with children about their sense of the role of meaning in spelling (including the example in this chapter with Kareem) demonstrated how this activity adversely influenced children's concepts of meaning and of root words. As far as we can see, this activity encourages children to play with a word at the surface level and to treat meaning as just a coincidence. Any word can be a root word when any "little word" is acceptable, whether or not it relates to the meaning of the "big word." Perhaps this activity creates an interest in words, or helps children develop personal mnemonics based on a word contained in the larger word, but we think that any such value is negated by the overall message about lack of a system in spelling, so we discourage it. (We make this bold statement fully aware that some clever teacher may have been able to use this activity in a way that develops real thinking and real understanding!)

Word Investigations to Uncover the Logics of Spelling

Word investigations are a good way to help children discover the logics of spelling. In a sense, word investigations are part of activities that use known-word lists. In fact, many of these activities are best when they include the known-word list as a source for word investigations. This embeds the investigations in what the children know already and ensures a continuing connection to the words children use in their writing. All word investigations have a common pattern. Children are encouraged to gather together a collection of words from particular sources and subject these words to specific analyzes, the intention being to uncover and articulate patterns that they discover in those words. To support these activities, teachers might consider two regular classroom features that make reference to word investigations.

1. Use some of the classroom display space for a word wall, or word display, on which words from the ongoing or most recent investigation are displayed to demonstrate the pattern, including the principle discovered by the children and expressed in their own language. The display may include a number of the children's versions. The creation of the display can be part of the investigation.

2. Include spelling problems if daily challenges are a regular part of children's classroom activities. Typically, these challenges involve brain-teasers from mathematics. It would be useful to include such problems as "How many words can you find today in which a *q* is *not* followed by a *u*? or "Which of these words doesn't belong and why: *nature, natty, native, natural*?" or "How many words can you think of that are from the same meaning family as *cover*?" These activities can be adapted for all age and ability groups.

When the children are young, explore places where words are used in the world. Children are bathed in print in their environment all the time. Even when children can't actually read the print as a sequence of letters, they read it as meaning and interact with it. As a three-year-old, Dennis's daughter, Tiina, got into her grandmother's new Chrysler K-car, saw the K-car logo on the dashboard, and asked, "Did Grandma buy this at K-Mart?" Here are some ideas for bringing the world of words into the classroom.

◆   Teachers might want to institute a regular classroom time when children bring in a word or phrase they have seen (a kind of show-and-tell of words). The child should provide the location of the word and, if possible, its meaning. If the class has a map of the neighbourhood or school, the location of the word can be noted. Other children can be invited to contribute their experience with that word, and perhaps the children can be encouraged to focus on the letters and sounds as well as the look of the word. For example, let's say a child brings in a drawing of a "No Parking" sign, with the letters copied out. Chances are that sign appears somewhere near the school. Have the child tell what the words say and where exactly the sign was seen. Others can be invited to think about where they have seen those words and asked whether they can name letters in the words. The teacher could focus a bit more on the word *No* and ask if anyone recognizes it. Some children may be familiar with the common admonition, "*N-o* means *no!*" The teacher can then ask, "Can anyone think of other signs that say, 'No something'?" A tour of the school might help locate other signs. The activity could be extended by organizing "word walks" in the neighbourhood, or by engaging in word scavenger hunts.

◆ Early investigations are likely to focus on the logic of sound. Children can search in their reading, writing, and environment for words that have a common sound. They can then note the different ways that a sound can be represented, and perhaps group words that use a common way of representing the sound. In some cases they may see reasons for particular representations being used in particular groupings, such as the place in the word the sound occurs.

◆ Poetry is a good source for investigations of sound because the sound of words is an important element in poetry. Isolating rhymes and looking at how they are produced or focussing on common opening sounds helps children see spelling patterns, but also alerts them to the craft of poetry writing. For example, children may learn that repetition of memorable alliterative sequences is a way poets use to make parts of the poem stand out in the reader's memory.

◆ Children can be encouraged to use sound when generating spellings by developing games of "rhyming ping-pong." One child starts by writing out and saying a word. The next child must write out as best they can, and say, a word that rhymes. The game can go back and forth between players or can go around the room. The writing of the words is a crucial part of the activity, but correct spellings needn't be mandatory early on.

Teachers will quickly want to move children to think of other logics besides sound. Letter patterns have a close connection to sorting by sound, but they prompt children to begin to focus on common visual features in letter order.

◆ Rather than looking for a sound, children can search for words with a common letter pattern, such as *ough*. Having collected these words, they can then determine how many different sounds this pattern makes and can group words according to sound.

◆ Children could be asked to seek out a feature, such as when *ei* makes the long *e* sound, and see whether they can determine a pattern in its use. Having discovered a pattern, or "rule," the children need to write it in their *own* words.

Very wide open cloze activities with lots of possibilities not only encourage children to think about how words go together, but can encourage children to discover some of the probabilities related to letter order.

◆ Patterns such as _p_____, _____t_, _____ly, and de_____, can all be used to discover features about words. Teachers can ask how many letters can go in front of the *p* or after the letter *t*, for example, or which letters can't.

◆ As children become familiar with these fairly open activities, teachers can use the approach to introduce fixed patterns, such as q_____. (We were surprised at how long it took many of the children in our study to learn the *qu* pattern.)

Whenever the activity allows children to generalize a pattern, they should be encouraged to generate a personal version. The class may work to create a shared rule, but this rule should grow out of, and relate to, the individual versions created around the class. It is clear from the confusion shown by the children in our study that rules merely passed on are often poorly understood or are poorly articulated. Having *children* create the rule and write it in their own words produces some clarity, gives the teacher insight into children's thinking, and provides a way to check each child's understanding of the rule.

◆ Although we are not thrilled by the imagery of the game Hangman, the concept of the game—that is, using knowledge of letter patterns, or probability, to make guesses about a word—is a good problem-solving activity. The game can be recast by having each guess add a piece to create a "doodle-bug," with a body, head, six legs, two antennae, two eyes, and a mouth. After a short while the game is best played by requiring that the blank spaces be filled in order. This moves the guesses from being about the probability of letters occurring in a word to attention to how letters go together. Adaptations of games like Wheel of Fortune or Scrabble can also be used to offer variety.

◆ Investigations can be developed around the use of prefixes and suffixes relating first to syntactic features (for example, *ing*, *ed*, *ly*) and then to semantic features (for example, *pre*, *ful*, *un*). These investigations should help children see that the features represent a unit of meaning, and that the unit may stay intact despite differences in pronunciation. The investigations should also focus on patterns for combining words—for example, how the letter *y* may be changed to an *i* in some situations or how a root word may either remain intact (as in *differently*) or be changed (as in *probably*).

Teachers can also include activities to help children think about meaning as a logic:

◆ Teachers can offer pairs of words that share a spelling feature, such as tele*vis*ion/*vis*ible, or dis*cover*/*cover*t, and ask the question, "Just a coincidence?"

◆ Teachers can also present a new invention, a particular emotion, or a situation and ask children to invent a word for it—for example, inventing a word for "the feeling of wanting to laugh and cry at the same time" or a word for "a beeper that reminds you to do your homework."

◆ Children should also look for examples from various families of words, paying particular attention to how each word adapts the meaning from the family and how the root is adjusted and built into the new words.

Learning How to Integrate Logics

The good spellers in our study were able to use the competing logics of spelling to generate alternatives and to make decisions from among alternatives. The stalled spellers seemed to include various logics in their spelling practice, but never really developed an understanding of how the logics worked together. When pressed, they almost always returned to sound as an explanation of their spellings. Moving toward correct spelling requires that children pay more attention to overall system in language. The influence of reading will cause more words that can't be explained by sound alone to appear in children's writing. The aim here is for children to begin examining the overall system and understand that there are reasons for how words are put together and that understanding those reasons will give them greater control over their own spelling. A good etymological dictionary is a useful classroom addition when children begin to explore these ideas.

The first thing to work toward is to help children realize that making spelling decisions involves considering possibilities and testing alternatives. Phenix and Scott-Dunne (1991) suggest developing the concept of "Las Vegas rules" to teach children that there are alternatives, and that these alternatives have various levels of probability. Ph and f are ways to represent the same sound but in English spelling, f is the more probable alternative and, therefore, should be the first one to try—in Las Vegas terms, it's the safer bet. The concept of Las Vegas rules may suggest to some children that the whole spelling game is a crapshoot, but it may help more children see that there are factors that control their choices. Children can return to their investigations of sound or letter pattern and determine the frequency of certain patterns in certain situations. Helping children think about spelling as a matter of probability is more useful than representing it in terms of "exceptions," which may encourage children to think spelling is arbitrary. In this sense, the language of "exceptions," which emphasizes the arbitrary nature of spelling, is replaced by the notion of what is "less probable" or "occurring in particular settings."

Children need also be encouraged to focus on the "Englishness" of the look of words. In our study children often generated words by analogy to sound patterns from different words (as Braden did in ATRACKSHON), but without seeming to notice that their spellings had combinations of letters that do not usually occur in English.

◆ Using nonsense syllables, children can create words that others can judge to be wordlike or not.

◆ A form of the word game Balderdash, in which one person out of three has to present a nonsense word as a real word, is a good way to play with the notion of how sound, look, and meaning fit together to make plausible words.

Children should be encouraged to see that their own problem spellings, or words that they look up in the dictionary, are often difficult because they may be spelled differently according to different logics. After correcting a word, or looking up a word, children should try to identify the logic that explains the spelling and, if possible, determine why that logic is the one followed. Why, for example, does English spelling have very few words with a double *i* yet call for a double *i* in the spelling of *skiing*?

As we conclude this section on investigating the logics of spelling we need to stress that the point of all these activities is to encourage children to approach spelling as a problem that they increasingly have the resources to solve. A significant part of accomplishing this is to *leave the problem with the children*. An important role for the teacher is to lead children to consider new possibilities about how spelling might work. Teachers may offer possibilities to children but, in the end, should not push the child into accepting a solution. Time and again we saw that children in our study who were on the verge of making new connections required time and opportunities to make those connections for themselves. We also saw that any short-term gain that might have been made by "rushing" children and trying to make the connection for them did not have long-term results. We believe that the goal of spelling instruction is to create situations and develop a discourse about spelling that will lead children to become aware of, and use, their own emerging understanding about literacy.

Working with Parents

When we started to look at the histories we had compiled of the children who became good spellers, we couldn't help noticing that when we asked them how they had learned specific things about spelling, every one of these children referred to their parents. The nature of the parents' help varied greatly. Alice lived out the artistic tension between creativity and convention. Her father was a writer; every day he met Alice at school and they walked home together, often talking about what Alice was writing or planning to write. During these talks she rehearsed and probed her ideas. As she completed her drafts, however, Alice shared them with her mother, who worked as an editor! Her mother enjoyed the stories, but also reacted to the organization and spelling. She talked about the problems Alice's readers might have and gave very explicit instructions about spelling. Obviously Alice's experience was exceptional. Then there was Hana, whose mother gave her very traditional spelling assistance, giving her word lists to study and then testing her and scrutinizing the results. For Hana, this was very useful experience, because she was very interested in how words were spelled, and this regular exposure to words and the evaluation of her errors gave her important information that contributed to her successful development as a speller.

Of course, parents are no more magicians than are teachers! Children who, by the end of our study, had not yet become correct spellers were also given lots of parental help. Interestingly many of these children also referred to this parental involvement as a memorable part of their learning to spell. Some parents saw regular library use and the habit of reading as key. Some read to their children or listened to their children read. Others provided computer programmes, particularly in the earliest years, which taught such things as the alphabet and letter shapes. Many, especially in Fulham and Black Ravine, supervised the direct learning and testing of a set of words, often involving an older sibling. Some required daily reading, or encouraged regular writing. Some proofread the children's writing and tried to teach them correct spellings to replace their misspellings.

Certainly, teachers should embrace this involvement and try to support it and guide it in effective ways. Many parents will become involved no matter what. It's best, therefore, that children hear a common message and receive instruction that is complementary. Judging from the children's comments, the kind of one-on-one attention that parents can give makes a difference. We haven't come across a single case where parents made things worse through their work with their children. Children are as resilient with their parents as they are with their teachers, and they usually only assimilate instruction when it makes sense to them. Alice reminded us of this in her recollections of learning to spell the word *said*. "My mom told me it was *s-a-i-d*, but for a while I still spelled it *s-i-a-d*, because I didn't believe her."

About the Programme

One of the greatest fears that parents seem to have is that schools don't teach spelling any more. We can't explore the sources or the truth of this, but teachers have to be aware that this concern will, for many parents, colour their discussions with teachers. The first thing teachers need to do when beginning to involve parents in spelling instruction is to demonstrate their own commitment to helping children become good spellers. That doesn't mean you have to be committed to using a commercial spelling programme or having weekly word study lists and spelling tests, or regular spelling bees. You *do* have to show how what you do will enable children to grow as spellers and to show that you have an instructional plan to both teach and monitor spelling.

The starting point at any grade level is helping parents see the links between spelling and the reading and writing programme. Parents can understand that reading is the number one source for information about spelling and for a growing vocabulary base. They may tend to see writing as more of a testing ground for spelling, but you can demonstrate that writing provides a problem-solving context that calls on children to use the knowledge gained from reading and make it part of their own spelling practice. Writing also provides the reason for learning to spell.

The next step is to talk with parents about how children need some specific instruction about spelling and involvement in the English spelling system in order to reach a high level of proficiency. Here you can share some of the activities you plan that will help children develop their understanding of spelling. For example, you might talk about the kinds of investigation that seem useful to children at a particular level and about the importance of encouraging a problem-solving approach.

You will also want to explain your approach to editing and your expectations for what the children do about spelling in drafts and in final copy. As we have pointed out, proofreading is an important process when children are going public with their writing, and it encourages them to take responsibility for their writing and become more aware of audience needs. At the same time, parents need to be aware of the importance of protecting and encouraging young writers. Parents should know what you expect your role, and the children's roles, will be. It would probably be helpful if parents have access to the list of features or words for which you hold the child entirely responsible. They should also know how you will foster and monitor that responsibility.

Finally, parents need to know your plan for ongoing assessment. They need confidence that something they value, and that they feel the world will one day use to judge their child's adequacy, will be monitored and will not fall between the cracks. So it is important that you share both the criteria you use in making judgements about spelling and the process by which these criteria are determined. Using a developmental feature list, like the one presented earlier in this chapter, may be a good way to demonstrate your concern about these issues. You can explain briefly that the list has been developed to provide insight into children's spelling strategies, so that their progress is not measured by the successful spelling of this relatively short list, but by the demonstration of a growing sophistication in their awareness of spelling—that is, by the child's ability to explain why a word is spelled the way it is. At the same time you can show how you use the children's own writing as a basis for assessment. Clearly, writing for an outside audience is the most authentic test of a person's spelling ability.

Ultimately, what you need to communicate to parents is that you think that spelling is an important aspect of overall literacy development, that you have a plan for helping children learn to spell better, that you monitor the effectiveness of your approach and the learning of your students, and that you will communicate clearly to parents about their children's progress and about ways to encourage them and help them improve.

About the Child

Parents' interest in teachers' programmes is of course very personal and grows out of a concern for their own child. Initially they may want to know what you plan to do generally, but very quickly they want to talk about their child. We think it is very important to approach parents as experts about their child. They have put in the time, shared triumphs and disasters, and generally know their child from a perspective that nobody else has.

As the teacher, you have a particular expertise and important insights into specific parts of their children's lives. As you share these insights, you are helping the parents broaden and clarify their own picture of their child. You can provide parents with insights into their children as learners, providing them with an understanding of how their children are creating a meaningful approach to using the English spelling system. At the same time, you can tap into the parents' expertise. They can talk about the children's entire history of literacy development. We found that sometimes children, such as Najali, were very involved in literacy activities around the home, and we only found that out when we talked with her parents.

The record of each child's spellings of the developmental feature list words is a useful tool for communicating with parents. It demonstrates the child's growth. The important thing is to stress the importance of the child's growth and the development of increasingly sophisticated strategies. Because the aim of the list is to prompt errors, parents should be encouraged to look beyond counting the number of correct words their children spelled and look instead at their children's thinking as reflected in all the spellings. Movement along the list is the most important point. Of course, it is also important to share concern when expected movement does *not* take place and, with the parents, investigate what is happening with the child. Sharing the feature list words with parents can create problems if they decide to give their children a boost by having them learn some of the words on the list; but because the list monitors understanding, not specific spellings per se, this will most likely prove to be a relatively short-term problem. You can return to the word or words a few months later, or substitute words that require similar understandings.

A more difficult challenge is that parents often want normative data— that is, they want to know how their child stacks up, and whether a particular level is good or bad for children their age. We don't believe this question can be answered with definitive, numerical certainty, but we think it's fair to give parents a sense of their child's development. Parents aren't stupid. They have a sense of how their children are doing. You can indicate to parents the range of words on the developmental feature list that applies to the class as a whole. That, at least, will show where most of the children stand.

Finally, it's important to discuss growth in spelling in relation to overall literacy development. We have described a few aspects of learning in reading that give children the basis for moving further in their spelling. Overall progress can be discussed in relation to these aspects. Remember, parents will have a good sense of their children's literacy development and can readily understand these relationships.

Commonly Asked Questions

Over our years as educators, many teachers and parents have raised questions about teaching spelling. In this chapter, we address some of those questions from the perspective of our study.

How Can Parents Help?

As we mentioned in the last chapter, all the good spellers referred to receiving help at home, and though the help took different forms, all of it appeared to enhance the children's interest in spelling. Parents are concerned about their children's education and want to help, but what kind of help is best for them to provide? We believe there are three areas where parents can help their children become better spellers: through creating and maintaining an environment that supports literacy; through helping their children become more actively aware of words; and by working directly with their children to help them learn to spell specific words.

When we met with parents to discuss their child's progress during the study, they often wondered whether they should encourage their child to cut back on their reading and writing for pleasure in order to focus more on specific spelling activities. We hastened to assure them that reading and writing for pleasure are keys to their children's development as spellers. Parents understand their need to introduce their preschool children to books, but they should be reminded that home-based literacy does not end when children enter school and learn to read. Early supports to literacy, such as reading to children and providing lots of books and writing materials, need to be built on as children progress through school. Parents can help identify children's reading interests and make sure they get access to new material that supports that interest. As children progress, parents need to share their own activities as readers and writers—for example, they can begin to "book-share" with their children, each talking about his or her current pleasure reading. Parents can also seek out opportunities for children to write at home. Letters to family, notes, directions, anecdotes on the back of family pictures, all provide meaningful opportunities for writing. The key to such home-based activities is that they be pleasurable and supported by one-on-one attention.

Awareness of words is one of the striking characteristics of good spellers. We have mentioned teachers using the environment as a source of information about words. Parents are in the more fortunate position of having a much less restricted environment available to them than teachers do. Parents are with their children as they drive through neighbourhoods, walk through stores, watch television, and find themselves in every other conceivable situation involving print. Early on, these opportunities can be used to simply point out words in the environment, but later on parents and children can look for misspelled words or for interesting words used in unusual ways. Parents can join children in collecting interesting words from the environment or looking for the different ways words are used to say essentially the same thing. These kinds of activities encourage children to consider the word as an artifact as well as a conveyor of meaning. This focus on words helps children become effective proofreaders. Word games, whether purchased or played with pen and paper, also develop children's awareness of words.

The parents we talked with were aware of these more general supports to literacy, but were looking especially for specific things they could do about spelling. Many had made up their own spelling lists and had their children copy words out ten times from the list. Clearly many parents have the interest, and will find the time, to help children learn specific words. One simple task is for them to monitor the known-word list. Periodically parents can select ten words from that list and give a spelling test. Because these are the words children are using and should know, it is also an activity that focusses on achievement rather than mistakes. Parents might also help children add to the list. Teachers can provide words from lists of commonly used words, or words from the child's own writing that would be advantageous to learn. In working with word lists, however, it is important for teachers to show parents a better method for learning specific spellings than having a word copied out ten times. Share with parents the following approach:

1. Say the word.

2. Look at the word.

3. Note any unusual or potentially difficult parts.

4. Imagine the word.

5. Try to write the word.

6. Check the word.

Explain how this approach gives children a chance to think about how a word is spelled and to compare their version with the correct spelling. Encourage parents, as they work on these words, to ask children why a word is spelled as it is, in order to encourage their children to use the logics of spelling and to think about system. On communications home—in school or class newsletters, for example—teachers may include word facts or results of word investigations that follow a derivation through a group of words or that demonstrate a common pattern. Teachers might remind parents that the appearance of letter-reversals, or apparent inconsistency in the use of lower- and uppercase in the writing of children in grades 1 and 2 is not unusual and should not be the focus of instruction.

Parents are also interested in proofreading their children's work, and here it is important to point out that the goal is to make children responsible for effective proofreading. This does not mean that parents should not work with children, only that the work of the parent should be to support the child. Parents can have children identify the words they think may be wrong and can lead them through discussions of their perceptions of the problem, having them think about how a word could be. Parents can check for misspelled words from the known-word list, give clues to finding misspellings from that list, and offer encouragement to reconsolidate that learning. They can encourage children to generalize from their use of correct words to think of correct words that share a pattern.

These kinds of activities help parents to support their children's learning about the systematic nature of spelling and help children produce correctly spelled words. If teachers share with parents a sense of how children's understanding of spelling develops, parents will be encouraged to help children shift their attention from sound, to look, to letter patterns, and finally to the syntactic and semantic features of meaning. This will come from teachers' successfully communicating their spelling programme to parents, so that parents can find their place within it. The kind of one-on-one instruction that is possible in the home has great potential in helping children become better spellers.

What About Children for Whom English
Is a Second Language?

English was a second language for several of the children we worked with, ten of whom were in the study to the end. Our observations of these children learning to spell suggest that having English as a second language was by no means detrimental to their development as spellers.

The lag in reading and spelling development that we observed in some of these children at the beginning of the study was no more than we observed in several of the children whose first language was English. Furthermore, in nearly every instance, that lag had disappeared by the end of grade 2 and, of all the children who spoke English as their second language, only one (Vang, who was one of the children who began school with no English at all) was having considerable difficulty in spelling at the end of the study. (And, as mentioned earlier, there were other, more pertinent reasons than the fact that English was not his first language to explain Vang's difficulties with spelling.)

It is notable, in this context, that at the end of the study, none of the group of poor spellers and only one of the group of early readers–stalled spellers came from homes in which English was a second language. In contrast, three of the good spellers and the three most promising of the in-flux group were all from homes where English was a second language. Also, the two children for whom English was a second language (as well as the child whose dialect and articulation might have created some difficulties) who were generally slow in their literacy development all made good progress once they were over their learning-to-read hurdle (they were in the late movers group). Clearly, it is possible for children who come from English-as-a-second-language homes, even those who come to school with very little or no English, to do very well as spellers.

In addition, although we don't want to overgeneralize about such matters, we did notice while working with the children that most of those who spoke English as their second language had very positive and conscientious attitudes about their learning, including their spelling, and were among those children who were most active in doing parent-initiated work on spelling at home.

What About Familiar Aspects of Classroom Spelling Programmes, Such as Spelling Activities and Word Lists?

As we suggested in the previous chapter on instruction, we believe there is a place for word games and activities that lead children to think about the logics of spelling. At the same time, many word games and activities encourage a spirit of play with language and support the kind of interest in words we have seen associated with successful spellers. There are some things to consider, however, when planning to use some of these activities. The first is time. Time is a precious commodity in any classroom. We would be concerned when time for reading and writing, the true essentials for spelling development, is squeezed out of the schedule while substantial time for "spelling activities" remains. In our view, no spelling activities adequately substitute for encouraging children to write and then working with them to investigate their own spellings.

It is likely, however, that time for some kind of spelling investigation can be included in the class schedule. We strongly support activities that lead children to general ideas about how spelling works. Such activities can lead to productive classroom conversations about spelling, whether the focus is on ways to represent sound, or on letter patterns or on rules for attaching prefixes, or on meaning relationships that are represented in spelling, or on the influence of another language on the spelling of particular words. Activities can focus the entire class, or large groups of children, on specific features. It's important to ensure that individual children have the opportunity to make sense of the activity or investigation and the opportunity to apply it to their own understanding about spelling. For example, teachers may ask children to write in their own words what they have understood or may have them review their known-word lists for words that demonstrate a particular pattern or to find examples where the pattern is disrupted by another factor.

Weekly spelling lists can be an effective part of a spelling programme, providing that the lists support the writing intentions and practices of the children. The lists need to be individualized to have any value and must be words that the child uses regularly. Words that are effectively learned should be added to the known-word list and become a part of the ongoing responsibility of the child as writer. In general, we think there may be limited value in using a set of "theme words"—that is, words involved in a classroom study—as the list of words to be learned because such words are often part of a specialist vocabulary; and although they will be in use during the period of study, they may not be used much afterwards. A far better use of a specialized list would be for word investigations, which allow children to examine any number of patterns within the words. Specialist words may often lead to etymological searches, which can lead children back to words they actually use, and that may have interesting links to the specialized vocabulary.

How Can We Help Children Who Are Slower to Get Started as Spellers?

The links between spelling development and reading and writing development are so strong that especially for children who are using pre-sound, or even early sound, spellings at the beginning of grade 1, the most useful "spelling" instruction is instruction that gets them started as readers and writers.

It is abundantly clear in our own study, and in the work of other spelling researchers, that without progress in learning to read, there will not be progress in learning to spell. None of the children in our study moved to using sound in their spellings before they had begun to develop a concept of words in print, and none moved beyond spelling by solely matching sounds and letters until they had become readers. So, in our view, especially for those children who are slow to move into literacy, it is better to devote as much instructional time and attention as possible to helping the children to read than to spend time on spelling per se.

At the same time, progress in spelling requires the children to have opportunities to generate spellings and reasons to experiment with new spellings as they become engaged in composing personally relevant text. For all children, then, and especially for the slower developers, it seems to us desirable that in the early years, before children become independent readers and fluent, engaged writers, teachers and parents have a high tolerance for invented spellings, as opposed to insisting on correct spellings, in all but those pieces that are to "go public."

If we want engaged writers, we need to encourage children to focus on messages they want to communicate in print, and to get those messages down on paper using whatever they know about spelling, without being restricted to using only the words they already know (or think they know) how to spell correctly. As we have said, it is important to protect young children from criticism about their spelling when they do go public with their writing, and also to encourage personal pride by having them produce some correctly spelled published pieces each year.

We also think it is vital, from the beginning, to build on what the children do know about spelling. Throughout this book we have suggested some ways to do that through, for example, building on each child's known spellings. Conversations with children about their spelling, using as a basis the kinds of feature lists we used or the spellings in the children's current writing, can help them think about spelling and what they know about it. Even explanations of spelling system can begin early, through the simple investigations we described in Chapter 9.

How Can We Help Children Who Stall as Spellers Despite Being Good Readers?

Of all the children in our study, those who were good readers, and who seemed highly motivated to achieve in school, yet who did not become correct spellers, troubled us most. As we analyzed their lack of progress, we came to refer to this group as being "trapped in transitional." This seemed to capture the frustration we could feel in their inability to break through to a better understanding of what spelling was all about. We are convinced that these children, who have demonstrated their ability as literacy learners through their reading, can be helped to progress as spellers.

It is vital that such children keep on reading, both purely for pleasure and with a greater emphasis on reading as writers and spellers. (We noticed a decrease in pleasure reading among some of these children as they moved through the later grades.) But we think that the major goal for these children should be to engage them as writers. For this to happen, time must be provided in the school day to allow them to explore their ideas and interests in writing. The writing needs to include the full range, from school-subject-driven research reports to personally selected narrative forms. They must be given authentic purposes and audiences for both reports and personal writing, so that they can experience the link with an audience and have a reason to focus on the style and form of their writing. Teachers may have to actively explore the outside interests of these children in order to find the topics and forms of writing that are most likely to help them see that writing can bring personal satisfaction.

Accepting responsibility for proofreading comes easiest when children are engaged in their writing and have a personal investment in its going public in its most presentable form. Teachers can encourage their students to take this responsibility by appealing to other kinds of motivation. For example, these children as a group are motivated to succeed in school. They can readily see that they cannot always rely on having a teacher-proofreader at their disposal, and that therefore they must learn to proofread independently. They also want to be seen as successful readers and writers, and when teachers remove themselves from the role of proofreader and redefine their role as instructors *about* proofreading, the children are more likely to attend to that instruction and proofread on their own.

The basis for instruction about proofreading could be the child's known-word list. As described earlier, such a list could be created by having children review their own writing to identify the words they use regularly and spell correctly. Teachers can expand this list by giving spelling dictation of commonly used words taken from word lists, spelling texts, or their own observations of the vocabulary in use in the class. Teachers who choose to use known-word lists should monitor the development of the list carefully. Children could test each other and then go over the tests together to see what problems they have. Teachers should watch for the correct spelling of these "known" words in all the children's work. Such careful focus on spelling will encourage children to think about the spelling of the words they are using. At the same time teachers can begin to provide strategies for working with spelling problems as children write. Children can be encouraged to identify words they are unsure of and can be led to focus on areas of difficulty and possible solutions. Direct visual comparison of words should be strongly encouraged. At the same time, teachers can ask children for reasons why an alternative spelling might be more probable, such as the word's similarity with another word or pattern, or the application of a spelling rule. Such conversations will also reveal where the children are confused about spelling. (Recall that children in the stalled groups in our study often had trouble explaining their spellings and struggled to articulate poorly understood principles.)

Group proofreading, with the writer as part of a group, rather than partner proofreading may also help pick up spelling problems. This activity might also lead to a group discussion about choices in spelling and provide opportunities for teachers to have discussions about spelling in small groups so that children can try to articulate their understandings to each other. These group discussions can also provide the opportunity for some specific word investigations, possibly involving the shared known-word lists. Here, children can revisit and confirm some of the generalizations about spelling that they may or may not be using. Teachers can intervene in these discussions and use the investigations to provoke the children's thinking about particular spelling features in order for the children to reconsider their own logics and approaches. Such conversations may help re-establish the notion of system and logic in the spelling of these "trapped" children and, coupled with the refocus on their writing, may offer a way out of their dilemma.

How Can Teachers Help Children Learn About the Logics of Spelling if Their Own Knowledge of These Logics Is Limited?

Conducting this study, especially trying to figure out how children make sense of spelling, has been the single most useful thing either of us has ever done to make us aware of the underlying logics of spelling. We did not begin, nor have we ended, as experts in how spelling works. We know that we have never given teachers a detailed understanding of English spelling. We are sure that it is from a position of seeking to understand how the language works that spelling instruction must begin. Inevitably, teachers will become better informed as they pursue this approach. Teachers can begin by being alert to the concept of the logics in spelling; then, as is happening with us, this consciousness will help develop understanding.

Engaging with children, either by talking with them about their spelling or by joining with them in spelling investigations, can lead to authentic research and learning. The position of the teacher's being a learner with the children is really a position of strength, because it allows the teacher to authentically model how one investigates some aspect of spelling. Questions about why and how spelling works can be jointly raised and answered. If our experience is typical, teachers will find that they have many pieces of knowledge to begin with and will start to see how these pieces and implicit understandings come together. As we talked about system and searched for it with the children, that system began to reveal itself.

That isn't to say that there aren't useful guides and resources. In particular, we found *Teaching Spelling: A Practical Resource* by Faye Bolton and Diane Snowball (1993) and *You Kan Red This!* by Sandra Wilde (1992) to be useful books that gave lots of information about the logics of spelling as well as ideas and information about the teaching of spelling.

Wilde herself recommends two books, *American English Spelling: An Informal Description*, by D. W. Cummings (1988) and *The Mother Tongue: English and How It Got That Way*, by Bill Bryson (1990), which are useful resources about the language as system. Good dictionaries are also a useful source of the history of words.

Teachers need not be put off by a fear of not knowing. They know more than they think, can search out more information, and, like their students, can find the investigation of language compelling.

Does Spelling Matter Now that We Have Computers?

Let's be honest. This manuscript was created on a computer and we made regular use of the spell-check feature. Computers have increased the possibility of creating better-spelled text, and, for writers whose handwriting is often illegible (like many children and ourselves), computers can aid in the creation of a finished product that can be shared with pride. So computers have a place in spelling, but can they replace the individual's knowledge of how to spell?

One advantage the ability to spell gives writers is the freedom to produce draft text relatively easily, or at least to read one's own draft text easily. On the one hand, to be so caught up in spelling that we constantly need outside help makes writing virtually impossible; on the other hand, to be (like some young writers) unable to read back what has been produced makes shaping and sharing writing unlikely. The operational standard for successful drafting is not perfect spelling, but there needs to be a basic comfort with and awareness of it.

As the technology currently stands, there are a couple of obvious problems as we use computers to prepare perfect final copy. Spell-check programmes cannot catch and correct all errors. Their biggest shortcoming is that they do not pick up misspellings that are correct spellings of the wrong word. This often happens with homophones, but we can teach ourselves to be alert for homophones. But if the mistake results from typing, not spelling—for example, when we type *form* instead of *from*—we aren't even aware of the mistake. For children using spell-checkers, problems often arise when they cannot spell a word closely enough to have the computer suggest a replacement, when the word they want is not included in the programme, or when they are unable to select the correct replacement from a list of suggestions.

Also, computers are not always available. Pen and paper are still more portable, cheaper, and more readily at hand. All but the most "plugged-in" of us will have tasks we still find necessary to do by hand, not because we can't use the technology, but because it can't do the particular job. Admittedly, research and development continues to push back the limitations in computer technology and use, but for now there are still compelling reasons why people need to be able to spell.

In addition, certain kinds of fundamental learning about words and text can occur best through direct problem-solving. Children can be brought to see relationships among words, to see the patterns in the building blocks that make up the language. Computers do not encourage this kind of thinking. Spell-check programmes currently focus on producing correct text. Unfortunately, like instruction that has the same focus, computers don't help children to think about the system and logics of spelling, and don't help them learn.

Can Teachers Help Good Spellers?

Can teachers help even good spellers? The short answer is yes. Even the best spellers in our study took a lot of time to progress, and still had more to learn about spelling at the end of the study. Taken as a group, however, they did not suggest that school instruction had played a key role in their development (although we suspect it was more important than they describe it as being). Class instruction tended to lag well behind their own learning. They were still being taught sounds as they moved beyond sound-only spellings, and were taught rules well after they had incorporated them into their spelling. But even for these children, the meaning logic of English spelling, especially derivational relationships, was confusing and difficult to grasp. At a minimum, then, teachers need to pay more attention to what good spellers are doing and try to make better matches between needs and instruction. The instruction should always communicate the sense of system; it would be dangerous to diminish the children's sense of system, because it is this that helps good spellers progress. The best approach is probably to ask questions that will encourage these children to extend their sense of a system in spelling. For example, we began asking children in the study about the role of meaning in spelling long before they appeared to use this kind of information, and certainly at a time when they denied its importance. Questions about meaning, however, did serve to introduce the possibility that meaning could be a factor and encourage them to consider it. As Hana told us, the questions led her to think more about it. Similarly, asking good spellers to reflect on the "why" of their spelling also appeared to help them develop a more explicit understanding of their knowledge, as well as a logic and a language to use in talking about and solving spelling problems.

If We Let Errors Stand Uncorrected, Won't Children Learn Incorrect Spelling? How Can We Allow Invented Spelling?

Without doubt, the spelling practice that has received the most negative attention is "invented spelling," the practice of encouraging children in the early grades to write by having them figure out, or "invent," spellings for the words they wish to write. "How can we get correct spelling if we allow children to write just anything?" critics often ask. Parents are unsettled when they see pages of unreadable text filled with misspelled words, and they wonder about the instruction.

The logical alternative would seem to be to keep children from writing until they have become independent readers and know how to spell a core list of words, or perhaps have them copy text from the board or from transcriptions of their own stories. It was clear to us from the study that, at least with the children we worked with, writing was an integral part of their learning to spell. In fact, none of the children moved away from spelling by letter-sound matching—that is, began to use the visual knowledge about print derived from their reading—until they had taken personal risks in their early, invented spellings. It seemed to us that, from the beginning, the very act of generating spellings is necessary for spelling progress because, in the act of deciding how to represent in spellings what they want to say, children have to draw on what they know about language. The need to share their writing with an expanding audience motivates children to pay increasing attention to language, and further develops their knowledge. Besides contributing to overall growth in spelling, writing using these early invented spellings also provides teachers with insight into their students' understanding of print and their awareness of letter-sound relationships.

At the beginning of our study all the children with the exception of Lorna, who was already well advanced as a speller, demonstrated the use of some sort of early, invented spelling, and we saw no evidence that they carried these early inventions with them for very long. Furthermore, there was no evidence that they considered these spellings correct; in fact, their early inventions were remarkably unstable and sometimes even changed within the same piece of writing. This is to be expected, given that young children are constantly receiving and processing new information about words that causes them to reform and elaborate their knowledge of spelling.

As we said at the beginning of this book, all spelling is "invented"; it is just a question of what information and understanding a person uses when inventing it. The instructional focus need not be on the correctness of early products, but on exploring and developing the children's understandings about spelling. Teachers should only be concerned when children do not demonstrate in their spellings an increasing understanding of literacy, when they do not reflect in their "inventions" knowledge gained from their experience as readers and writers.

How Can I Talk to Children About Their Spelling?

As discussed in Chapter 8, we believe that important prerequisites for productive and authentic conversations with children are that the adults have a genuine curiosity about the children's perspective and confidence in the children's ability to talk about their own thinking. In many ways our own lack of expertise about how children learned to spell helped us to ask questions sincerely and to treat the children as the true informants they were; we were learning about spelling alongside the children. Unlike many classroom questions, there are no right answers to the kinds of questions we were asking in our conversations. Our goals were to try to understand the children's reasoning as they generated and monitored their spellings.

It's often difficult to remember one's reasoning for doing something once time has passed, so the best time to have conversations about spelling is while the children are actually engaged in the process. As mentioned earlier, we found it best to talk with the children while they were spelling words from our dictated feature list or when they were making spelling decisions during composing. But we also had informative conversations about spelling during writing portfolio conferences, especially once the children were familiar with the kinds of questions we raised in other spelling conversations. The important thing is to ensure a context for the conversations, by using a spelling or set of spellings the children have done very recently or are in the process of generating. That way you and the child have something specific to refer to, rather than trying to discuss spelling in the abstract.

We found that the most informative conversations took place when we kept our questions simple, open-ended, and related to what the children were doing and saying. For example, when referring to specific spellings teachers might ask, "How did you do that?" or "How does that work?" or "Why do you think it works that way?" An advantage of such simple questions is that they help to ensure an authentic conversation, because the questions are so easy to remember that there is no need to refer to a list of written questions. Another benefit is that if you repeat the same kinds of questions each time, there is more predictability (and security) in the situation for the children. They may even begin to think about these questions and their spelling logic between conversations—as we found happening in our study. Certainly such conversations can provide children with a language to think and talk about spelling. It's important to keep asking those basic questions even if at first a child may not be very responsive to them. Just leave the questions with the child to think about, rather than rushing in to provide the answers yourself. Remember that an informative conversation is one where the *child* does most of the talking!

Our conversations worked best when we tried to keep our responses to what the children were telling us short, open, and nonjudgemental. This is not necessarily the best time to try to correct the child's reasoning in a direct way. We found that when we tried that approach, any apparent change in the child's thinking was short-lived! Also, if you correct them regularly, the children may get the impression that the goal of your questions is to show them how wrong their reasoning is, and they may, as a consequence, be less inclined to tell you what they are actually thinking or may try to second-guess what you want them to think and say. Either reaction is counterproductive to your goals.

At the same time, don't be afraid to nudge the children's thinking a little to create some dissonance when appropriate (we talked about that in Chapter 9), in order to encourage them to consider alternative possibilities. Nudging is *not* the same as telling; it is more a matter of offering some new information or an alternative way of looking at a spelling situation and leaving the child to think about it. For example, when you see inconsistencies in reasoning or different approaches to similar spellings, you might ask such questions as "Why would it be like this [spelling] *here*, and yet like that [spelling] *there*?" or "How do you decide which way to spell that?" Again, do not worry if the children do not have answers; just leave them to think about the problem. If you tell the children that you'll return to that question on another occasion, they will be encouraged to think about it in the meantime.

While there are obvious advantages, for both the teacher and the child, in one-to-one conversations, we believe that useful conversations can also take place in small group situations. These, however, would be more productive after the children have become familiar with the basic questions and issues in one-to-one situations.

Because the nature of these conversations involves responding to what the children are doing and saying, it is difficult to suggest the exact wording of the questions. Besides, we all have different ways of expressing questions. Just remember to make your wording as natural as possible. We hope we have given enough information here, in Chapters 8 and 9, and in the actual conversations we have shared throughout the book to encourage such conversations in your own classroom. We believe that, like us, you will find them truly rewarding.

What Surprised You in Your Study?

DENNIS: Without question, what surprised me most was the amount of time it took for even our good spellers to move beyond spelling solely by letter-sound matching to spelling correctly. For most of the very best spellers the process took a full four years, and they were still learning. To me, this demonstrated the complexity of the spelling system. There is clearly much to be learned, first about the various logics, each of which works to determine spellings in different ways; then about how to integrate understandings of these various logics; and finally, about how to become at ease with a vocabulary-rich language. What we haven't answered is, if this is how long it takes the *good* spellers to learn, how long will it take others? Shifting instructional approaches may hasten this process, but I think we must recognize that learning to spell extends well past grade 6. Unfortunately, experience suggests that as the children move into higher grades there is less opportunity to read and write in the engaged way that appears to support spelling and less opportunity for systematic language exploration. Spelling instruction tends to become much more focussed on correcting and rewriting text. Ironically, this focus may come just at a time when many children are better able to handle approaches that encourage explicit analysis and generalization. If spelling is indeed a priority, and something we wish to do more than complain about, we have to recognize its complexity and give it more developmental time throughout a child's years at school.

My second, and pleasant, surprise was the unequivocal support the study gave to the role of writing in learning to spell. It was my interest in children's writing in the classroom that led me into this research. I could see that writing would support learning to spell by providing a meaningful purpose for spelling. I hoped that writing might have something to do with success in spelling. I was not prepared for the degree of its importance we discovered. Without exception, sustained progress in spelling was not made without an accompanying engagement in writing. We can speculate that such progress could take place without writing, but we never saw it. As I look back at the chapters in which we contrast those children who stalled with those who moved, I am struck by the clarity with which the children show us that writing matters.

MARGARET: When I look back at what surprised me, I'm now surprised at what *did* surprise me. In retrospect, what was surprising at the time now seems so obvious! For example, I think I was first surprised by how informative the children could be about their spelling processes and just how valuable that information was in helping us understand the nature of spelling and how it is learned. I remember being amazed by how articulate and insightful Lorna was in that early grade 1 interview when she talked about her interest in words and how she learned to spell by watching her dad as he read to her. At first I thought Lorna was unique, but over the years I was continually astonished by the reflectiveness and sense of engagement the children displayed, as they explained what they were doing and why. As we had anticipated, analysis of the children's spelling did help to inform our thinking, but there was no substitute for what the children taught us through their talk. For me, the conversations with the children were the most pleasurable and memorable parts of the study. It's not surprising, then, that as we wrote this book we tried to make sure that the children's voices were present on every page.

Another surprise was the degree of consistency we found in the patterns of learning to spell. As we said in Chapter 1, we expected to see change over time as the children learned more about spelling, but we set out with no commitment to any particular pattern of growth, or even the idea that there would be common patterns. What we discovered was a lot of commonality in the knowledge children used and how they used it. Especially during early development, when the children were using sound as their spelling logic, differences were more a matter of the timing of development. We saw numerous examples of the same misspellings produced by many different children. Even when the children moved away from using sound as their only logic and showed more diversity in the way they integrated new logics (or *not*, as the case might be), it was surprising to me how easy it was to see common patterns of attitude, behaviour, and growth, which crossed classroom and school lines as we looked at the various groups of good, poor, and stalled spellers. We believe that these patterns can help teachers better understand spelling development, although we have tried to show that such patterns are not a required route for growth. We still need to pay attention to the uniqueness in each child's spelling development.

I was also surprised that learning to spell was such a high-level, problem-solving, sense-making activity, so much like other processes of language learning. I admit that when we began I believed that, if not totally a rote-learning activity, spelling was a relatively lower-order thinking process when compared with learning to talk or read or compose text, and I had definitely not understood the reciprocal relationship between spelling and those other processes. I came to see how much learning to spell is like the other parts of language learning. It requires children to use what they know about English language from their experiences, first as speakers and then as readers; to make sense of, and find system in, English spelling; and to test out their understanding as they generate text. I also came to realize that, whether at the early letter-sound matching level or the derivational meaning level, the understandings about how language works that come from figuring out spelling can greatly enhance the child's reading, writing, and even talking.

Finally, both Dennis and Margaret were surprised that studying how children learn to spell could prove to be so fascinating.

References

Bolton, Faye, and Diane Snowball. 1993. *Teaching Spelling: A Practical Resource*. Portsmouth, NH: Heinemann.

Brown, Roger. 1973. *A First Language: The Early Stages*. Cambridge, MA: Harvard University Press.

Bryson, Bill. 1990. *The Mother Tongue: English and How It Got That Way*. New York: William Morrow.

Chomsky, Carol. 1972. Write Now, Read Later. In Courtney B. Cazden, ed., *Language in Early Childhood Education*, pp. 119–126. Washington, DC: Association for Education of Young Children.

Clay, Marie M. 1979. *The Early Detection of Reading Difficulties*. Portsmouth, NH: Heinemann.

Cummings, D. W. 1988. *American English Spelling: An Informal Description*. Baltimore, MD: John Hopkins.

Ehri, Linnea C. 1985. Movement into Reading: Is the First Stage of Printed Word Learning Visual or Phonetic? *Reading Research Quarterly* 20: 163–179.

Gentry, Richard. 1982. An Analysis of Developmental Spelling in GNYS AT WRK. *The Reading Teacher* 36: 192–200.

Gillet, Jean Wallace, and Charles Temple. 1986. *Understanding Reading Problems*, 2d ed. Boston: Little, Brown.

Goodman, Kenneth S. 1970. Behind the Eye: What Happens in Reading. In K. S. Goodman and O. Niles, eds., *Reading Process and Program*. Urbana, IL: National Council of Teachers of English.

———. 1973. Miscues: Windows on the Reading Process. In K. S. Goodman, ed., *Miscue Analysis: Applications to Reading Instruction*, pp. 3–14. Urbana, IL: ERIC Clearinghouse on Reading and Communication Skills and the National Council of Teachers of English.

Graves, Donald. 1983. *Writing: Teachers and Children at Work*. Portsmouth, NH: Heinemann.

Halliday, Michael A. K. 1973. *Explorations in the Functions of Language*. London: Arnold.

Hanna, Paul R., Jean S. Hanna, Richard E. Hodges, and Erwin H. Rudorf, Jr. 1966. *Phoneme-Grapheme Correspondences as Cues to Spelling Improvement*. Washington, DC: U. S. Office of Education. (ERIC Document Reproduction Service No. ED 128 128 835).

Henderson, Edmund H. 1985. *Teaching Spelling*. Boston: Houghton Mifflin.

———. 1990. *Teaching Spelling*, 2d ed. Boston: Houghton Mifflin.

Henderson, Edmund H., and James W. Beers, eds. 1980. *Developmental and Cognitive Aspects of Learning to Spell: A Reflection of Word Knowledge*. Newark, DE: International Reading Association.

Henderson, Edmund H., and Shane Templeton. 1986. A Developmental Perspective of Formal Spelling Instruction Through Alphabet, Pattern, and Meaning. *Elementary School Journal* 86: 305–316.

Hodges, Richard E. 1981. The Language Base of Spelling. In Victor Froese and Stanley B. Straw, eds., *Research in the Language Arts: Language and Schooling*, pp. 203–226. Baltimore, MD: University Park Press.

Morris, Darrell. 1983. Concept of Word and Phoneme Awareness in the Beginning Reader. *Research in the Teaching of English* 17: 359–373.

Phenix, Jo, and Doreen Scott-Dunne. 1991. *Spelling Instruction that Makes Sense*. Markham, Ontario: Pembroke Publishers.

Pringle, Ian, and Aviva Freedman. 1985. *A Comparative Study of Writing Abilities in Two Modes at the Grades 5, 8, and 12 Levels*. Toronto, Ontario: Ontario Ministry of Education.

Read, Charles. 1975. *Children's Categorizations of Speech Sounds in English*. Urbana, IL: National Council of Teachers of English.

Smith, Frank. 1978. *Understanding Reading*, 2d ed. New York: Holt, Rinehart and Winston.

———. 1982. *Writing and the Writer*. New York: Holt, Rinehart and Winston.

Wilde, Sandra. 1992. *You Kan Red This! Spelling and Punctuation for Whole Language Classrooms, K–6*. Portsmouth, NH: Heinemann.

Zuttell, Jerry, and Timothy Rasinski. 1989. Reading and Spelling Connections in Third and Fifth Grade Students. *Reading Psychology* 10: 137–155.